The Sport of Kings

The Sport of Kings is an ethnography of the British racing industry based upon two years of participant observation in Newmarket, the international headquarters of flat racing. Racing in Britain provides a lens through which ideas of class, status, tradition and hierarchy can be examined in an environment which is both superficially familiar and richly exotic. This book explores concepts about 'nature' specific to thoroughbred racehorse breeding, and pursues the idea that in making statements about animals, we reveal something of ourselves. It explains the action that takes place on racecourses, in training yards, on studs and at bloodstock auctions. It analyses the consumption of racing through betting on the racecourse and in betting shops, and it proffers an insightful description of a unique class system: that of the humans and animals involved in the production of British flat racing.

REBECCA CASSIDY is Lecturer in Anthropology at Goldsmiths College, University of London.

The Sport of Kings

Kinship, Class and Thoroughbred Breeding in Newmarket

Rebecca Cassidy

Goldsmiths College, University of London

CAMBRIDGE
UNIVERSITY PRESS

PUBLISHED BY THE PRESS SYNDICATE OF THE UNIVERSITY OF CAMBRIDGE
The Pitt Building, Trumpington Street, Cambridge, United Kingdom

CAMBRIDGE UNIVERSITY PRESS
The Edinburgh Building, Cambridge CB2 2RU, UK
40 West 20th Street, New York, NY 10011-4211, USA
477 Williamstown Road, Port Melbourne, VIC 3207, Australia
Ruiz de Alarcón 13, 28014 Madrid, Spain
Dock House, The Waterfront, Cape Town 8001, South Africa

http://www.cambridge.org

First published 2002

Printed in the United Kingdom at the University Press, Cambridge

Typeface Times 10/12 pt.   *System* LaTeX 2_ε [TB]

A catalogue record for this book is available from the British Library

ISBN 0 521 80877 4 hardback
ISBN 0 521 00487 X paperback

Contents

Preface

Riding across Newmarket Heath on some shiny specimen of thoroughbred perfection I often thought to myself, 'I must be the luckiest anthropologist ever.' Studying horseracing enabled me to fulfil a number of ambitions, including riding racehorses, taking a yearling through the sales ring, seeing a thoroughbred foal born and, ultimately, leading up a winner at Newmarket's July Course. My relationship with my informants in Newmarket was influenced by the passion for horses that I shared with most of them, to the extent that no study would have been possible without it.

Newmarket is a town of seventeen thousand people and four thousand racehorses (Newmarket Tourist Information Centre 2002). It is located on the Suffolk–Cambridgeshire border, and its windswept Heath has been the site of horseracing in a multitude of forms, from the scythed chariots of Boadicea to the massive finances and internationalism of flat racing today. It is often assumed that the history of Newmarket *is* the history of horseracing. It is occasionally stated that Newmarket *is* horseracing.

Newmarket epitomises English racing. It is not typical of, nor entirely different from, other racecourse towns and cities. What makes Newmarket interesting is that it was the site of the codification of horseracing in the eighteenth century, and became the favoured location for the most powerful opinion-makers in horseracing society at that time. Newmarket still accommodates the Jockey Club Rooms. The result of this concentration of power has been the identification of the town with a single industry that still dominates its landscape, daily routines and social relations. Amongst racing professionals and aficionados Newmarket has earned the nickname of 'Headquarters'.

This book is a case study of a 'specific class system' – that of the trainers, owners, breeders, bloodstock agents, racing administrators, stallion men, lads, farriers, stud-workers and work-riders who contribute to the production of racing as a sport, industry and betting medium, referred to throughout as 'racing society'. It offers a characterisation of this system as well as an explanation of how it is maintained in dialogue both with those who bet and visit the racecourse, and with the aristocrat of the animal world, the English thoroughbred racehorse.

Fieldwork in Newmarket

I arrived in Newmarket in October 1996, an experienced rider, but a relative newcomer to the world of racing. I enjoyed going to the races, but I did not know anyone with a professional involvement in racing. During my undergraduate degree I had acquired the habit of driving over to Newmarket to watch the horses on the Heath, and it was during this time that I began to notice the interesting characters surrounding the practice of horseracing.

As later chapters reiterate, my pre-existing knowledge of horses and my ability to ride and handle them was one of the most significant factors influencing my fieldwork. Evans-Pritchard famously said, '"cherchez la vache" is the best advice that can be given to those who desire to understand Nuer behaviour' (1940: 16). Of course, in relation to Newmarket Evans-Pritchard's advice would read instead, 'cherchez le cheval'. My acceptance by many racing people depended upon my ability to perform tasks involving horses with the minimum of difficulty and fuss. On meeting people for the first time, I was often asked to 'just grab hold of that old mare for me', or 'hand me that scraper will you?' Though the manner was casual and the task usually straightforward, its completion often depended upon a confidence with horses and a knowledge of their specialised equipment, which indicated to 'horse-people' that I was 'one of them'.

This book is based upon fifteen months' fieldwork in Newmarket. Although Newmarket was the primary site of my fieldwork, my object of study was in fact 'racing society', a collection of people involved in the production of racing, found in high concentration in the town. I also gathered data from a variety of locations outside Newmarket, specifically, from racecourses all over Britain, from the Ascot and Doncaster bloodstock sales, from racing's service providers in Wellingborough (Weatherbys) and London (the Jockey Club and the British Horseracing Board) and from Lambourn, the centre of National Hunt racing in Britain.

I began my fieldwork in the autumn, when most of the important sales take place at Tattersalls Park Paddocks in the centre of Newmarket. The breeding season for English thoroughbreds runs from February to July, and all thoroughbreds share a nominal birthday of 1 January. Foals are the produce of a particular 'dam' and 'sire', a mare and a stallion. Female racehorses are referred to as 'fillies' up to and including the age of four, after which time they become 'mares'. If the filly is 'covered' (mated) before she is five, she automatically becomes a mare. A 'stallion' refers to a male horse at stud, a 'gelding' is a castrated male horse, a 'colt' is a male horse up to and including the age of four years who is not at stud or gelded. A 'horse' is a male horse over the age of five who is neither gelding nor stallion.

Most English thoroughbreds are sold as yearlings, ready to go into training and to race the next season as two-year-olds. Yearlings are either brought straight from the stud on which they were born to the sales, or go through a 'preparation' with a sales agent. The sales run until the end of the year, and once they had finished I began working on a stud, at the beginning of 1997.

My experiences of working as a stud hand are described in detail in chapter eight. The early part of the year was dominated by foaling and then by 'covering' (mating). Once the foals had been born and the mares covered, the emphasis changed and the turf flat season began (all-weather flat racing continues throughout the winter, but is not as prestigious or valuable as turf racing). My fieldwork also moved, from stud to training stable, where my own initiation into riding racehorses began. My experience of working as a 'lad' is described in chapter seven. The yearlings bought at the sale are sent to the training stables chosen by their owners. Racehorses are trained on behalf of their owners by professional racehorse trainers, who may board between six and two hundred 'horses in training'.

Once a yearling has been placed with a trainer, it becomes a 'horse in training', and is 'backed' and 'broken', that is, accustomed first to a bridle and saddle, and then to a rider. Two-year-olds may be too 'backward' to race and need time to grow before they can withstand the pressures of training. Others are quick to learn, growing into what is referred to as an 'early' two-year-old. Once the two-year-old is broken, he will be 'tried' against his peers, to see whether he 'shows' any speed. A two-year-old who is 'showing' at home will be tried in a race, the outcome of which will determine his future. The majority of two-year-olds will be given several chances to race as they may not show their ability due to being 'green', i.e. lacking in experience. At three, the racehorse is thought to be mature enough to have 'shown' his ability although there are some who are 'slow to come to themselves' and continue to develop. Once a racehorse has established his ability, after several runs at two and three, it is unlikely that he will ever run in a better 'class' of race, and will run at the same level until he loses his physical 'soundness' or 'form'. At this point the horse may be retired or tried over jumps. Mares are likely to be 'put into foal' whilst only the best bred and most successful colts become stallions.

The major phases of my fieldwork were thus spent working on a stud, in a training yard, on the racecourse and at the sales showing yearlings. In addition, I met members of racing society who were eager to describe their families. These interviews were conducted throughout fieldwork, at the races and in informants' homes. My association with the professional punter, who explained a great deal about gambling, stemmed from an introduction by a racecourse commentator with whom I spent a day. Over the course of fieldwork I also spent time with breeders, owners, farriers, vets, bloodstock agents, Jockey Club officials, racing correspondents, bloodstock experts, local councillors, the local

Member of Parliament, the London Racing Club, and at Weatherbys, the Jockey Club and the British Racing School.

I choose not to describe this thesis as an example of 'anthropology at home'. In Newmarket, I was 'at home' in relation to my nationality, skin colour, upbringing and affinity with horses. I was also, of course, not 'at home', because I was always a member of a community of anthropologists, that membership being the purpose of my presence in Newmarket. Writing up has reinforced this separation. If 'anthropology at home' refers to a purely geographical notion of 'inside Britain, Europe, or North America', then it is merely uninformative. However, if it implies something more profound, such as a sharing of concepts significant to the conduct of anthropology in that area, then I believe that it is misleading. It is not necessary to leave the society in which one feels 'at home' in order to question the founding principles of that society, whilst, as McDonald has argued, it is possible to go to any distant society, only to return with fulfilled and unquestioned expectations. ('We now realise, I think, that some anthropology never left home, or never really returned with its home categories and values seriously challenged in any way other than that in which we expected them to be disturbed. We expected the natives to have lots of ritual, religion, kinship, metaphor, myth and meaning, and that is what we found' (McDonald 1987: 123).) I would prefer to emphasise Cohen's statement that, 'any mind beyond the ethnographer's own is Other and, therefore, requires to have interpretive work done on it' (1990: 205).

Whilst it no longer seems necessary to rail against exoticism within anthropology, it does appear that some societies remain more suitable subjects of anthropological enquiry than others. In particular, anthropology seems suited to understanding the most under-represented and least powerful societies. Part of the purpose of this study was to discover whether anthropology was equally well suited to characterising a Western, aristocratic elite. I feel that anthropology met this challenge, with the anticipated benefits to the relationship between fieldworker and informant. Shovelling muck at 6 a.m. one freezing morning, with a broken finger and a strapped ankle, covered in horse secretions of various sorts, I pondered my place in the scheme of things that was my fieldwork. I was shaken from my reverie by a loud blast from 'the boss': 'Rebecca! Get your anthropological arse out here!' As Ortner said of her high-school colleagues whom she made objects of study, 'it's healthy to be in this more symmetrical position vis-à-vis my informants. Nobody can accuse me of silencing *them*' (1995: 271).

Those who might feel that horseracing is too technical and specialised a world to comprehend from so short a piece of work have succumbed to the exact state of befuddlement that racing knowledge is intended to induce. No understanding of the handicap weighting system or the tongue-strap/blinkers controversy is necessary in order to approach this book. I hope that it will become obvious that the technicalities of racing are strangely unfounded, and therefore that their significance lies less in what they enable an individual to *do* and more in the appearance of knowledge they communicate. This awareness is intended to help the reader to concentrate less on what they do not know about horseracing and more on what I can tell them about the people who have racing lives.

Acknowledgements

The major period of fieldwork on which this book is based took place during an Edinburgh University Studentship. I am very grateful to the university for their support, and to the people who helped me to secure the award. The PhD that formed the basis for this manuscript was written under the expert guidance of Janet Carsten, and examined by Tony Cohen and Sarah Franklin. All three of these people have been great sources of inspiration to me. The writing-up process was completed during a British Academy Postdoctoral Fellowship held at the department of Social Anthropology at Cambridge University under the enjoyable mentorship of Stephen Hugh-Jones. I am very grateful for the support I have received from the British Academy. Needless to say, numerous people at both Edinburgh and Cambridge have contributed to the book in different ways, and I thank them all. Of course, I must also acknowledge my debt to my friends in racing, human and equine, not least Waders, Homer and The Golden Anorak. I didn't know that it was possible to have so much fun until I met them.

Whilst I hope that the description of peoples, places and events is an accurate reflection of the period when I conducted my fieldwork, some changes will inevitably have taken place since 1996, and readers should not assume that what was, to the best of my ability, a true record at the time, is necessarily still so.

1   Introduction

A brief and selective history of flat racing in Newmarket

> The earliest English horse race of which we know, took place, not at New-market, but at Weatherby in Yorkshire, in the reign of the Roman Emperor Severus Alexander (a.d. 210).
>
> (Lyle 1945: 1)

This book does not concern itself with identifying the first ever English horse race or with tracing the ancient history of racing generally. It is concerned with the modern period of horseracing, from the time at which it was codified in the nineteenth century, to its contemporary form. The main impetus for this codification came from the Jockey Club.

The Jockey Club was established in 1750 as a gentlemen's club, meeting most often in the Star and Garter in Pall Mall. The Club also met at the Corner, Hyde Park, owned by Richard Tattersall. When Tattersall moved to Knightsbridge the Jockey Club moved into the Bond Street residence of their agents, Weatherbys (Black 1893). This trio of institutions – the Jockey Club, Weatherbys and Tattersalls – are still dominant forces in English racing, though their roles have changed since the formation of the British Horseracing Board in 1992.

The records of the Jockey Club do not reveal its original purpose, and there does not seem to be any explicit statement of intent to control racing. Membership was almost exclusively aristocratic. The term 'jockey' referred, at the time, to the owner of the horse, rather than its rider, and so it could be said that the Club was, initially, a racehorse owners' association. In 1752 the Jockey Club leased a plot of land in Newmarket, and the original 'Coffee Room' was built. According to their own history, the Jockey Club was soon approached for advice where disputes arose on 'the turf' (Jockey Club History 1997: 1).[1]

Horseracing at Newmarket had been established well before the Jockey Club chose to locate itself on the High Street. Newmarket's place as the 'HQ' of racing developed with royal patronage, beginning with Richard II, 'But it was under James I that the village really became Royal Newmarket' (Lyle 1945: 4). This royal association culminated with Charles II, who famously conducted the court from Newmarket during autumn race meetings:

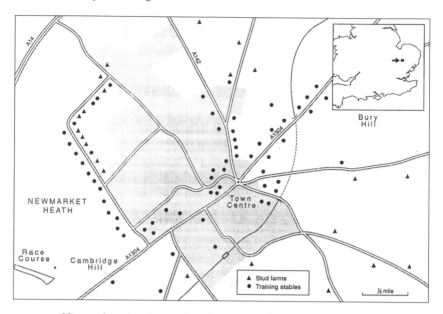

Newmarket, showing the locations of stud farms and training stables

Thus we find the turf, rising like a Phoenix from the ashes on the accession of Charles II, thoroughly reinstituted as our great national pastime during the Merry Monarch's reign... To this resuscitation the king extended his powerful patronage and support. (Hore 1886: 92)

Newmarket's royal patrons reinforced the existing association of racing, and the horse itself, with prestige and status. As James I wrote in his *Religio Regis*, or *The Faith and Duty of a Prince*, 'the honourablist and most commendable games that a king can use are on Horseback, for it becomes a Prince above all Men to be a good Horseman' (quoted in Lyle 1945: 7–8).

In more recent times, Princess Anne has ridden in amateur races and the Queen is and the Queen Mother was substantial racehorse owners. Britain remains the most prestigious of all racing nations, and although its prize money is lower than in France and America, the five annual Classic races still attract the richest owners in the world, most obviously, the Dubai and Saudi Arabian ruling families. Royal patronage remains one of the strongest influences over the image of British racing. This influence was partly preserved by the work of the Jockey Club in codifying the rules of racing according to aristocratic ideals.

The Jockey Club famously established the right to 'warn off' in 1821, when a tout known as 'Snipe' was banned from Jockey Club land (Black 1893: 82). The practice of 'warning off' whereby the individual is forbidden from entering any Jockey Club land remains. Two men were warned off for ten years in 1998 after collaborating in the formation of an allegedly fraudulent syndicate. There is no right of appeal, and a 'warning off' ends any professional involvement in racing. The Jockey Club retains the right to end individual careers where it feels racing has been brought into disrepute.

The authority of the Jockey Club began to extend beyond Newmarket after 1832 when a notice in the Racing Calendar effectively called the bluff of all other local authorities by announcing that the Club would only adjudicate on New-market races, as those elsewhere were run under such a wide variety of rules.[2] This was a first step towards the standardisation of the rules of horseracing, and the contemporary Jockey Club notes with satisfaction that it has 'finally culmi-nated in reciprocal agreements with the Jockey Club, and Turf Authorities of practically every country in the world where racing takes place today' (Jockey Club History 1997: 3).

The introduction of a series of revised rules of racing after 1858 reflects the rapid period of change undergone by racing at this time. Although the old rules had remained unchanged for over one hundred years, the new rules lasted until 1868, only to be revised again in 1871 (Jockey Club History 1997: 2–3). Where race meetings had been a haphazard affair with the atmo-sphere of a local fair or carnival, they were now becoming highly organ-ised with formalised procedures for starting, weight allocation and judging. Of course, the increased sophistication of the rules of racing succeeded in reinforcing the role of the Jockey Club and its place in the government of racing.

Weatherbys employees still describe themselves as the 'Civil Service' to rac-ing. Weatherbys is a family business, its current head being Johnny Weatherby, descendant of the original agent of the Jockey Club. Weatherbys holds the records of owners' colours (the unique colour and design of the silks worn by the jockey on a particular owner's horse), names (horses' names must be regis-tered with Weatherbys before they may race) and financial affairs for the Jockey Club. It takes entries for races and deals with the administration of licences and permits. It has recently registered as a bank and can provide a variety of finan-cial services in addition to handling racing accounts which pay entry fees and Heath tax, and hold winnings.

Richard Tattersalls, the original host of the Jockey Club when they held their meetings at the Corner in Hyde Park in the 1750s, founded his own dynasty of thoroughbred racehorse auctioneers (Orchard 1953: 1). Tattersalls is no longer family-owned or run, but remains perhaps the most prestigious bloodstock auctioneers in the world, located in Park Paddocks in the centre of Newmarket. Tattersalls attracts the best bred yearlings to the annual Houghton Sales, where 215 horses were sold for a total of 34.5 million guineas[3] over three days in October 1999 (Tattersalls website 2000).

The role of the Jockey Club has changed since the inception of the British Horseracing Board in 1992. The Board is now responsible for racing's finances, political lobbying, the form taken by the fixture list, marketing (an innovation) and training:

> The BHB will strive to maintain significant improvements to the finances of Flat and Jump horseracing, as an important spectator sport, leisure industry and betting medium. It will aim to do this for the benefit of all those who invest in Racing and derive enjoyment from it, and in order to enhance British Racing's competitive position internationally. (British Horseracing Board Annual Report 1993: 1)

The Jockey Club retains responsibility for discipline, security, 'the conduct of a day's racing' and the licensing of racecourses and individuals; its current role has been described as racing's policeman. Membership of the Jockey Club is still internally elected and retains its male-dominated, aristocratic emphasis; thus in 1997, of 112 members, 89% were men, 44% were titled. Of the fifteen honorary members, five were British royals, four Sheikhs, two held military titles and two were Weatherbys.[4]

In addition to regulating racing, the Jockey Club is the major land owner in Newmarket. The Jockey Club estate extends to 4500 acres in total, of which 2800 are training grounds, plus three stud farms, a farm, seventy-five residential properties, twenty commercial properties and The Jockey Club Rooms. This portfolio includes both the Rowley Mile and July Racecourses, the Links Golf Club, the National Stud land, the National Horseracing Museum, twelve leasehold training yards and, in a surprising diversification, two Happy Eater restaurants. Trainers pay a Heath tax to the Jockey Club (£69 per horse per month in 1997), that entitles a horse to use the training grounds.[5] The Jockey Club has defined its new role as 'setting and maintaining standards for racing' (Jockey Club Annual Report 1997: 1).

The funding of racing in Britain has developed in accordance with its executive growth. The Horserace Betting Levy Board (HBLB) was instituted in 1963 in order to assess, collect and apply the 'monetary contributions from bookmakers and the Totaliser Board (the Tote)'. Until January 2002, a levy was raised on all legal bookmaking, at a level of 1.25% of turnover (approximately £50 million annually). Betting off-course had been liable to General Betting Duty, at 9%, of which the government took 6.5% (approximately £300 million annually). Betting on-course was tax free. Racing also has its own betting enterprise, the Tote, the profits of which (£4,457,000 in 1999) go directly into racing. The HBLB spent £29,471,000 on prize money in 1999, which constituted 49% of expenditure (Horserace Betting Levy Board 2000).

Racing is therefore, for the time being, funded primarily by contributions from the betting public, collected by bookmakers and distributed by the HBLB.

Many owners complain that ownership is unprofitable, and that bookmakers should pay more for the privilege of using racing as a betting medium in order to boost prize money and thereby sustain what is the sixth largest industry in Britain. The bookmakers invoke the plight of the punter and say that he should no longer subsidise what is a rich man's sport. The impact of off-shore and internet betting operations further complicate these arguments as the levy becomes increasingly difficult to gather in a de-regulated betting market. The structure of the funding of racing is set to change in the near future, from the present levy system refereed by the government to an independent system based upon payments made by bookmakers for media rights to television pictures and information on runners and riders.[6]

Both French and American racing developed 'in conversation with' the British tradition. In France, the Jockey Club was founded by Lord Seymour, in 1833 (Slaughter 1994: 4), and this link was concretised in the language of racing, which still includes 'le Jockey Club', 'le yearling' and 'le turf'. In America, the Jockey Club was formed by August Belmont I, in 1837, and the Stud Book was opened in 1896. The same equine bloodlines are followed in America, and as August Belmont IV was elected chairman of the American Jockey Club in 1982, it may be suggested that similar concerns also appear to inform the human contingent of racing in the States (see Bolus 1994).

Thoroughbred racing in America is standardised in a way that the British racing establishment finds unseemly. The majority of American races are held on dirt (as opposed to turf), and race 'tracks' are all tight, left handed ovals. In Britain courses are sufficiently wide and sweeping to facilitate manoeuvres which make the draw less important. British racecourses are all different, some are left-handed, some right-handed, undulating or flat, narrow or wide, they are thought to offer a more thorough test of a horse (and therefore of its breeding). Furthermore, American horses are permitted to run on drugs including Lasix and Bute, which disguise bleeding and lameness respectively. No drugs are permitted in Britain, further encouraging British breeders to assert the superiority of their bloodstock. In Britain, thoroughbred racing enjoys a virtual monopoly, whilst in both America and France, trotting and harness racing are also popular. These forms of racing employ non-thoroughbred racehorses, and were scorned by my British informants.

Apart from the intrusion of more recent forms of racing, perhaps the most important difference between Britain and France or America is the system of wagering. France enjoys a Tote monopoly, a pool betting system which returns its profits to racing. In America, bookmaking is only legal in Nevada, and the majority of betting is with the American Tote (Munting 1996: 111). All bets with the Tote are settled at odds calculated according to the weight of support for each horse. They do not, therefore, involve the personal contact on which the wager with the bookie depends:

Nowhere have bookmakers come to play such an important role in the betting market as in Britain and Ireland, though they remain legal in many other parts of Europe and the world. (Munting 1996: 110)

The relationship between the bookmaker, the punter and the producers of racing is unique to British racing, and is a reflection of broader dynamics within British society. In 2000, 7422 races were held during 323 days racing at the 59 British racecourses. Fourteen thousand racehorses in training ran for £72 million in prize money. According to the British Horseracing Board's website, five million people went racing. Racing remains the most televised sport on British terrestrial television, and a huge ten million people watched the Grand National in 2000. Racing and breeding employs 60,000 people, or one in eight agricultural workers in Britain. It provides an estimated 70% of income for the betting industry that employs some 40,000 people. In the year 1999–2000, £7 billion was bet off course in Britain's 8500 Licensed Betting Offices, generating £344 million for the government in betting duty. In addition, £94.5 million was bet on course with the Tote. In the breeding paddocks of the UK and Ireland, 30,000 mares and 1000 stallions produced approximately 14,000 foals in 2000, the next generation of champions.

Making connections

Although kinship was central to anthropology throughout the twentieth century, English kinship was not the focus of any sustained or influential study until the 1980s. Even after this time, as Cohen indicates, it did not receive the same attention as more 'exotic' kinship systems/patterns might:

We seemed to be apologetic for taking up readers' time with descriptions of systems and processes which were manifestly less elaborate, exotic, mysterious and, therefore, intellectually demanding than those to be found in Africa, Asia, the Pacific or the Middle East. In short, we were defensive. (1990: 218)

Part of the explanation for this defensiveness can be extrapolated from the centrality of kinship to the classic anthropological texts and its perceived peripherality 'at home'. The proper subject of anthropology before the latter half of the twentieth century was 'primitive society'; studying kinship 'at home' required an explanation where studying elsewhere did not. In more recent anthropology, however, 'primitive society' has been revealed as illusory, a construct fashioned in opposition to the society to which early social anthropologists belonged.

Kinship had been presented as the source of sociality in those societies that apparently lacked an institution which anthropologists could equate to either a state or a commercially driven division of labour. Thus unilineal kinship governed politico-jural affiliations in, for example, Evans-Pritchard's *The Nuer* (1940). English kinship, described as 'cognatic' or 'bilateral', apparently lacked the ability to do so. The main organising principles of 'Western' or 'civilised' society lay elsewhere: kinship was a purely domestic affair, concerned only with the nuclear family. Cognatic kinship, conceived in opposition to unilineal reckoning, became a sort of 'non-kinship'.

English kinship, recast as the study of the family, was the province of sociology, rather than anthropology, a division of labour that reinforced the belief that kinship was somehow more fundamental in non-Western societies:

[Anthropologists] have investigated kinship in more primitive societies where it is of so much greater importance than our own that the study of society is sometimes in large part the study of kinship. (Willmott and Young 1960: 187)

The sociology of the family traced a historical progression from a pre-modern era in which roles were ascribed by birth and tradition was looked to as an authority for the present, through a modern period in which tradition was replaced by scientific rationality, faith in progress and individualism. The nature and even the name of the third stage of this progression, most commonly described as 'post-modern', remains contested. The relative fluidity of the second phase was the subject of Bott's work on *Family and Social Networks* (1957).

the individual constructs his notions of social position and class from his own various and unconnected experiences of prestige and power and his imperfect knowledge of other people's . . . He is not just a passive recipient assimilating the norms of concrete, external, organised classes. (1957: 165)

Though these observations seem unremarkable now, they make a stark contrast to Jamieson's descriptions of the pre-modern era:

the intimacy of close association did not necessarily result in empathy, because this was a highly stratified social world in which each knew his or her place in the social order . . . Marrying and having children were economic arrangements and the relationships which resulted were ones in which men were assumed to rule and own women and children. This was sanctioned by religion, law and community norms. (1998: 11)

These descriptions reproduced the common-sense version of 'progress', from a society in which social position was fixed, determined by birth, to a society in which the 'individual' created a unique lived trajectory, unhindered by social mores and restricted only by hugely depleted structural limitations, a version of progress reproduced by one of Bott's informants in 1957:

It might have been simple in the Middle Ages, everything being so definite you know exactly what your place was and did not expect to be anything else. Now it is all uncertain and you don't even know what your place is. (1957: 174)

Bott, working amongst the middle class, was reluctant to correlate class status with extra-familial kin contact. Firth, however, was prepared to reproduce, however apologetically, a sweeping framework in which upper and lower classes were characterised by the greater importance of extra-familial kin, whilst the middle class exemplified the Parsonian nuclear family:

Crudely generalised, such views seem not too implausible. They place the kinship attitudes of the middle classes somewhere between the interest – both co-operative and competitive – in perpetuation of economic and political assets shown by the upper classes and the warm protectiveness of the propertyless working classes. (1969: 16)

Firth concludes that extra-familial kinship amongst the middle class is 'expressive rather than instrumental' (1969: 461–2).

The dismissal of cognatic kinship and the accompanying reduction of English kinship to family and class was halted in the late 1970s and early 1980s with Fox's *The Tory Islanders* (1978), and Strathern's *Elmdon* (1981). Whilst Tory Island kinship provided a framework, manipulation of which could enable the distribution of scarce resources in a harsh setting, Strathern went further in showing that:

Village and kinship together provide images of class. It is not just that they are about particular classes in the direct way in which Elmdoners experience their situation, but they are about class in general. A person's own particular position need not totally determine his view of the overall structure. (1981: 200)

The sociological work that attempted to find correlations between 'family', 'extra-familial kin' and 'class', was thus replaced by an anthropological method sensitive to differences in the meanings of the terms themselves.

Whilst mainstream social anthropology until the middle of the last century concentrated upon the 'other', recent work has attempted to redress this balance by considering the tools of anthropology as similarly 'constructed'. In particular, the 'natural facts' of kinship – of biology and reproduction – have been scrutinised by anthropologists wishing to stress their contingency.[7] This study uses local ideas of relatedness in Newmarket in order to illustrate how kinship looks when the biological 'facts' of pedigree that support it are exposed.

Nature in Newmarket

The idea that relationships with animals can tell us something about relationships between humans is not new within social anthropology, as Evans-Pritchard's comments about the Nuer confirm. Recently, however, the study of animal–human relationships has enjoyed a period of intense attention, partly due to an invigorating cross-fertilisation between academic disciplines, particularly history, philosophy, cultural theory, biology and anthropology.[8] Recent studies of human–animal relationships have consequently shown a greater awareness of changes through time, environmental and political factors, and the place of animals in human systems of discrimination, be they based upon race, class or gender.

The breeding, buying, selling and racing of horses in Newmarket make visible the ideas that govern human relations within racing society. In order to understand this contention, the origin story of the thoroughbred racehorse must be understood. The English thoroughbred is a breed of racehorse which originated with three imported stallions; the Darley Arabian, the Godolphin Arabian and the Byerley Turk, and a number of domestic mares in the late seventeenth and early eighteenth centuries. It has been 'selectively bred' since this time, so that all of the present generation can be traced back to these three stallions through the General Stud Book, which has recorded every mating and its produce since 1791. It is the fastest breed of horse in the world over any distance further than a quarter of a mile. Racing in Britain is concerned almost exclusively with thoroughbred racehorses, which became a specific breed in the era in which racing society began to define itself, the two developing in parallel.

The idea that nature is everywhere and always the same thing and that it always stands in opposition to culture has been dismissed by anthropology. As Strathern states, 'No single meaning can in fact be given to nature or culture in Western thought, there is no consistent dichotomy only a matrix of contrasts' (1980: 177). Ideas of nature to be found in Newmarket include its separation from humans as the object of human efforts directed towards its improvement. The thoroughbred racehorse has been selectively bred for three hundred years, in the belief that racing ability is hereditary and therefore one must 'breed the best to the best to get the best'. Nature, in this context, is perceived as a recalcitrant but talented child who refuses to fulfil its own potential and so must be strongly directed. However, the opposite notion, that animals, particularly horses and dogs, are fundamentally the same as humans, and that all are part of nature, is also present, facilitating an intersubjectivity between the thoroughbred and its human attendants.[9]

In addition to the contextually sensitive ideas of nature in Newmarket, I should add that racehorses are polysemic. In relation to racing society, the racehorse is an ambivalent creature. Not animal, not person, not object, not subject, not entirely artificial and not entirely natural. The obtaining relationship between horses and racing society, in which racehorses are sometimes part of 'nature' to be improved, sometimes part of a 'nature' that includes humans, is comfortable. During fieldwork, processes that encouraged members of racing society to articulate these organising principles included the General Election, the ban on British beef and the bomb threat at the Grand National. More generally, racing society confronts outsiders, including those who bet and attend race meetings, in ways that highlight their own uniqueness. These encounters are discussed in chapter three. However, it was the 'literalising process' (Strathern 1992b: 4–5) implied by the technologies of Artificial Insemination (AI) and cloning which led racing society to explain their ideas about nature with greatest force.

Summary

Chapters two and three of this book describe Newmarket and its inhabitants, and, in particular, those people involved in the production of racing. In chapter three I describe the means by which racing people are reproduced. I concentrate upon the elite of racing society, those who see themselves as 'real' Newmarket families, and claim a familial connection to Newmarket and to racing. A particular family, and their ideas about their own 'pedigrees' and those of others, is described in order to suggest that racing is thought to be 'in the blood'.

Chapters four and five engage with the public side of racing, but go beyond the image presented on television or by the tame racing press. Chapter four is a guided tour of the racecourse, where racing is made public. I discuss segregation on the racecourse, the differences between the variously priced enclosures of the racecourse and their correlation with sumptuary distinctions and dress codes. Chapter five discusses the consumption of horseracing by punters in the betting ring and in Licensed Betting Offices. Betting on horseracing is the dominant form of gambling in Britain.[10]

Chapter six describes a different kind of gamble: the action that takes place in the auction ring, where pedigrees are articulated financially in the sale of yearling thoroughbreds. The purpose of the chapter is to present the ideology of pedigree in the context in which it is most fully played out, amongst horses when they are being treated as objects. Chapter seven describes the apprenticeships experienced by lads in Newmarket.

Chapters eight and nine combine to describe the ideology of pedigree in greater detail. The intersubjectivity between humans and animals that makes pedigree such a powerful organising principle in Newmarket is examined. Chapter eight takes as its starting point Ingold's assertion that, 'Contrary to the normal assumption, the borderline between humans and animals is anything but obvious, clear and immutable' (1988: xii). In chapter nine I identify the 'natural facts' of reproduction assumed by the ideology of pedigree. I examine the sales catalogue as the site of graphically reproduced ideas of heredity and procreation and therefore of kinship, gender and class. The impact of AI upon the racing industry, and the means by which it are opposed are discussed in order to suggest that the blood of racehorses is perceived as gendered, noble, finite and English by its human custodians.

NOTES

1 Huggins (2000) reassesses the role of the Jockey Club and argues that its influence was not felt until much later, 'In reality, up to and sometimes beyond the 1860s, outside Newmarket and a minority of elite courses, the Club was ineffective, with some influence but little actual power, except in parliament . . . But by the later nineteenth century the Jockey Club's response to changing economic imperatives gave it much more influence over major "recognised" meetings' (2000: 174).

2 Huggins dates this extension of influence a little later, 'The first truly effective move to extend the Club's power beyond Newmarket came in 1870 when new rules were introduced and more attempt was made to ensure that the majority of major courses would use them' (2000: 182).

3 Racehorses are still sold in guineas, units of a pound and a shilling. The shilling originally paid the fee of the auctioneer and the auction house.

4 These percentages are calculated from the list of members provided by the *Sporting Life*, on 10 November 1997.

5 Huggins identifies the role of the Jockey Club as Newmarket land-owner as the source of a great deal of its historical influence, 'Any original power the Jockey Club possessed lay almost entirely in the control it exercised over Newmarket . . . all trainers there were required to be licensed. Licenses had been refused to several trainers, putting others under more pressure to conform or lose their livelihood' (2000: 176–7). The same pressure can be seen in operation today

6 At the time of going to press the British Horseracing Board was celebrating the completion of what has been referred to as the 'Go Racing' deal. On 25 June 2001 the BHB website trumpeted, 'BHB reaches historic decisions on Go Racing Contract and Future Funding Plan'. The Go Racing consortium (later renamed 'Attheraces') of Arena Leisure, BSkyB and Channel Four, have made a media rights deal with 49 of Britain's racecourses worth £307 million to racing plus £80 million for marketing (Ashforth 2001: 6). Racing will be televised on a free to air policy in the format pioneered by Channel Four, in order to exploit new digital technology that will enable armchair punting. The relationship between betting turnover and televised coverage is extremely strong, and it is the existing audience of terrestrial viewers that the consortium will hope to build on through marketing and betting innovations. This sort of interactive television betting produces margins of around 10%, the reason for Go Racing's eagerness to invest in racing, the most popular betting medium in Britain and the world (Broen 2001: 7). The effects of this change in the basis of the funding of racing, and in the nature of the betting experience, will be profound, but it will also presumably affect the bloodstock industry if the demand for racing increases and so more horses are needed to service this demand. In essence, the effects of the deal may spread throughout the industry.

7 See also Haraway 1989, Carsten 1999, Strathern 1992a, Bouquet 1993, Yanagisako and Delaney 1995.

8 For an overview of this process see Mullins 1999.

9 A similar arrangement to that described by Schneider, 'The formal category of nature, as it is defined in American culture, includes within it both man and animal. Yet in another context, the meaning of the word "man" is sharply differentiated from the category of nature and set apart from it' (1968: 110).

10 In the year 1998/9 the National Lottery's turnover was £5.2 billion, compared to a turnover of £7 billion for off-course betting (National Lottery Commission 2000).

2 Headquarters

Introduction

The nature of a first encounter with Newmarket is determined to a large extent by the season and the time of day at which the unsuspecting visitor arrives. Arrive on a wintry afternoon and an eerie calm permeates the town, the most energetic activities being shopping, pensioner-style. Late at night, particularly during the summer, the stable lads venture out into the town. One may find a brightly clothed, noisy mass of people moving between the four nightclubs and numerous pubs of the High Street, buzzing with excitement and creating an atmosphere described by locals as 'like a street party'. Arrive in Newmarket early on a spring morning, however, and something of its true purpose will be revealed. The hundreds of racehorses who spend the rest of the day hidden away in the stables that are tucked into every corner of the town take over, and standing amongst the milling horses one is reminded that this is a town in which, as I was told, 'everything is horse'.

This chapter is based upon a discussion of landscape, language and appearance. I shall begin by introducing the town of Newmarket through a historical account of the development of its link with horseracing. This account reflects the dominance of racing voices amongst the historians of Newmarket. I have not found a history of Newmarket told independently from that of horseracing, and my own account reproduces this symbiosis and is thus 'bad' history, but consciously so. This is followed by a description of contemporary Newmarket that attempts to communicate the influence of the racing industry upon its daily and seasonal rhythms.

The landscape of Newmarket and the surrounding countryside will then be discussed in order to illustrate the attempts to improve the environment that appear as the corollary of controlling the processes involved in breeding and training racehorses. The landscape of Newmarket is that of immaculate hedges and white painted fences, raked gravel driveways and chessboard lawns. Attempts to control nature disguise the minimal human ability to explain, and therefore repeat, many of the breeding and training successes thrown up by the industry.

The language of racing, and its capacity to include and exclude, will then be considered. Racing language not only serves to distinguish between insiders and outsiders, but also offers a field of expertise in which knowledge is scarce or even absent. Proficiency in breeding racehorses, perhaps unobtainable, may thus be replaced with fluency in the language associated with this proficiency. As the people called upon to explain why a horse ran badly, jockeys must be experts in this language, or, as champion Frankie Dettori has stated, a jockey 'must be able to bullshit'. Communication maps class relations amongst the insiders of racing society.

The distinction between upper class and working class in Newmarket is resilient. There is no straightforward career path between, for example, working as a lad and training, and the two roles are created as separate social spaces, across which communication and mobility are generally discouraged, as a trainer explained to me:

> The best lads know their place . . . they tell me what I need to know in order to do my job and get on with the rest themselves. This is what good lads should aspire to, just as I aspire to training winners.[1]

Physical appearance, including factors such as weight and body shape, as well as dress, will also be considered. Racing society is obsessed with weight. Part of the explanation for this obsession lies in its importance to those who ride, for whom it is preferable to be below nine stone seven. In addition, the language of weight is a constant preoccupation to those involved in racing due to the attribution of a 'weight' to each horse by the 'handicapper'. The amount of weight carried by a horse in a race is intended to reflect its ability, such that a pound in weight is said to equate to a distance of three lengths, and horses running in a handicap race should all cross the line at the same time if the 'handicap' has been accurate. A horse will go 'up or down in the weights', the handicapper may be 'on top of it', i.e. giving it sufficient weight to prevent it from winning, whilst a winning horse is said to be 'ahead of the handicapper'. Discussions of weight are thus both part of the structure of racing, and also the concern of a society obsessed with appearances.

The chapter is an attempt to account for the means by which racing society reproduces itself within such a self-evidently hierarchical structure, taking into account Willis' insight in relation to working-class kids:

> We need to understand how structures become sources of meaning and determinants of behaviour in the cultural milieu at its own level. Just because there are what we call structural and economic determinants it does not mean that people will unproblematically obey them. (Willis 1977: 171)

Newmarket's history

Running across Newmarket Heath and beyond is an enormous defensive rampart, called the Devil's Dyke. Excavations of the Dyke have revealed something of the early history of the Heath. People frequently thought that I was studying the Dyke, on the grounds that anthropology was 'about digging up bones'. The past is important to Newmarket people, and is constantly employed as a source of justification for the present, as in this description by the *Racing Post* bloodstock correspondent Tony Morris:

Racing has developed from a pastime for the few to a massive global industry since Herod, Matchem and Eclipse established their reputations at Newmarket. Forty generations on from the founding fathers of the breed, the town's unique status is preserved, its history and traditions preserved, its commitment to the sport and the industry more vigorous than ever. (1998: 4)

Newmarket's history is perpetually told through its association with thorough-bred horseracing and royalty, thus the first figure of Newmarket history is that of Boadicea, Queen of the Iceni, the chariot-racing Roman rebel of the first century. Heath opinion states that lasses still model themselves upon her warrior-like tendencies. Boadicea was based in Exning, a small village just outside Newmarket, and it is thought that she used the Heath for hunting and racing. The origin story of Newmarket itself has two versions, the romantic and the pragmatic. Morris cites the 'wooing and winning' of Cassandra de l'Isle by Sir Richard d'Argentine in the thirteenth century as initiating 'a truly momentous sequence of events' (1998: 4), whilst Newmarket historian Robert Lyle emphasises a plague that forced the relocation of the population of Exning and the establishment of a 'new market' (1945: 2).

From romance to disease, historical accounts of the growth of Newmarket's importance to the racing industry progress via a consideration of royal patronage, focusing particularly upon James I and Charles II. James I's first visit is dated as 27 February 1605 by Lyle, 'From that moment began Newmarket's rise from a little wood built hamlet to the metropolis of the turf' (1945: 4); Charles II's influence is also highlighted by Morris:

An accomplished horseman, he rode in races, winning his share, shifted the royal stud to Newmarket, had a palace and racing stables erected there, and turned the town into the unofficial capital of England, with the entire court in residence there for long stretches of time. His neglect for his nation and fondness for East Anglian fun were neatly summarised by the sardonic poet Alexander Pope: Newmarket's glory rose, as Britain's fell. (1998: 4)

Historical portraits tend to linger over Charles II's affair with Nell Gwynne, whose house was apparently attached to the palace via an underground tunnel, and the sporting exploits of the King and his followers, as in this description by the nineteenth-century historian John Hore:

Take him all round he was a thorough English sportsman, who could hold his own against all-comers in the chase, on the racecourse, at angling, shooting, hawking, billiards, tennis; none could excel him in his morning walk from Whitehall to Hampton Court. (1886: 93)

Charles II even took his nickname, 'Old Rowley', from his favourite horse. Contemporary Newmarket historians discover in their predecessors the qualities they admire in themselves, qualities admired by all Newmarket men, who should express their masculinity by being charismatic, 'sporting', good horsemen and successful lovers.

The topography of Newmarket and in particular of the Heath, combined with a proximity to both Cambridge and London, promoted royal patronage initially stimulated by the hunting and hawking possibilities on offer. The town's association with racing was consolidated by the relocation of the Jockey Club from the Star and Garter in Pall Mall, to the Coffee Room on the High Street in 1752. The Jockey Club gradually became the governing body of racing, resolving disputes and determining the rules of racing, as described in the introduction. Newmarket's status as the 'HQ' of racing since the eighteenth century has been subject to fashions, such that, at times, the Heath was considered too hard, the climate too drying to provide good ground on which to train, leading to injuries and lameness. However, this association has been resilient, and has reached a peak in recent decades.

Contemporary Newmarket

More than two thousand racehorses are currently trained on the sixty miles of Newmarket gallops by sixty-eight trainers. Racehorses travel between gallops and stables on the fifty-seven miles of 'horsewalks' (concrete paths that criss-cross the town, with trigger-operated traffic lights at rider height at every road crossing). Despite the horsewalks, racehorses can also be seen on the roads every morning, weaving in and out of cars and jogging along paths reluctantly deserted by pedestrians. Newmarket residents complain bitterly that whilst the horsewalks are strictly maintained the roads themselves are pitted and in disrepair. As the horses head for the gallops and the commuters head to work, the antagonism between the two kinds of road users is often in evidence. Petulant horseriders smoking cigarettes cross roads in front of cars without acknowledgement, assuming that drivers will give way. Cars squeeze through lines of horses, separating stable mates and causing panic amongst the horses, before careering off at top speed in anger at having been held up yet again.

Surveying the town from the top of Warren Hill, one sees an expanse of trimmed green, scarred by artificial gallops, separated by white plastic rails and dotted with hundreds of horses and riders in all colours. The sight is suggestive of order on the brink of chaos. Horses are easily startled and 'shy' at anything from puddles to suspiciously shaped leaves. Moreover, when one horse 'shies' in this way, the adjacent horses will often follow suit, the fright travelling like a shock wave across the Heath, occasionally dislodging riders in the process. Riders are particularly vulnerable whilst waiting for their turn to travel up the gallop, when horses become excited in anticipation of their run. On winter mornings, when the turf is frozen and the horses must use the artificial surfaces, backlogs of circling horses build up at the bottom of the gallop, like queues of skiers waiting for a place on the lift. The potential for chaos is enormous, and yet most mornings pass without incident, the rhythmic movement of horses travelling up and down and to and from the gallops that is repeated six days a week, in all weather. Rates of attrition on the Heath are higher for horses than humans, although there were two human fatalities on the gallops whilst I was riding. The Jockey Club provides emergency phones on the Heath, as well as two horse ambulances and a carcass collection service. Newmarket in the morning is a surreal place, buzzing with the activities of hundreds of centaur-like figures, nonchalant but serious, as though unaware of the danger and absurdity of answering rich men's whims by teaching racehorses to run faster.

Contemporary Newmarket fields, on average, just under a third of all British race winners in a season, and these wins are often concentrated in the better races, referred to as 'Group' races. In 1996, for example, Newmarket-trained horses won 72% of English Group One races and 60% of Group races overall. They also won all five of the English Classics (Jockey Club Annual Report 1997: 42). Newmarket is conscious of its status as a flagship and centre of excellence. Despite the rivalries that exist between individual yards in Newmarket and all of the other training centres, such as Lambourn, competition between racing centres is mainly along the axis of Newmarket versus the rest. Yard rivalries may be ritually resolved in organised football matches, or less formally in scraps after closing time. Rivalry between Newmarket and other training centres focuses upon results and the quality of the lads. A Northern trainer told me that: 'Newmarket lads are the worst in the world, ham-fisted yobbos', whilst Newmarket lads told me that other lads had no idea of the modern job and were: 'playing a different game to us', seeing themselves as the standard-setters for the industry.

Landscape

In Britain, the best example of a town which is intimately identified with sport, and owes its raison d'être and visual character to it, is, in my view, Newmarket, home of British horse racing . . . My own impressions are that it is somewhat more 'horsy' than Saratoga, New York.

(Bale 1994: 137)

Every possible resource necessary in the training of racehorses is available within the town, from two racecourses and the gallops to the three public equine swimming pools. Newmarket is the focus of veterinary research of relevance to racing, in particular, the Animal Health Trust, the Equine Fertility Unit and the Horserace Forensic Laboratory. In addition, it houses Tattersall's sales ring in Park Paddocks where many of the most expensive thoroughbreds are sold, and the British Racing School where jockeys and lads are taught their trade. Newmarket also boasts the Jockey Club Rooms, five saddlers, a specialist cobbler, several corn and hay merchants, manure disposal services, specialist accountants and solicitors, and farriers. Every corner turned in Newmarket reveals further examples of the dominance of racing in the town. Residential streets conceal stable gates that swing open first thing in the morning, spewing strings of racehorses into the centre of the town. Less directly, the four nightclubs and numerous pubs and restaurants service the needs of both lads and also trainers who wish to entertain their owners, the town centre generally providing the focus for the former, and the outlying villages that of the latter.

Even those retail outlets and services with no apparent connection with rac-ing maintain links of sorts through their names: 'The Gift Horse' (gift shop), 'Golden Horses' (take-away), 'Chifney's' (restaurant). Others feature menus or advertising slogans which make reference to racing, such as the menu in the White Hart that offers dishes 'in the starting gate' (first courses), or 'Derbys' (main courses). Mobile telephone companies urge customers to 'Place your bets on us!', the football team is, of course, called the 'Jockeys'. The Clocktower Cafe pays photographic homage to the famous racing people who have break-fasted on fry-ups throughout its history. The local newspaper, *The Newmarket Journal*, advertises itself as, 'A Thoroughbred staying the distance in the New-market field for more than 124 years'. Ubiquitous in all shops and pubs are the inevitable racing prints, seeming particularly incongruous in the Wimpy on the High Street, where, it is joked, some of their less-fortunate subjects may be consumed.

The training stables themselves differ in scale and particular layout, but often share the common features of courtyards and clocks. The structure of the courtyard enables the gregarious horses to see each other, and also the head lad to keep an eye on his juniors. Just as the High Street is headed by a huge clocktower, clocks loom large in the yards themselves, governing the activities of horses and lads. Horses are creatures of extreme habit, hypersensitive to any change in their routine, such that a feed an hour late or early can induce colic in the most fragile. Yards strive for efficiency, slow lads are continually chided for falling behind and holding everyone up. 'Going like clockwork, sir' was a favourite response to trainers enquiring of the lads as to how the morning was progressing.

As feeding presents a possible opportunity for the security of the yard to be compromised through the introduction of drugs which may 'stop' a horse, feed stores are locked and feeding is the task of the trainer himself or his trusted head lad. The trainer is responsible for, and must explain, the presence of any illegal substances in the samples of any of the horses in his charge. The Jockey Club may enforce the ultimate sanction of a 'warning off', should the trainer fail to provide a convincing explanation as to the origin of the drug in question. The fortunes of the yard can be judged according to the state of the paintwork on the stable doors, and by the appearance of the lads in the yard. The most successful yards have colour co-ordinated jackets, caps, rugs, bandages and stable doors, the least successful make do with peeling paint and whatever moth-eaten jacket and hat come to hand.

Riding on the gallops suggested to me that a familiarity with the landscape was expected and even demanded. I often had no idea where I was going when told that we were heading for 'the back of the flat', or 'the woodchip', names referring to particular gallops that were learnt by experience. Thus my instructions were often something like: 'Trot round the rings first, then go half way round the sand, canter up to the four furlong marker, pull up and come back down the woodchip.' Which sand? Where is the four furlong marker? Which woodchip? Am I in control? I remember the exasperation of my colleagues when I asked for directions, before I had worked out which paths were referred to in each vague instruction. As Gow found in Western Amazonia:

Such imprecision has a precise meaning. Once you already know where 'Over there' is, or where old Julio Felipe is making his garden, you can locate the spatial meaning of the incident. If you do not know, how could it matter? You, as a listener, are not implicated in the landscape in which these things happened, so can only relate to them in the abstract. (1995: 51)

In keeping with Gow's suggestion, old-timers preferred to give instructions in the form of 'you know, where we took the new filly for her first blow', or, even better, 'you know, where Sophie fell off!' In most cases these instructions depended upon a perspective on the landscape gained from horseback.

Although the town and the surrounding gallops are the focus of these activities, it could be said that 'Newmarket' is equally the network formed by the stud farms and racing stables of the surrounding countryside. Horses are present in almost every conceivable form wherever one looks in the town itself, in sculptures, shop names, paintings and in the flesh, but the surrounding environment is no less a reflection of the monoculture of the area.

Studs, in particular, require more land than training stables where horses are generally permanently stabled. Villages within a ten-mile radius of Newmarket, such as Cheveley, Dullingham, Exning and Fordham, house many of the forty-two 'Newmarket' studs. The landscape changes once the outskirts of the town are reached, the unsegregated land use of the town itself giving way to the striped green expanses, clipped hedgerows, painted fences and sweeping driveways of the stud farm.

Driving from Newmarket to Cheveley one exchanges urban landscape and the purpose-built artificiality of the gallops for some of the neatest country-side imaginable. During the breeding season in the spring, in particular, the hedgerows and verges of all the major studs in Cheveley are pristine, as if to say: 'We humans are in control here.' The fields are cleared daily of droppings by enormous vacuum cleaners mounted on tractors, leaving a striped effect like a cricket pitch or bowling green, a reminder of the obsession with the removal of those products that betray the presence of horses. Stud grooms, where possible, like to put mares and foals in the field adjacent to the car park so that visitors will see them on arrival, and thus be reminded of the purpose of paying their bills, whether 'their' foal has been born or not.

A stud groom explained the importance of the appearance of the perimeter of the stud in the following terms:

> Punters need to believe that they can send their mare to us and she will be safe, for a start. But just as important, we want to reassure them that we take at least some of the guessing out of a mating. They have to have confidence in us.

By calling the client a 'punter', the stud groom reveals the risk shared by betting on and breeding racehorses. He also implies that by mowing and clipping, the stud is communicating its ability to manipulate the environment, a message that he hopes owners may extend to the process of breeding. The pitiful inadequacy of this gesture is a reflection of how much influence the stud can actually exert upon the outcome of a mating. The landscapes of the countryside surrounding Newmarket have thus become an analogue for the genes that the stud farms are attempting to map.[2]

Language and communication

In order to 'belong' in Newmarket it is necessary to be able to 'talk racing', or to at least 'talk horse', as Jack Leach notes:

> Get a crowd of racing people together and they will talk horses for sure and with such extreme gravity that many parties to it forget that racing is a sport and sometimes confuse themselves with normal people. (1970: 21)

Fieldwork taught me that when racing people get together they do indeed talk about racing, often in an incomprehensible language, filled with references to horses, people and places of which I had little or no knowledge. I was fortunate in being able to 'talk horse' before I arrived in Newmarket, and it was onto this related, but simpler, language that I grafted the pieces of racing vocabulary that I managed to pick up in the field.

The most commonly identified purpose of jargon is to exclude outsiders from that which does not concern them whilst enabling insiders to communicate with greater efficiency, as Burke states: 'The use of jargon is one of the most potent means of inclusion and exclusion' (1995: 14). In Newmarket, however, any practical benefit gained by excluding outsiders is overshadowed by an ideology of exclusivity as intrinsically valuable. As Barth's analysis of Baktaman ritual suggests, 'it is their secrecy and exclusiveness, not their potential for enlightenment, that give them value' (1975: 221). Status in Newmarket is often determined by access. Access to the training yard is determined by wealth. Access to the Jockey Club is subject to wealth, success and pedigree. The more exclusive the institution, the more highly it is valued by Newmarket racing society. The style and content of the language is also significant, because communication is not only intended to exclude, but also to create the impression that the interlocuters are in possession of greater power than is actually the case. The content of the language serves to mystify the outsider or newcomer by implying that the speaker holds powers over uncontrollable processes.

The language of racing thus offers opportunities for mystification on two levels: primarily through the use of a specialised vocabulary, and secondarily through discussions of whole relationships that are taken for granted by racing society. Thus, discussions of 'stayers', 'sprinters', 'tongue straps', 'blinkers' and 'prickers' initiate the distancing process of excluding outsiders, a process that may be completed by whole conversations based around 'the influence of the going on a field of maiden hurdlers with good flat form but unproven jumping pedigrees'. Whilst the specialised language of equipment for horse and jockey seems warranted, much of the discussion of the taken-for-granted relationships within racing are contradictory, and even absurd. The complexity of the vocabulary and style of the language of racing conceals the uncomfortable truth that fluency will not enable the speaker to predict which horse will win a race or which stallion will produce champion racehorses. I would suggest that the language of racing serves to conceal the unknowable aspects of the industry, replacing proficiency of action with that of speech. This explains the tendency of racing conversations to alternate between highly technical and entirely mystical notions, the one often unfamiliar, the other completely untestable. Like Baktaman discussions of ritual, racing conversations are exercises in mystification, 'instead of developing a "theory" of growth and health and fertility, the Baktaman develop a "mystery" of these themes' (Barth 1975: 221).

Successful communication of accomplishment in racing is role-dependent. Thus lads learn at the British Racing School or during their apprenticeship that 'keeping schtum is usually the best option'; jockeys speak in clichés, changing horses' and owners' names, distance or other variable whilst keeping interpretative variables fixed, and trainers speak with self-assured composure, slowly, whimsically, often turning the question back onto the interviewer, delighting in their own cunning. In all cases, as if to prevent the realisation that nothing definitive can be stated with complete certainty regarding the ability of a horse, information is restricted. In this way, the horse's performance cannot contradict pre-race statements, thus undermining the role of trainer and jockey, and explanatory 'space' is always left in order to accommodate whichever excuse may be called into play to account for the horse's poor run.

Jockeys' explanations of failure invoke the variables of distance, ground and style of running, '(S)he needs a trip (further) / (S)he didn't stay. (S)he didn't like the ground, needs more cut / it was too soft. (S)he needs blinkers / to be held up / to be in front.' The vast proportion of debriefings after a race take this form. Explanations such as 'The horse was slower than the others / not fit / "dogged it" (gave up)', are avoided because the jockey hopes to retain the ride and these explanations are implicitly critical of either the trainer or his horse. These explanations are particularly avoided within earshot of the owner, since they may prompt the sale or movement of the horse out of the trainer's yard. The trainer may receive one explanation from the jockey and give the owner another, less fundamental excuse, suggesting a problem that can be solved 'at home'.[3]

'Talking racing' in Newmarket involves displaying a familiarity with the significant places, horses, people and relationships that exist locally and throughout the racing world. All discussions of racing involve casual references to individuals whose fame rarely extends beyond this limited social world. Particular sentiments and modes of expression are role-specific, and thus capable of expressing the relations that obtain between different sections of Newmarket's insiders. Lads are seen but not heard, jockeys are heard but only within a strict framework that does not permit them to compromise the position of the trainer to whom they refer as 'the boss', or 'the guv'nor'. Trainers impose restrictions on who *hears* what they say, in order to limit the damage of ambitious predictions.[4] Communication prefigures association as an indicator of social equality. It is therefore possible to map social equivalence by analysing interactions.

It is amongst racing pundits that 'talking racing' assumes its most comprehensive and thus most absurd composition. Calculations as to which horse will win a race are routinely undertaken in the light of comments such as: 'Well, if you ran the race five times you could get five different winners', or 'It's a wide open race and it just depends whether the filly is having a bad day or not.' Pundits ponder unknowable factors, and in doing so sound knowledgeable and well informed. They can 'talk racing'.

Appearance and embodiment or 'the body for the job' (Bourdieu 1984: 191)

There are two obvious body shapes valued by Newmarket racing society, and they can be described in mutually opposing terms. A friend who visited me in Newmarket, and commented that: 'It's just like Gulliver's Travels', was referring to the contrast between the body shapes of the jockey or work rider and the trainer. Bourdieu's argument that class is literally embodied, is almost too obviously illustrated in Newmarket. The ideal jockey is short, thin, tough, quiet, hunched, reticent. The ideal trainer is tall, elegant, straight-backed, self-assured and charismatic.

The lad's body is not valued at all, and is generally lightweight, but not sufficiently so to be a jockey. His hands are rough and large, his face chapped and windburnt. Lads often look tired from their early mornings and late nights, but they are not credited with any definitive qualities. When I asked my trainer the favourable shape for a lad he replied: 'Nondescript'. And so, 'one can begin to map out a universe of class bodies, which (biological accidents apart) tends to reproduce in its specific logic the universe of the social structure' (Bourdieu 1984: 193).

The oppositions between the important bodies in Newmarket extend to the culinary preferences that enable the body to express these differences. Trainers were often associated with expensive and scarce foods, which are difficult to prepare and perhaps an 'acquired taste', for example, seafood, particularly shellfish, game, salads, olive oil, balsamic vinegar, high-quality preserved meats and vegetables, champagne, gin and tonic, and whisky. Jockeys are limited to small, low-fat meals of chicken, fish, dry toast, salad without dressings, black tea, mineral water and, occasionally, champagne. Lads eat crisps, tinned soups, sliced bread, chocolate and take-aways and drink beer and fizzy drinks. The prevalence of smoking amongst all of the groups is stunning, and was often associated with weight control. It was suggested to me that genetic engineering had been extended to humans in Newmarket, but of course the body is worked on by society rather than being simply biologically determined. The sixteen-year-old son of a former jockey, for example, who weighed 4 stone 4 lbs fully clothed, and had gone straight into a yard at fifteen, told me that he would much rather have finished school.

Jockeys were originally boys, thrown up onto horses at a time during which a premium was placed on weight rather than strength. Racing has become increasingly tactical and modern jockeys must be strong as well as lightweight. Strong jockeys can 'anchor' keen racehorses at the beginning of the race in order to preserve their strength for a fast, hopefully winning finish. In addition, a jockey must be able to 'ride a strong finish', squeezing the last ounce of effort out of his horse by pushing with his hands and legs, and by using his whip. Modern jockeys are thus incredibly strong, fit and athletic, capable of riding out in the morning as well as riding six races in the afternoon, all on a negative calorie count. Naturally lightweight jockeys have less of a struggle than those who are tall or heavy, but almost all jockeys have to 'waste', a combination of dieting and sweating, that is potentially debilitating. Ex-jockeys told me that their appetites were permanently affected by their need to waste. In one case the jockey had gained four stone when he gave up race riding through bingeing, returning to ten stone through a diet of oysters, jalapeno peppers and raw onions. This individual had retained something of an obsession with his weight, and told me that he had found himself disgusting when he weighed fourteen stone.

The most recent high-profile case of a jockey experiencing problems with weight was that of Walter Swinburn, nicknamed 'the Choirboy' because of his angelic looks. Swinburn's high-profile fall from grace was attributed to an eating disorder and a resulting intolerance of alcohol. After a near-fatal fall in Hong Kong in February of 1996, Swinburn lost control of his weight, culminating in an assault on the owner of a popular Newmarket Italian restaurant. In his defence, Swinburn said:

Wasting does get you down and I was fasting for two days and then eating. When you haven't eaten for two days, you suddenly eat too much. I want to get back to eating like normal people. (Morreau and Taylor 1997: 1)

Similarly, jockey Richard Pitman told journalists that:

the thought of going into another sauna to lose weight makes him physically sick . . . 'I always had it in my mind that I would ride until I was 30 but I couldn't continue to put myself through that regime of keeping myself so light, it wasn't natural to be that thin'. (Smurthwaite 1997d: 22)

The health food shop in Newmarket's shopping centre was packed with weight loss products, and energy supplements. I used vials of guarana root in order to give a boost of energy for the early mornings, which were apparently very popular amongst lads, jockeys, and those members of racing society who had no practical need to regulate their weight but were still obsessed with dieting, yoghurt energy drinks and wonder drugs. Perhaps these members of racing society were modelling themselves upon the racehorse itself – lean, fit and muscular, thus making sure that the racehorse could be seen as created in the image of its 'connections'.

Jockeys' bodies are routinely damaged by the accidents common to race riding, particularly over jumps. The death of jump jockey Richard Davis in 1996 prompted an inquiry into safety, but the foregone conclusion was that riding over jumps is a potentially fatal occupation. Jockeys routinely break bones and speak of their injuries in terms of how long they will take to return 'to the saddle'. Flat jockey Lorcan Wyer, for example, was kicked in the face during a fall, and suffered a smashed cheekbone, a split palate from the top to the bottom of his mouth, a fractured pelvis and collarbone, two broken eye sockets and a broken jaw. He returned to riding after three months, and said:

I don't want to sound like a punch-drunk jump jockey full of bravado but I don't feel my confidence has been affected in any way. More often than not this game gives you up before you give up the game, but, though it's a brave shot for me to say it, I don't think that's happened yet. (O'Ryan 1997: 10)[5]

Retired jump-jockeys to whom I spoke cited injury as the reason behind the end of their career, and always attributed to others a loss of 'bottle'.

Dress

Physical differences amongst racing society that betray class affiliations are embellished by the additional markers of dress. An obsessive preoccupation with weight extends to all sections of society in Newmarket, but those who ride face the particular challenge of wearing appropriate clothing, which is tight and unforgiving. Jodhpurs and chaps are tight, following the contours of the body in order to prevent the chaffing which loose material generates as it accumulates between the body and the horse or saddle. On the Heath, jockeys often wear jeans and boots, and brightly coloured jackets, perhaps emblazoned with a prestigious international meeting such as The Breeders Cup. They wear jeans because very little of their leg will be in contact with the horse at any time. Trainers wear jodhpurs because their legs are long, and they have long stirrups. On the Heath, which is really the domain of the horse and jockey or lad, the trainers look ridiculous, they do not have the right body in this context. The absurdity of the trainer out of his element is completed by his horse, referred to as his 'hack', that is usually of a different type to the thoroughbreds he helps patrol. Hacks must go calmly away from their stable mates so that the trainer may gain a vantage point from which to watch his string. They must then stand motionless whilst the other horses gallop by, something few thoroughbreds would tolerate. Thus the hack is often a thicker set type.

Trainers on the Heath employ two techniques in order to deflect the impression that they are, in fact, out of place. The first of these is that attempted by the more confident trainer, who seeks to make a virtue of his physical difference, by riding flashy, spotted or patchy ponies whilst wearing colourful and outlandish clothes which jockeys or lads would 'not be seen dead in'.[6] Alternatively, the confident trainer may adopt the traditional role of trainer, wearing breeches modelled on the fashions of circa 1930, combined with a dark hacking jacket and hat, on a sombre and solid coloured large hack, probably a retired racehorse. His tack is English whilst the outlandish trainer may prefer to take a chance with a Western saddle.

In opposition to those trainers who seek to make a virtue out of necessity are the actions of those who detract from their discomfort in this setting by being extremely casual, thus dissociating themselves from any active attempt to fit in, as though preserving the excuse that should they try, they also could move unnoticed amongst the jockeys and lads. These trainers are scruffy, and may have one glove, a cigarette, a scruffy old hack of indeterminate age, breed and colour, stirrups of unequal lengths, and no riding skill whatsoever. One morning, as I stood on the Heath with a scruffy trainer on his mangy old hack a traditional trainer who had just won the Derby rode over and berated him for his appearance. When ignored, the traditional trainer found purchase in a hole in my friend's jodhpurs and tore them from hip to knee. He rode away saying, 'Get yourself some new jodhpurs. You're a disgrace to the Heath!'

The difficulties of the trainer on the Heath should not suggest that the clothes worn by jockeys and lads, those who are in their element, are somehow devoid of symbolic impetus. Lads on the Heath often wear caps that bear the trainer's colours, and may also wear uniform jackets. Lads with aspirations to race riding wear their stirrups far shorter than those who have given up this dream. Most obviously, jockeys wear the silks of the owner of the horse they are riding during a race. 'Colours' are unique to their particular owner, and still retain an element of the significance of the livery worn by servants from which they originated. They signal ownership of the horse, and an element of control over the jockey, who must doff his cap to the owner as he enters the paddock and the winner's enclosure. As Hoffman states, 'dress communication is always a mirror of the social condition' (1984: 11).

The importance of clothing also extends to that of the horse in Newmarket. Whilst it has been suggested that clothes fuse the biological and cultural bodies, merging private and public (Tarlo 1996), in Newmarket, animal and human bodies are also merged. Riding a horse fuses the two bodies so that it is difficult to establish where one ends and the other begins, both are wearing whatever either is wearing. All racehorses wear rugs during the winter when they are ridden out, which bear the trainer's monogram. Often they may need several rugs as well as the towel and pads which fit beneath the saddle. All of these items must be put on in a specific order, and folded back from the shoulder in accordance with strict conventions, which vary between trainers and must be learnt. The horse must always be immaculately clean, as I discovered when I left the yard with straw in my horse's tail. The trainer for whom I was riding jumped from his horse and brushed it clean, saying sharply, 'Do you want me to be the laughing stock of the village?' The horse is thus an extension of the rider's body as are clothes, but the horse is also an extension of the trainer whose reputation and monogram he carries. This explains the role of clothing in Newmarket, which is important because, 'clothes are frequently perceived as expressions and even extensions of the people who wear them' (Tarlo 1996: 16).

The horse's clothing reflects its status throughout its career. The racehorse is naked whilst a foal, and before it is sold as a yearling. Once a yearling, the racehorse is most closely worked upon by its human handlers, and begins to wear rugs in order to control growth of its coat. These rugs must be tolerated and mark a point from which the horse will wear rugs for the majority of the rest of its career. Only rarely are racehorses left 'naked', even when stabled. One of the horses in our yard was adept at removing his rugs during the night, after which he would delicately pull all of the fluff from one of his woollen blankets with his teeth. When his lass found him 'naked' each morning she would blush, as though he was being inappropriate in some way, and say: 'Oh gosh, he's undressed himself again!' Perhaps the most significant horse clothing of all is the rug presented to the winners of big races; usually brightly coloured and bearing the name of the race and its sponsor, the horse carries its status on its back.

What of those members of racing society who are not giving away their status as such by riding a horse or shouting at people on the Heath? It is still possible to discern racing elements amongst the shoppers in Newmarket. Racing society in mufti does not submit to sociological exposition, but is rather an overall impression forced upon the observer, as Le Wita found in Paris, where 'ethnographic observation did for its part offer an appreciable glimpse of the "existential reality" of the bourgeoisie' (1994: 25).

The ability to recognise racing society grows from an accumulation of small experiences which gradually fuse into a single semiotic pattern. For example, watching the tall, middle-aged man who drives his Mercedes Estate (the Mercedes is the trainers' car) along the High Street, swings into a miraculously appearing parking space and rushes into the bank. The first impression is of his height, which is above average. He is wearing a yellow V-neck pullover (definitely no logos or brand names), and light moleskin trousers, a solid blue shirt, open at the neck and suede Gucci loafers (essential). In addition, he has a healthy, but not too obvious tan, straight white teeth and smells clean but not of scent. He is in a hurry, does not lock his car and leaves it running. His expression is preoccupied, although when, as is inevitable, he is hailed by an acquaintance, he breaks into a smile, shakes hands and offers excuses to hurry on with his mission.

Details are obviously where the fine distinctions within racing society can be made. New shoes are not a good sign, whilst a trainer friend spent a week in mourning for his deck shoes which were pinched whilst he was in the sauna at the gym, 'You know Rebecca, I'd just got them to that perfect worn stage, I hadn't undone the laces *ever*.' New clothes are also undesirable, clothes that are worn in, without being scruffy, are favoured. New clothes may provoke some sort of judgement by others, whilst older clothes go unnoticed. New clothes imply an investment of energy and taste that reveals something of the wearer, whilst older clothes do not express an active choice which can then be scrutinised, and possibly found wanting. The detail on a shirt can be significant, particularly the collar which must be wide cut and should not be button-down. Ties are silk, and often decorated with horses' heads, bits or stirrups, in a style that echoes not only equestrian links but also the traditional or classic, 'The obsession of the gentleman is to avoid all extremes at all times' (Lurie 1983: 130). The penchant for the traditional extends throughout racing and reflects an innate conservatism that naturalises class membership by making it apparently effortless.

The best place to see racing women is in Waitrose on the High Street. A trainer's wife described her diminishing fortunes to me thus: 'I used to shop in Waitrose, but now I go to Tescos'; I nodded in sympathy. Newmarket is the smallest population in Britain capable of supporting a Waitrose, and its stock reflects its place in racing life as a source of food for racing families who have to entertain visiting owners at short notice. Thus the freezers are full of vast seafood platters, to be defrosted at a moment's notice, and ridiculously luxurious desserts, with curled caramel trimmings and fantastic price tags. Racing women are usually what I was repeatedly told was 'petite', which seemed to mean short and slim. Many trainers' wives ride out, thus in the morning they are to be found in boots and jodhpurs, short jackets and perhaps a neck scarf. Their boots are particularly well fitted, and old enough to have adopted the precise curve of the ankle and calf without being the least bit scruffy. The leather is soft and well treated, self-evidently expensive. They are usually picking up a few rushed things in the morning such as butter or eggs, orange juice and bread.

Later in the day jodhpurs have been replaced by jeans, and, as in Paris, 'there are jeans and jeans' (Le Wita 1994: 64). Women's jeans are tailored and cut fairly tight in the ankle. Jeans in Newmarket are certainly not unisex, thus whilst men may wear Levi's or Wrangler, women told me that they preferred Moschino, and a specifically 'feminine' cut. During my stay in Newmarket the staple top of the racing woman, the polo neck, had been embellished with tiny patterns, often of animals or flowers. This style was championed by Lesley Graham, the female presenter of Channel 4 Racing, and trainer's wife. These polo necks were sold from a stand at a Fair held just before Christmas on the racecourse, which sold out. Jewellery is simple, restricted to discreet earrings (not hoops), watch and wedding ring. Handbags are leather, plain but smart, again of good quality and classic rather than fashionable shape. The same rules apply to shoes. Jackets are Puffas or Goretex, often of a strong single colour, rather than earth tones, which are avoided due to their association with the waxed jacket that has been appropriated by people outside racing and is thus rejected.

The dilemma of the racing man or woman is that the rules of their dress code dictate that they must look wealthy, whilst at the same time remaining discreet and understated, because being wealthy and displaying wealth are aspects of two opposing value systems. The motivation to express wealth is particularly strong in racing society where success translates directly into wealth, via the mechanism of prize money. The fine line between being obviously wealthy without appearing vulgar is negotiated by the wearing of items of high quality but of conservative styles, thus appearing effortlessly and therefore 'naturally' of high class. The display of wealth thus becomes almost accidental, and the desired effect is achieved. Where brash styles are preferred, wealth is obviously on display, reflecting the cardinal sin of racing society: insecurity. In order to function successfully as a badge of high class, wealth must literally be worn lightly.

Conclusion

The reproduction of the two important types of body in Newmarket is facilitated both genetically and socially. Jockeys' children are more likely to be short and lightweight, whilst trainers' children are often tall and well built. However, both are likely to 'inherit' their father's occupation because of the expectations generated by their involvement in racing. This chapter also introduced themes of landscape, language and appearance. The introduction to the landscape of Newmarket and its environs identified a concern with the improvement of nature. Controlling nature yields prestige and status through selective breeding which enables racehorse breeders to claim credit for the English thoroughbred as 'man's noblest creation'.

The specialised language of racing can serve to exclude outsiders, but it also reflects distinctions within racing society. Communication maps class boundaries in Newmarket, and terms of address, silence and body language all reflect negotiations between classes. In its most extreme form, lads of all ages may be classified as children by their trainers, in accordance with the Victorian principle whereby they are 'best seen but not heard'. In addition, racing language serves to obfuscate the scarcity or even absence of knowledge. In keeping with the emphasis on appearances, competence in racing talk can compensate for an absence of real knowledge. Throughout my fieldwork, maintaining the appearance of confidence and expertise got me into all sorts of interesting situations for which I was entirely unqualified. However, although I could 'talk racing' or at least 'talk horses' with no effort at all, my body was on the margins of acceptability, being what was described as 'horizontally challenged'.

Although I was sufficiently light to ride racehorses, I was seen as overweight and therefore desirous of every weight loss pill and potion available in Newmarket. I received tips about weight loss constantly, and was practically force fed a variety of high-energy, low-fat supplements whilst working on the stud and on the training yard. Whenever I was under physical pressure, such as when a horse was pulling with me, or generally misbehaving, I would hear the inevitable comment, shouted from the following horse: 'That'll sort you out!' On an early morning gallop up a hill, Bill, who was on the lead horse, complained about the sun having been low and in his eyes, whilst Mick, who was behind me, retorted that he had been fine because my backside had eclipsed the sun.

The obsession with appearance amongst racing society is one mechanism by which 'pedigree' is elicited from the racehorse. It arises from the importance of embodied knowledge as the mechanism by which pedigree is translated into class. Knowledge is expressed as talent, not learnt, and therefore, an individual's future is envisaged in accordance with his breeding. This is the 'natural' order in Newmarket, and belonging there depends upon knowing one's place and on perpetuating the mechanisms guaranteeing both that place and also the hierarchy of which it is a part. The following chapter examines these connections in more detail.

NOTES

1 A similar separation was found amongst agricultural workers in East Anglia by Howard Newby in the 1970s. Interestingly, it is again the system of inheritance that appears to support the division of labour responsible for the character described by Newby as 'the deferential worker', 'most farmers have not achieved the ownership of their land or their position as employers by demonstrating their expertise in agricultural skills but because they have inherited their property and the rights and powers attached to it from their fathers. Their dominant position in the local social structure is therefore based upon the almost unquestioned acceptance of the right of the farmer to acquire his farm on the basis of birth. Since the possibility of upward mobility from farm worker to farmer is so remote in East Anglia as to be virtually non-existent, employer and employee roles tend to be ascribed rather than achieved' (1979: 420). In the case of the trainer, the inheritance of the *means* to train is de-emphasised, and what is stressed is the inheritance of the *ability* to train.

2 As Bender observes, 'the landscape is never inert, people engage with it, re-work it, appropriate it and contest it. It is part of the way in which identities are created and disputed, whether as individual, group or nation state' (1993: 14).

3 This is just one of the mechanisms by which unsuccessful trainers remain unsuccessful. Forced to retain useless horses rather than forfeit their training fee, they run hopeless races and cement their association with losers. The sale of even a useless horse produces a time of insecurity for the trainer during which he faces the potentially disastrous possibility that the horse may not be replaced. As I was told, 'Better a useless horse with a good paying owner than no horse at all.' Uselessness is, of course, relative.

4 The significance of the information withheld by the trainer does not reside in its practical value, but in the fact that it is concealed, as in Bellman's discussion of the Poro, 'Secrets cannot be characterised either by the contents of the concealed message or by the consequences and outcomes that follow exposure; instead they are understood by the way concealed information is withheld, restricted, intentionally altered and exposed' (1984: 143). In Newmarket, secrecy often communicates class difference, thus the content of the secret is almost always secondary to its status as such.

5 According to Newmarket myth, Wyer's surgeon came to speak to his wife after repairing her husband and told her that the operation had been a success and that they had even managed to save the gap between his front teeth. Nora Wyer, somewhat surprised, asked 'What gap?', and Lorcan was wheeled back into the operating theatre.

6 This approach may have been borrowed from American trainers who sit on the track on beautiful Quarter horses, the quintessential cowboy's horse. The most successful American trainers make an impressive display of belt buckle, ten-gallon hat, silver-dollar bridle, and shiny white teeth. Few trainers on Newmarket Heath would be able to carry this off.

3   Keeping it in the family

Introduction

In this chapter I discuss those people who identify themselves as 'real' Newmarket families. These are individuals involved in the training, breeding, buying and selling of racehorses, and I shall refer to them as the upper class of racing society. They are the primary source of ideas of pedigree, and it is their position in the social structure that is safeguarded by this ideology. In Newmarket there are a number of interconnected families who could be named by most people involved in the racing industry. The true extent of the dominance of a few families in Newmarket is not the focus of this chapter, but rather the source of this image of dominance and its purpose.[1] I use a composite case study in order to illustrate the ideology of pedigree as it is employed by members of these families. The case study is supplemented by more general observations.

I begin by introducing the family I have chosen to present as a case study, and describing the methods I used in order to record them. I draw upon informants' discussions of marriage and, by extension, their ideas of gender. The male dominance of the sport of racing is described, and suggestions made in order to explain its resilience. In the second section of the chapter I deal with death. In relation to the ideology of pedigree, death represents a loss of blood, and is thus opposed to possible gains through marriage. This loss is less pressing when the individual in question has fulfilled the ideal life path and reproduced. Those who fail to do so are seen as incomplete, ideal candidates for ghosts, whether in the memories of the living, or gliding around the stables of Newmarket.

The 'connection' crystallises notions of identity and relatedness that recur throughout Newmarket society. In racing parlance, 'connections' refer to the humans associated with a particular racehorse, its trainer, owner and jockey. Thus access to the exclusive zone of the paddock is restricted to the 'connections of horses in the present race'. In this way, a 'connection' has come to signify an object as well as a relation. It is interesting to note that a connection is a particular type of person made such by a relationship with a horse, a reversal of the convention whereby animals depend upon an association with humans in order to gain status.

Whilst 'connections' may refer to the owners and trainer of a particular race-horse, an association which confers prestige, connections as relations can also be made to apply to kin, to good business, and to Newmarket itself. Both being a connection and also being connected in and to Newmarket are intrinsically valued. Those who describe themselves or others as 'Newmarket families' identify two important connections. The first of these is to Newmarket itself, described in the third section of this chapter. Newmarket families also claim connections with racing via individuals successful in its sacred arena, the race-course. I shall consider the resilience of this particular system of relatedness in the fourth section of the chapter.

Finally, I shall examine the response of Newmarket families to outsiders (those perceived as lacking connections to Newmarket or to racing) in the context of events which framed my fieldwork in 1997; these were the bomb scare at the Grand National, the General Election and the ban on British beef. Though these seem unconnected events, the response to them was consistent. Informants resented any force that they considered a threat to their freedom. Thus, the Referendum Party provided a refuge from European invasion, animal rights activists 'should all be shot', and banning beef was the act of a 'nanny state': 'I'll eat what I bloody well like!'

This chapter is not a systematic description of the kinship practices of Newmarket's racing families, although I believe that it gains coherence from the idea of pedigree as a way of imagining connections between people. It is fieldwork led, in that it focuses upon those concerns repeatedly articulated by informants, as in Strathern's study of Elmdon:

In so far as my account imitates a case study in the traditional anthropological sense, its main line of enquiry takes its cue from what Elmdon people themselves seem to be interested in. (1981: xxxi)

A 'real' Newmarket family

Charles was introduced to me in the local pub as a fourth-generation racehorse trainer and member of a Newmarket racing dynasty. I told him that I was an anthropologist studying racing in Newmarket, and he immediately began to tell me about his family, much to my surprise. The technique I found myself employing, described by some anthropologists as 'talking family' (Bouquet 1993: 46), was immediately hijacked by Charles, and became a means of 'talking family trees'. My own wariness of the genealogical method became an irrel-evance as Charles called for paper and pen from the landlord, and began to scribble. The relationship between anthropologist and informant assumed a heightened symmetry as he quizzed me on my knowledge of 1940s Classic winners and their associations with his family, attempting to locate me within his own frame of reference. By the time I had known Charles for just over an hour he had plotted several generations of his family on a beer-stained napkin, and pressed it into my hands, pointing out discrepancies where the pen had smudged or blotted. The detail imparted with each family member was remarkably consistent; names of stables, horses, owners and significant races, all connected by the inevitable trunk and branch formation.

Charles is currently training, fairly successfully, in Newmarket. He trains from a famous old stable, and had approximately fifty horses in training when I visited him, and around fifteen staff. Charles is authoritative, confident, impatient and serious. He talks about his family as though this information is a matter entirely fitting for the public realm, since these are his racing credentials. He frames the information as genealogy, as this is the recognised form taken by evidence of heredity by racing families in Newmarket; as amongst the bourgeoisie of Paris studied by Le Wita, 'genealogy makes a title of social function, thereby transforming it into privilege' (1994: 5).

'Talking family' was, for Charles, the same as 'talking racing', and did not involve doing violence to his idea of what sort of information could be shared with a virtual stranger. 'Talking family' was imbued with power, but the power was Charles'.[2] I was stunned by the breadth and depth of his knowledge of connections and every individual he introduced drove home his point, which was that racing ability was somehow bred into his family, it was 'in their blood'. That I should wish to map this precious blood was not in the least bit extraordinary to him.

I recorded approximately five hundred individuals of nine generations in many sittings with various members of this family who found it natural that I should want to know about them. Not surprisingly, I tended to be introduced to those members of the family who were involved in racing. A lot of family tree had already been recorded, in a format that revealed a preoccupation with those individuals who had cultivated a career in racing.

The abridged family trees of many Newmarket dynasties, showing the links between seven original racing families, are reprinted in the historian Richard Onslow's book, *Royal Ascot* (1990). This family tree is set alongside two others; the first of these records those members of the British royal family who have been credited with an association with Ascot racecourse, and the second is a trace of the male line of a particular stallion from the nineteenth century to the present day. No comment is made upon the mixing of species, and the symbiosis between royal patronage and famous racing families, both human and equine, is neatly captured in three pages.

The stories of Newmarket families are told almost exclusively from the perspective of the family's association with racing. Links created by male lines, particularly those associated with racing, were pursued, whilst female links were neglected unless they initiated contact with a significant racing line. This tendency was reflected by the trace of surnames which were lost by marriage 'out of racing', whilst marriage 'into racing' could introduce a brand new association.

Marriage

During my stay in Newmarket, an important wedding took place, between champion jockey Frankie Dettori and Catherine Allen, the daughter of 'Twink' Allen, a Cambridge University equine fertility expert. Their wedding in the centre of Newmarket reflected many of the features of the networks of kin and connections common amongst racing families. Horizontally, the wedding list was described as a 'who's who of racing'. Dettori is the son of the former champion jockey of Italy. He was sent to Newmarket as an apprentice to Luca Cumani, the Italian trainer, with £300 in his pocket, and has been incredibly successful, particularly as the retained jockey for Godolphin.[3] He is currently the most famous and popular jockey in Britain, rising to stardom by riding all seven winners on the card at Ascot in 1997, costing the bookmakers an estimated £25 million.[4]

This was racing's wedding of the year, and it was reported in all of the newspapers in exactly the same way, concentrating far more upon 'racing' than on 'wedding'. The concentration of racing people was highlighted, to the extent that some of the papers reproduced partial guest lists that recorded only this category of guest. The anecdote most frequently recounted of the wedding was that Dettori had been pleased to lose a bet of £50, that the day would be sunny. Also quoted were members of the two hundred and fifty-strong crowd of well-wishers who gathered around the church, telling the journalists how much money the jockey had won for them through bets.

The public reporting of this wedding concentrated solely upon its significance for racing. Reassurance as to the 'horsy' nature of the bride, a strong show from racing folk, a wager on the weather, all of these things submit easily to the idioms in which racing identities are expressed. Outside the public eye, my informants' discussions of their own relationships focused upon compatibility, which is a family matter. Despite the variation in celebrations arising from marriage, I was struck by the constant relevance of family to their predicted outcome.[5]

Discussions of the likely success or failure of a marriage amongst informants were conducted within a familial frame of reference. Most commonly, the parents of the couple were discussed. Where either of the couple had divorced parents this was identified as a possible threat to their future. This belief was summarised by a farmer friend, 'like begets like', and has been fully explored by Simon Barnes, a journalist with *Horse and Hound*:

Serious horse people look at the breeding, for today's aspirant or hero is merely the culmination of the mingling of bloodlines; of the collision between dam and sire. Sire:

a champion jockey, a single-minded man who demanded respect which crossed the boundary of fear. Dam: a trapeze artist. Produce: Frankie Dettori, out of a show-off with perfect balance and a love of danger, by a ruthless 'sonofabitch'. (1997: 24)

Along with those who had shown a tendency towards divorce and infidelity, parents with no affinity with horses were seen as a potential weakness, particularly where the individual in question lacked this affinity him- or herself. All discussions of compatibility were skewed towards considerations of the compatibility of women with men. The man was the fixed point in many of these conversations, and women were characterised as suitable or unsuitable in relation to him. The dominance of men in racing's most powerful roles is overwhelming, to the surprise of one male racing administrator:

We get quite a number of women trainers and there are no restrictions in operation. I don't really know why there aren't more women, they have equal opportunities. There are a lot of female administrators, 11% in the Jockey Club for example. It manifests itself more in the press room, when on a day to day meeting you wouldn't get a single girl.

That the 11% female membership of the Jockey Club was singled out as an example of a field in which there are 'a lot' of women reflects their virtual absence from other racing spheres. The highest concentration of women in racing occupations is, predictably, amongst 'lads', the least prestigious role. The ratio of male to female 'lads' through the years 1991 to 1995 ranged from 1712:1395 to 1473:1202 (The Racing Industry Statistical Bureau Statistics 1996: 210). At apprentice jockey level, the ratio of men to women (or 'boys' to girls' as the industry would prefer) is greater than five to one for these years. Even this ratio is not upheld into the professional ranks. In December 1992, the Jockey Club had licensed 112 flat jockeys, 8 of whom were women, and 148 jump-jockeys, 8 of whom were women. By contrast, amongst apprentices on the flat, 43 of the 205 were women, although over jumps of the 160 apprentices only 7 were women.[6]

Racing is controlled by men, and this situation is self-perpetuating. Accordingly, women in racing are often perceived as strident and self-assured, having struggled against this bias:

She's a truly awful woman Rebecca, you wouldn't like her one bit. One of those women with a terrible chip on her shoulder, you know. Always on the offensive. She knows her stuff, sure, but she's fallen victim of this terrible business whereby successful women seem to need to push it down your throat. You know? (Senior racing administrator)

Predictably, powerful men in the racing industry, such as the administrator I have quoted, are wary of these successful women, labelling them 'brash' and in particular, 'unfeminine'.

The resilience of this dominance requires an explanation. Racing society is wealthy and traditionalist, and presents change as a bourgeois quality. Impermanence is seen as evidence of weakness, and institutions gain authority with age. Tradition is thus invoked as a justification for practices that are subject to criticism. These beliefs have had practical consequences for women in racing, whose position has changed far less than those outside. For example, it was not until 1966 that women were able to take out training licences (Jockey Club History 1997: 7), though a few women trained before this time in the names of their head lads. The Honourable Mrs George Lambton discussed the possibility of women being granted licences in 1950:

the Jockey Club have always been adamant over this question, and I must say I think rightly so; once the door was open and women allowed into the sacred precincts of the weighing room on the official footing as trainers, what is to stop them from becoming jockeys too? No doubt many in these days have that ambition, but although there are plenty of embryo 'National Velvets' in the making, I think it will be a long time before feminism asserts itself to this extent; in fact, the Turf will remain a last ditch! (quoted in Bland 1950: 181)

Jockey's licences have been granted to women since 1972 (on the flat) and 1976 (over jumps) (Hargreaves 1994: 276). However, attitudes towards women jockeys remain largely unchanged, as the Director of the British Racing School observes, 'There is no doubt that you will find more male chauvinism in racing than in any other industry, apart from male bastions like coal mining' (Rory MacDonald quoted in Lovesey 1994: 32). The Jockey Club's former Chief Medical Officer offers this explanation:

It is perceived in racing that women are weaker. Therefore if you have a strong horse and you want it to be ridden hard, there is, as I understand it, a reluctance on the part of owners and trainers to put up a woman jockey when the chips are down. (Michael Turner quoted in Lovesey 1994: 32)

The place of women within racing has been determined by a theory of gender based upon physical attributes, made evident in this quote from ex-jockey and Channel Four racing presenter Lord Oaksey:

To say that the Sex Discrimination Act came as a shock to the British racing world would be an understatement. A large majority of the men who make their living in that world are, to say the least of it, conservative by nature and their reaction to the idea of female jockeys ranged from genuine horror to chauvinistic mockery – with a fair amount of ribald humour in between. Lester Piggott, never a man to use two words when one will do said simply, 'their bottoms are the wrong shape', and, as usual, he had a point. (1978: 7)

I was given a similar explanation by a trainer, who told me that, 'In relation to jockeys, it's obviously a physical difficulty.' Not all trainers prefer lads, however, those who prefer 'girls' use a similarly stereotypical idea of both men and women in order to justify this choice. So, I was told, for example, 'You know what lads are like, they want to be jockeys day and night, so we stick to girls, they really care about the horses and do a good job.'

Characterising women as 'the weaker sex' has enabled men to justify their exclusion from the roles of jockey and stallion man. Women are thought to require protection from colts and stallions, which were likely to become aroused by the scent of a woman and to cause her harm as a result.[7] I would suggest that using a primarily physical idiom of gender has eased the crossover of ideas from animals to men and women, so common in Newmarket:

There's no difference between a woman and a mare, except that a mare is more agreeable. The mare is a self-contained foaling unit and nursery, and that's all a woman would be if she didn't talk so much. (Bloodstock agent)

Men compare women to horses and horses to women, a tendency observed by almost all racing's observers:

I have always been fascinated by the way   and it's simply a habit, not an insult – [racing people] refer to women as though they are horses. I remember once asking Fred Winter what he thought of a certain trainer's mistress and he replied, 'Oh, she's very moderate'. Another trainer described a woman as being 'of little account'. I suppose the best sort of woman to spend a day at the races with would be described by Mr Winter and his colleagues as 'promising, useful, scope'. (Bernard and Dodd 1991: 58)[8]

At first glance, these comments may appear to support Ortner's idea that women's physiology makes them seem closer to nature (1974). Ortner arrives at this contention by asking what every culture devalues, believing that there is only 'one thing that would fit that description, and that is "nature", in the most generalised sense' (1974: 72). However, Ortner's characterisation of nature as universally demeaned in relation to culture is a simplification that masks more than it reveals in Newmarket. Women are associated with birth and nurturing, perceived as 'natural' processes, but 'nature' is also powerful and violent and, in this guise, associated with male virility, as the following description indicates:

The business of women and horses reminds me of Roger Mortimer's theory that a stallion needs to be something of a shit to be a success at stud. He even predicted that Mill Reef would be better at stud than Brigadier Gerard because he was nastier, and he was absolutely right. (Bernard and Dodd 1991: 58)

Physical explanations were not so commonly evoked in discussions of the dominance of men in the roles of trainer, agent or administrator, although the explanations I received were similarly uniform. I was told that men were more numerous than women in racing roles due to the unequal opportunities that existed in the past, but that these things were currently changing. When I pressed men as to who they would rather employ, these changes were often attributed to a 'future' which involved people other than the individual in question, for example:

I'd rather have a man simply because at the moment we deal mainly with other men. But, as I said, things are changing, and in the future, who knows, I may need to employ women too. (Bloodstock agent)

The idea that men and women communicate more efficiently with members of the same sex was institutionalised in the maddening convention by which women chatted in the kitchen before supper whilst the men enjoyed a whisky in the lounge. Talk in the kitchen was often of the children or other domestic concerns, whilst conversation in the lounge was of business (so I'm told). These ideas were raised in a number of my interviews with women, for example:

My official role is to look over the stable door and say 'Ahh'. It is a sexist industry, and it is because of being a woman. I don't fit in because I have my own career [as a teacher]. I won't stay in and answer the phone and polish the step like the last two stud groom's wives. This world isn't like a job, it's a culture or a way of life. (Wife of stud groom)

This woman identifies the expectation of racing society that a woman's status, occupation and lifestyle will be determined by that of her husband. The only variable capable of transcending this discrimination in racing is class, as Hargreaves states:

The few women who broke into horse-racing were exceptional and from middle or upper-class backgrounds. Lower-class women only held supporting, subservient roles such as stable girls, cloakroom attendants, payers-out at the Tote windows, barmaids, trainer's wives, daughters and sisters. (1982: 120)

Thus, for example, the Queen is perceived as an authority on racing, despite the fact that she is a woman, because her status 'compensates' for her gender.

The dominance of men in all of the most powerful roles in racing encourages the perception of marriage as consisting of women 'marrying in' to racing and thus being responsible for adjustment to a racing man. The exception to this rule arises where a woman's class status is capable of 'neutralising' her gender. This exception is a further source of the resilience of the male dominance of racing, since status is only granted to those women who have an existing family association with racing and no mechanism exists whereby women can begin to create this association, except through their alliances with men.

Death

The retrospective appreciation of fellow members of racing families reveals traits valued amongst the living. Deaths are greeted with tributes to life in the form of riding skills, training skills, risk-taking and good humour. Racing triumphs are always mentioned, greatest winners listed in newspapers and on television, associations with good horses recalled, whether jockey, trainer or bloodstock agent. The individual's contribution to the particularity of each race in which he had an involvement, his influence upon the accumulated history of racing, is acknowledged.

Speaking to family and friends at racing funerals one will find the same traits attributed to the deceased: horsemanship, generosity and good humour. These are the qualities associated with being a good racing person, as made clear by this obituary for Bob Ruttle by trainer Peter Walwyn:

A beautiful horseman, Bob is well remembered for riding a talented but wayward filly, Scarf, as a hack, setting off as many as thirty two-year-olds at the bottom of the Bury Hill canter, before following them up, with a long rein and not a care in the world . . . One of his great expressions was that when a difficult horse appeared, he would say: 'I'll ride it.' And he did! (1997: 4)

Primarily, one must have an affinity with horses. This affinity may take the form of 'an eye for a horse' in the case of a bloodstock agent, an ability to 'keep them sweet' in a trainer or an 'eye for a stride' in a jockey.

Generosity is valued because it reflects both success and also nonchalance, an absence of anxiety about the future, the confident undertaking of risk and liability. All members of racing families are expected to take risks without revealing discomfort, and successful risk-taking is the means of advancement in all racing occupations. Taking risks is seen as indicative of self-assurance, such that one's place in the racing hierarchy is secure, achieved effortlessly, and not in the least bit threatened by one's behaviour. Those who do not take risks are regarded with suspicion.

Humour in racing is dominated by anecdotes that relate those mishaps which originate in taking risks, an excess of alcohol which culminates in potentially compromising exposure, for example. Humour is usually derived from indiscretions of a sexual or financial nature. I would suggest that this humour serves to increase the distance between racing society and the outside world by revelling in the irresponsibility facilitated by involvement in such an isolated, unaccountable industry. Tales of drunk driving, in particular, were met with admiration for the protagonist: 'Bloody hell, three times over – that's pretty good going!' These tales involved defiance of the law and of the police, the authority of whom was explicitly dismissed as 'irrelevant to us', 'for the masses' and 'meant for joy riders'.

The death of a member of racing's upper class, as in the case of the death of a successful racehorse, represents a loss of blood – a gap in the genealogy of a particular 'family'. The sudden deaths of popular horses are greeted by behaviour that can only be described as mourning. The death of Red Rum, for example, was followed by a television tribute to an 'equine hero'. The death of One Man live on television was accompanied by the tears of his seemingly hard-bitten jockey, prompting a flood of letters and sympathy to the BBC.

The death of even a mediocre racehorse is, to his stable, a tragedy. My own experience of the death of a horse in the yard revealed that racehorses are mourned as though they are individuals and, explicitly, persons. The dead horse was discussed, his personality re-evoked and his quirks recalled. These discussions focused particularly upon the things that this horse did that made him distinctive in the way that people are. The horse's straw was left in his box for several days until the lad who looked after him was able to remove it herself. I was told that this was something that could not be rushed, she must do it 'when she is ready', as it was 'part of the process of saying good-bye'. Though this process could properly be described as anthropomorphic, there is no question that the grief expressed was real.

Some horses have always been buried in Newmarket, and many of the older yards have equine graveyards and headstones. The reactions of racing professionals to the fatal injuries occasionally sustained by horses whilst racing and training have undoubtedly changed due to the industrialisation of racing and of the animals themselves. However, despite the increased commercial pressures of the modern sport of racing, accidents were dreaded for more than financial reasons. Almost all of the people working in racing profess to some affinity with horses, and most to much more. Accidents to horses caused great distress to those who care for them in particular, but the ripples of this grief spread well beyond the lad who collected his horse's bridle from the racecourse vet, to every connection of the stricken animal.

Similarly, attitudes towards horses who had reached the end of their racing lives due to either injury or loss of form varied widely between yards. Some seemed to find 'retirement' homes for even their most useless and unappealing failed racehorses, whilst others merely wanted to see the back of the offending creature on the grounds that 'a hack eats as much as a champion'. Some racehorses are undoubtedly unsuitable for rehoming due to either physical or mental defects and these animals are sometimes destroyed on the basis that it is a more responsible end for them than a life of neglect. Old lads and trainers told me that this has always been so . . . some horses are lucky enough to be associated with owners or trainers who are committed to them for life, others are less fortunate and can be removed from yards for a nominal payment. Of course, it is the talented who are most likely to survive, carefully preserved for their reproductive promise.

The importance of ancestors, now deceased, in determining the ability of the present generation, provides fertile ground for ghosts of both species. Newmarket is riddled with the ghosts of trainers and jockeys, perhaps the best known of which is that of Fred Archer described by ex-jockey and racing journalist Marcus Armytage:

they say . . . (cue hairs rising on the back of your neck) . . . Fred's still around. 'The lads say they see him from time to time,' says the trainer. 'The older we get, the more whisky we drink, the more ghosts we see. The lads tend to see him on a Friday night.' When the lads called him up on an Ouija board, Fred told them to back Unblest the following day (he won at 6–4), where his grave was and where he committed suicide. Sounds like we could all do with a benevolent ghost. (1997: 32)

Fred Archer was the most famous jockey of the second half of the nineteenth century, and he makes a perfect ghost because he had a hard life and met a tragic end. Archer shot himself whilst suffering from a delirious fit brought on by wasting to reduce his weight. His suicide was made more poignant as it fell upon the anniversary of the death of his wife during childbirth. The son to whom she gave birth also died. I would suggest that Archer cannot rest because he did not leave an heir. He is still implicated in Newmarket in numerous ways, due to the presence of his ghost, a street named Fred Archer Way, and the sinister cabinet in the Racing Museum dedicated to his memory, which contains his diary, his tiny boots, and the gun with which he shot himself. Even as a ghost Fred is a good racing sort, however, as his winning tip confirms.

Claiming a connection to Newmarket

Many informants credited their family with an association with Newmarket, and the title of 'Newmarket trainer' is generic, and used in opposition to, for example, the 'Northern trainers'. The association of various racing figures with Newmarket has been codified in the street names of the town, to the extent that many of them bear the name of a jockey, race or trainer, as in the case of Fred Archer. Beyond an association with Newmarket itself, many families have developed links with particular yards, as reflected by the description of Machell Place offered by the Newmarket Open Day Guide:

Machell Place, built in 1884, was named after Captain Machell and was bought from him by Tony Hide's Grandfather-in-law, Col Leader. When Col moved to Stanley House, as private trainer to Lord Derby, Ted Leader moved in, followed by Jock Halsey, Charlie Elliott, Jack Watts – who trained Indiana to win the St. Leger – Brian Lunness and now Tony Hide, who started training in 1977 on returning from Italy, where he trained the winners of their 2000 guineas, 1000 guineas and Oaks and the second in the Derby. Whilst at Machell Place he has sent out Group winners in France, Germany and Sweden. (Newmarket Open Day Programme 1996)

The significant features of this description are those which are introduced in order to convey prestige, by association, upon the present occupant of the stable. Thus the relationship between Tony Hide and the Leaders is featured, because the Leaders trained for Lord Derby, and all classic winners (even Italian) get a mention. Prestigious winners are listed as though they still exert an influence over the present-day fortune of the yard, as in the following example:

Park Lodge is one of the oldest yards in Newmarket and is now the most central operational yard in the town. Many famous horses have been trained here including

Blue Peter. Sir Jack Jarvis, who trained Blue Peter and many other classic winners trained here from the twenties to the sixties. (Newmarket Open Day Programme 1996)

By mentioning the Leaders and Jack Jarvis, both of these descriptions signal an association (to those 'in the know') with a major racing dynasty. Similarly, when recording family members who trained, informants always specified the yard they occupied. Some yards remained in families throughout generations, and the sale of these yards is always regretted, whilst their possession is remembered with great nostalgia.

The relationship between the established Newmarket families and the latest influx of trainers is captured in the difference between the old established yards and the yards built during the 1980s. The stories associated with the newer stables do not concern past glory, or association with famous equine and human figures, but rather the sadness of the recession which caught out many of the new trainers. One yard remains unfinished, with weeds growing through the concrete, and an uncertain future. Even more sad is the story of the horse left in a deserted yard by his trainer as payment of a debt to his landlord. Speaking of the more recently established yards, a trainer told me:

They haven't got the horses in the boxes to talk to the horses and the trainer in the house to talk to the trainer. No history speaks to them, and they're in a vacuum, trying to make history out of nothing.

Some families can claim a connection to Newmarket through residence in, and ownership of, the historic training yards. However, recognition of this connection is contingent upon the success that marks racing people. Thus, whilst an unsuccessful trainer may have spent his working life in Newmarket in a yard on the Hamilton Road, he has failed to make a connection. The daughter of a jockey who has never lived on a yard but can trace an association with a historic yard through her uncles is, in contrast, proprietorial about its fortunes, and is acknowledged as having a connection. Connections are thus activated by success, because someone involved in racing who does not ever achieve success does not require explanation in terms of pedigree. Likewise, one may choose not to activate one's connection to racing, but one may not choose to have such a connection. If successful in racing, a connection will be envisaged, but it will take the form, not of a choice, but of a 'natural fact'. The next section examines in more detail how these 'natural facts' are envisaged by racing people.

Making connections

Whilst recording relatives with members of a family of informants I noticed that they were omitting people from our record. When I asked about this I was told that they had been missing out those people without any known involvement with racing. Informants were happiest when the ratio of 'racing' to 'non-racing' people was as high as possible, and even suggested that I should devise an equation capable of calculating this concentration.

Eventually, they settled for running a diagonal pencil line through 'non-racing' people, so that my diagrams would be very confusing to an anthropologist, depicting people seemingly reproducing from 'beyond the grave'. This is racing's answer to Schneider's question of, 'What, then, determines whether a relation will exist or not?' (1968: 72). Amongst members of 'real' Newmarket families, the most significant factor influencing whether a relative will be recognised as such appears to be their racing credentials.

Memories of connections amongst these families are entirely selective. 'Social interest' is highly focused, so that those with racing credentials (however distantly 'related') will not be forgotten, whilst those without such credentials (however closely 'related') will be recalled reluctantly and in passing, or not at all. Furthermore, those with sufficiently strong racing credentials may have biological links envisaged for them. Where these biological links seem lacking at first glance at an individual's immediate family, they will be attributed to his or her unrecorded 'past'.

Informants describing the contemporary relations between Newmarket families thereby delineated themselves from newcomers. The desire to include some and exclude others became almost farcical, as the transcript of our conversation reveals:

Informant: The Candys go back, and the Easterbys in Yorkshire are all connected. There are huge families in Epsom too. The Tollers . . . Tom is in transport, and James' nephew Mark is from a racing family too. There's a possible connection between the Yorkshire Watts and the Watts via Yvonne. Harry Wragg's father married into a racing family. Harry Carr the jockey married Joan who was connected to the Wraggs, or was it the Barlows? Of course, Frankie Barlow's sister Carol married Kipper Lynch so that joined up the families through sisters marrying jockeys. James Eustace's wife's brother trains in Hong Kong.
R: Are the Baldings all related too?
Informant: Yes, that's right, Toby [trainer] and Ian [trainer] are cousins, and Peter trained for the Queen after the Rickaby and Marsh time, and then Colonel Robin Hastings is chairman of the BBA, now isn't he the one who can be traced back to Robin Hood? I think there is some connection there.

In order to claim people as family members, informants envisaged connections. These connections were both vertical (moving through generations) and horizontal (moving across generations), either will do and when one is absent the other compensates. Thus the Candys 'go back', whilst the Easterbys are 'all connected'. This is an example of the Alltown phenomenon identified by Edwards and Strathern whereby, 'Connections appear intrinsically desirable' (1999: 152). The connections informants were prepared to acknowledge depended almost entirely upon the individual concerned, and whether they wished to admit him or her to their ranks. Thus although a recent recruit to training had a father who had been a major owner, they did not permit this connection. In other contexts, in order to provide a link between two major families, for example, this connection was permitted. The purpose of claiming such connections is not simply to identify a particular individual as part of racing society, but also to stress the image of racing society as highly interconnected.

As Edwards and Strathern note, in their study of kinship in a British town, 'biology is never the full story' (1999: 160); however, this leaves open the question of exactly what, in Newmarket, constitutes 'biology', and 'society'. In the case of Newmarket, biology is imagined through 'racing blood', whilst 'society' is success in the sacred arena of the racecourse. An 'interdigitation' (Edwards and Strathern 1999: 158) thus occurs between the ideology of pedigree and the reality of the successes of those who do not qualify biologically for such achievements. Where links neglect to provide success in racing they are killed off, thus biology is banished by the diagonal line through non-racing relatives. Where success occurs without biological connection such a connection is imagined or assumed.

I am not suggesting that this is a particularly exceptional feature of kinship particular to Newmarket families, since kinship is often highly selective in this way. What is specific to this context is the ideology that family cannot be separated from occupation and thus class, all are implied by birth. The fluidity of racing ideologies, such as 'the big win', and that 'all men are equal on the turf and under it', that anyone can back a horse and therefore become rich, the camaraderie of the racecourse and the idea that everyone in racing has more in common with each other than with anyone outside racing emphasises what is shared at the expense of what separates, blurring the reality of class distinctions. Thus, whilst modern Britain may be perceived by some as having separated class from birth, the dominant ideology of pedigree in Newmarket is a double bind. What appears fixed (kin) is actually relatively fluid, though what seems to be mobile (class) is fixed. The 'natural facts' are recognised only selectively, and are subordinate to the fixed social reality that without success one cannot be a member of a racing family. 'Success' is a composite notion involving appearance, residence, connections and winning, a way of 'being in the world' which offers (self-fulfilling) proof of the theory of pedigree.

Reactions to outsiders

A contrast was drawn between 'newcomers' and 'real' Newmarket families in the same way as was made by 'real Elmdoners' (Strathern 1981) and 'Muker people' (Phillips 1986).[9] Newmarket 'before the war' was characterised as a place in which everyone really was related to each other, where bicycles featured heavily, and a policy of helping one's neighbour held sway. Newcomers were distinguished from 'real' Newmarket people by two things: their money and their lack of breeding. As a female informant told me, 'They were already millionaires, what on earth would they possibly want with training racehorses? That man has twenty-six phones in his house!' The newcomers were described by those with Newmarket roots as 'businessmen rather than horsemen', and I was told that the nature of training horses had in fact changed from the days when a trainer would have a maximum of forty horses. Newcomer trainers with strings of two hundred horses were thought to be training as a 'business' rather than 'for the love of it'. 'New money' was thus cast as destabilising the 'old order' to the extent that the nature of training itself was actually seen to be changing, 'Training used to be hands on, you know, feeling legs, knowing the horses. But now it's more about PR and money. Getting the business in' (Trainer).

However, whilst the relationship between Newmarket families and outsiders is often antagonistic, the boundary between the two is permeable, and kinship performative. Thus by proving oneself to be 'the right sort' one may be assimilated into Newmarket society by revelations concerning one's own family. Although the primary mechanism available for infiltrating Newmarket society is birthright, biology is entirely subordinate to social performance. Thus, whilst birth into a racing family appears the obvious means by which a connection may be claimed, it is not a necessary or sufficient condition of entry, since 'natural facts' can be conjured up for insiders, whilst those who remain outsiders by performance will remain so by birth. In other words, both marriage and birth only serve to connect where proof of a connection exists in the individual's performance.

This section raises questions regarding my own relationship to informants during fieldwork, and my place in their perception of 'insiders' and 'outsiders'. My entry into this society depended on my ability to display my affinity with horses. Being comfortable with horses is perceived as an absolute quality that does not admit to degrees. Thus, when I complained that my riding ability was limited, I was told that some people would never be able to do this thing. My ability was a matter of degree, and would improve with experience, but I was already on the right side of an absolute divide between those who could ride and those who could not. This ability was often explained in terms of my breeding, despite my insistence that I could not recall any racing ancestors. My Irish surname made this specificity unnecessary, because according to most of my informants, all the Irish have 'racing in their blood'.[10]

Discussions of outsiders amongst myself and informants assumed, from quite early on, my complicity with members of racing families. When a bomb scare forced the postponement of the Grand National and the evacuation of the course, the response in Newmarket was extreme. Some informants told me that they had considered emigrating because they believed that, 'you can't do anything in this bloody country'. The belief that animal rights activists had disrupted the race infuriated them. Animal rights activists are perceived to be ignorant of the countryside, town dwellers with abstract ideas rather than empirical knowledge, prompting comments such as, 'What do they know about the countryside? I suppose they've read something in a book.' The contempt in which intellectual or 'bookish' learning is held stems from its contradiction with lived knowledge as embodied and inherited. As I was told on a number of occasions, 'racing people don't think, they *do*'.[11]

The ban on British beef which followed the BSE scare was also seen as an infringement of an individual's right to choose by a government too weak to stand up to European pressure. Farmers were seen as natural allies. Refuge was sought in the policies of the Referendum Party in the General Election, which received double the national average of votes in Newmarket. James Goldsmith's video was widely circulated in Newmarket, and its message cherished. Bumper stickers supporting British beef could be found in abundance in the trainers' car park of racecourses all over Britain in the nineties, whilst my vegetarianism was a constant source of irritation to many of my informants, 'Oh God, she's a bloody vegetarian. Better pass the rabbit food.'[12]

Although the beef ban, the Grand National and the General Election brought ideas of peripherality, and even persecution, into focus, these ideas are a continual undercurrent. The most frequently cited justification for racing's antagonistic relationship to the government at the time of fieldwork was the level of General Betting Duty, which was seen as prohibitively high. Racing was often described as a goose laying golden eggs for the government. Although betting duty was cited as the prime example of the inability of outsiders to comprehend the problems facing the industry, I would suggest that it is indicative of a more general attitude towards outsiders. The self-image of the upper class of racing society as an exclusive, inter-related, highly specialised minority promotes 'peripherality as a self-image' (Cohen 1982: 7).

Conclusion

In this chapter I discussed the 'upper class' of racing, that is, the individuals preoccupied with the training, owning, breeding, buying and selling of racehorses, who sometimes identify themselves and each other as 'Newmarket families'. I have attempted to establish that tracing connections in Newmarket families depend upon a combination of both 'social' and 'biological' factors. Furthermore, both social and biological facts can determine each other. Biology is in no sense the prime mover in this form of relatedness, despite its explicit reification in the ideology of pedigree. Thus Newmarket trainers embody Newmarket by being successful, whilst parts of Newmarket embody particular Newmarket trainers by absorbing their good fortune into their bricks and mortar.

The self-fulfilling operations of the ideology of pedigree in Newmarket, such that in order to be successful one must be well connected, and in order to be well connected one must be successful, are mirrored in numerous small ways, but particularly through appearances. In order to be successful in Newmarket, one must appear to be successful. This preoccupation with appearance extends to racing residences. Yards assimilate the fortunes of their occupants and come to be associated with particular successes or failures. A yard steeped in history (perhaps with a resident ghost) is more prestigious than one of the new developments on Hamilton Road, associated with disappointment and financial ruin. Older yards with their ancient walls, clocktowers, roses and ivy appear more permanent than the Hamilton Road equivalents which change hands every season, devoid of the connections necessary to keep them solvent. Training yards are associated with their owners to the extent that the fortune of one affects the fortunes of the other. A successful yard will continue to embody the successes of a previous occupant though the occupant may have left long ago. Training yards are not fully alienated from their human owners or their equine inhabitants.

It seems that being related to a Newmarket family by what the anthropologist Rivers and his intellectual descendants might characterise as a 'descriptive' blood relation is not a necessary or sufficient condition of claiming a connection. In order to be a member of a Newmarket family one must be active in racing, and if one is active in racing one may find that connections are created in order to account for this involvement. The flexibility of this system does not threaten the ideology of pedigree in the least, since its greatest exponents practise interdigitation between biological and social factors as a matter of course.

NOTES

1 As Strathern notes, 'When Elmdoners say, then, that so-and-so is a real village person, or a newcomer, that real Elmdon families have been there for generations, we should ask not so much whether it is true, but why it matters' (1981: 17).

2 I mention this because it is in contrast to the experience of 'talking family' described by Bouquet, 'Talking family is charged with latent violence quite as much as affectivity ... It is a discourse that deserves comparison with sorcery which as Farret-Sada shows, is about power rather than knowledge or information' (1993: 46). In my case, it was me who was bewitched, as my informant ran genealogical rings around me.

3 Godolphin is Sheikh Mohammed's highly successful breeding and training operation.

4 In 2000 Dettori survived a light plane crash on Newmarket racecourse along with fellow jockey Ray Cochrane. Their pilot was tragically killed.

5 The two weddings I attended in Newmarket couldn't have been more different. One was a traditional church wedding, the other a registry office followed by a meal in a curry house.

6 Of the 2791 jockeys licensed to ride in the USA, Canada and parts of Mexico in 1992, 447 were women. In Sweden, two women have been champion jockeys, an unthinkable achievement in Britain. Berneklint was champion with 71 wins from 357 rides in 1991, whilst Nordgren was champion in 1982 with 61 wins from 232 rides (Lovesey 1994: 31–2).

7 The rape of a woman by a horse was often described euphemistically by men who advocated the protection of women from colts and stallions. It represents another example of the tendency to elide human and animal categories.

8 Believe it or not, these remarks come from an essay entitled 'Sizing up a filly', and epitomise the tendency of men who discuss women in this way to dismiss its importance by describing it as a 'habit'. By so doing, they make any resulting offence taken by a woman inappropriate, the result of a misunderstanding. Such offence is invoked as evidence of the greater 'sensitivity' of women relative to men, and so the cycle is complete.

9 In Muker, for example, 'the idea that "everyone's related to everyone" is a collective representation of the local community which Muker people represent to people from the outside world. Kinship is depicted as being at once a mechanism of inclusion in, and exclusion from, the core set of locals' (Phillips 1986: 143).

10 My role was further complicated by the demands of some of the tasks I undertook with horses, which required immediate responses. Reflection whilst performing these tasks could actually be dangerous. It was essential to get through some days merely following instructions, really being a stud hand or lad.

11 It was about the time of the bomb scare that I was 'caught' reading a book in a quiet and sunny corner of the yard, and it was funny to see the obvious physical relaxation of my trainer when I explained to him that it was simply a jockey's autobiography. I turned the cover photograph towards him to reveal a photograph of a horse and he let out an audible sigh of relief.

12 However, I have been struck by recent changes in attitude. At the 2001 Guineas meeting at Newmarket, for example, I ordered the vegetarian option for lunch and was surprised when my male companion did the same. I questioned him about his choice, as I had always thought of him as a beef-eating, red-blooded Englishman (on his insistence). In reply, he asked me the rhetorical question, 'Well who eats meat any more?'

4 At the races

Introduction

In this chapter I focus upon the racecourse, because it is here that the supply side of racing, including members of the class described in the preceding chapter, encounter racing's consumers. I have spent dozens of days at racecourses during the past four years, and travelled all over Britain, from Mussleburgh to Brighton. I have been racing in a number of different roles, including those of lad, trainer's assistant and owner. As a spectator I have been racing with gamblers, touts, groups of friends and virtual strangers. On all these occasions I spoke with as many people as possible, recording as much information as I could in note-books, and on an assortment of betting stubs, racecards and cigarette packets.

It is not surprising that some of the most famous, successful and well-connected trainers dislike going racing. It is at the racecourse that the client base that sustains the industry is to be found: the spectators and, in particular, the punters. The central paradox of horseracing is that it is a sport intimately associated with, and some would say driven by, the betting activities of the lower classes whilst many of its professionals (excluding most jockeys) are members of the upper class.[1] The obfuscation of this uneasy symbiosis is achieved through the conventions that occur on the course.

Both the supply and demand sides of racing collude, at times, in the naturalisation of class distinctions on the racecourse. The supply side of racing focuses upon the owner in order to obscure the fact that it is providing a service for consumers of betting. The spectators and punters are patronised by clichés of equality perpetuated by those who depend upon their custom. My fieldwork suggested that some racing spectators collude in their own subordination on the racecourse because their attraction to horseracing lies in its prestigious associations. This association precludes their involvement in its central rituals, but permits their presence on the periphery. Exploring segregation on the racecourse, for example, and particularly its origin in class distinctions and the contemporary form these take, makes relations on the racecourse explicit. This sort of inquiry was therefore a source of discomfort to almost all of my informants, regardless of their structural position in the racing world.

Racing is made public at the racecourse, but what it reveals is systematically obscured by secrecy, impression management and a perverse rendering of
chance and risk as skill and calculation. Racing is supposedly a simple contest
in which horses run around a field and the fastest horse wins. Crowds dress
up and cheer the winner home, praising the bravery of horse and jockey, the
skill of the trainer and the beauty of the scene in a world where it is always an
English summer day at Ascot. How does this image of racing fit with the recent
allegations of doping and race-fixing?[2] How does this image fit with revelations
of 'coups' and the punishment of 'non-triers' by the Jockey Club, and with the
revelations of 'coups'(however unrealistic) by disgruntled and unlucky regulars
in betting shops?

The racecourse circumscribes the majority's experience of horseracing. In
fact, most will think that this is all racing 'is'. I hope to present an alternative
perspective to those writers who focus upon the racecourse as the culmination
of the efforts of the racing industry. What is really being revealed, and obscured, at the racecourse only becomes evident when one has a certain amount
of knowledge about the industry and its professionals, enough knowledge to
puncture the ideology faithfully reproduced at each racecourse, every day of
the year. This chapter functions as a guided tour, moving inwards from the
fringes of the racecourse boundary, via non-members and members, in order to
reach the paddock, the centre of the racecourse universe. I shall describe what
happens within all these areas, whilst drawing upon knowledge from outside
the racecourse to 'make strange' that which is taken for granted. Possible explanations for this systematic obfuscation will be suggested, themes which will
recur throughout the ensuing chapters.

Inside the racecourse, the 1997 Epsom Derby

> As much of America surfaces in a ball park, on a golf links, at a race track, or
> around a poker table, much of Bali surfaces in a cock ring.
>
> (Geertz 1973: 417)

No matter how far I leant out over the rails at Epsom, I couldn't separate Benny
the Dip and Silver Patriarch as they flashed past the post in the 1997 Derby.
I swung round, leant on the winning post and looked at the crowds behind
me. The favourite saying of the racing fraternity that 'all men are equal on the
turf and under it' drifted into my mind, and I tacked on the relevant qualifying
phrase, 'however, some are more equal than others'. Inequality is a defining
feature of racecourses, but at Epsom on Derby Day it was particularly rife,
expressed spatially, and through dress. Top hat and tails: Queen's Stand, suit
and tie: Club Enclosure, t-shirt and jeans: Tattenham Enclosure, bare chests and
bikinis: Centre of the Course. 72,000 people made up the Derby crowd, and they

were spread out in front of me, in zones, categorised according to how much they were prepared to pay to see the biggest race of the European flat racing calendar.

The 1997 Derby provided me with a fantastic opportunity to observe segregation on the racecourse at its most extreme, as the dress code reproduced on the racecard shows:

Dress Standards at Epsom
While we try to keep restrictions to a minimum, we would be very grateful if all customers could be guided by the following:

Queen's Stand Derby Day
Morning dress or service dress is obligatory for gentlemen, ladies should wear formal day dress with hat.

Queen's Stand other days
Suits, or jackets and trousers, with shirt and tie, are preferred for gentlemen. Denim or shorts are not permitted.

Club Enclosure (Derby meeting only)
Suits, or jackets and trousers, with shirt and tie, are preferred for gentlemen. Denim or shorts are not permitted.

Other Enclosures (all days)
Reasonable standards of dress are expected elsewhere. Customers in all enclosures are reminded that the removal of shirts is not allowed.

Although everyone is welcome at Epsom, we do reserve the right in extreme circumstances to either refuse admission to, or to eject any person from, any enclosure or the racecourse. (Official 1997 Vodafone Derby Racecard)

Although there are more and less expensive seats available in most arenas, it is difficult to think of another sport in which the spectators are required to conform to such strict dress codes. Segregation is one of the most striking features of the racecourse, and can be seen as an effort to overcome the paradoxical structure of the racing industry, driven by betting, mainly in off-course shops, patronised on the racecourse by the aristocracy and the upper class. As long as the horse-owning public does not need to encounter the betting public at the races they can maintain that racing is a sport funded by their contributions for their enjoyment, rather than an industry sustained by and for two-pound punters in smoky betting shops in cities all over the country. Conversely, punters can 'back' their judgement, and in doing so oppose members of the upper class, thereby achieving brief ascendancy over them.

Segregation at the racecourse is no longer primarily based upon membership of the course or the Jockey Club as it was in the nineteenth century. However, rather than do away with the category of 'member', racecourses have provided a contemporary perspective thereon. Whilst membership used to involve being forwarded and seconded, and paying a large fee for the privilege, 'member-ship' now resides in the payment of a fee to the racecourse. The category of 'day member' provides the racecourse with a convention whereby they may extend the privileges of membership to those prepared to pay extra on the day. The predictable effect of this is that day members now dominate the category of members, and life, annual or Jockey Club members are provided with smaller but even more exclusive facilities and benefits. Tickets are in all cases called 'badges' suggesting something less transient than the equivalent 'ticket' bought for the cinema. Members' badges fall into the categories of Life (metal), Annual (metal) and Day (cardboard). These badges offer access to the majority of the racecourse enclosures and facilities, and are correspondingly more expensive than the non-members' badges, which have a variety of inoffensive names such as Lonsdale or Tattersalls, and offer limited access to enclosures and facilities on the racecourse. Thus, whilst membership was once a meaningful concept whereby individuals were vetted before being granted their badge, 'member-ship' now means only 'prepared to pay more'.

Dress standard requirements at the Derby are complemented by the appro-priate cuisine within each enclosure. Thus whilst the Queen's Stand boasts a Pimm's bar serving champagne, Pimm's, fresh orange juice and soft drinks, plus a Ben and Jerry's ice cream cart, the Grandstand and Vodafone Village prefer traditional hog roast and sausage baguettes, cider on draught, jazz bands and Cockney dancers. The correspondence between dress, badge price and as-sumed preferences and tastes reveals the racecourse administration's perception of its customers and their group characteristics. The wealthy are to dress up, appreciate the racing and enjoy 'sandwiches, cakes, tea, coffee, cold drinks and other light snacks', whilst 'the masses' can go to the fair (outside the race-course), eat roasted meat in bread and toast their recent peasant ancestry with scrumpy. The racing administrators reproduce the story of the working class told by, for example, Hoggart in the 1950s:

'Something tasty' is the key phrase in feeding: something solid, preferably meaty and with a well-defined flavour. The tastiness is increased by a liberal use of sauces and pickles, notably tomato sauce and piccalilli. (1957: 37)

This stereotypical view of working-class tastes as conservative and unrefined has, of course, been rejected as simplistic by more recent studies that emphasise the dynamic quality of consumption, its historical contingency and potential as a process for self-definition (see Miller 1993).

Sumptuary discrimination is present at all racecourses, in that seafood and champagne bars are the quintessential owners' and members' snack, with fish and chips being the most common form of sustenance found in non-members'. Seafood and champagne have become institutionalised as the celebratory meal par excellence for owners and trainers:

in the working classes fish tends to be regarded as an unsuitable food for men, not only because it is a light food, insufficiently 'filling'... but also because, like fruit (except bananas) it is one of the 'fiddly' things which a man's hands cannot cope with and which make him childlike. (Bourdieu 1984: 190)

Fish is attractive to the elite of racing society for the very reasons that Bourdieu argues it was unattractive to the French working class.[4] Fish is low in fat, comes in small portions, and is fiddly to eat, therefore less is eaten, pleasing ultra-weight-conscious racing society. Furthermore, fish, and particularly shell-fish, requires specialised knowledge of conventions as to which parts are eaten and how they are prepared, and therefore serves to distinguish insiders from outsiders.

Seafood on the racecourse is expensive, and the price of champagne is a continual gripe amongst those with something to celebrate. Celebrations of betting wins generally take the form appropriate to their subject's enclosure. Those with a big win in the non-members and day members are likely to be men in male company, and are celebrated with rounds of drinks. Men accompanied by their families in these enclosures tend to bet in small quantities and might spend winnings on ice cream or chips. Betting wins amongst the members or owners and trainers will not necessarily provoke any sort of celebration, as they may be large and unpublicised, as in the case of professional punters. Smaller wins may be celebrated with champagne, certainly with some form of alcohol, and quite often with another bet. The importance of alcohol at the racecourse can hardly be over-emphasised.[5]

Not all racegoers adhere slavishly to the pursuits attributed to their particular enclosure, however. Even before entering the Derby, creative and suggestive forms of consumption were in evidence. The car park culture of American-style 'tailgating', a picnic technique, was interpreted in various, sometimes extreme, ways by racegoers and others who were simply there in order to eat and drink in the extensive grassed areas. The two extremes of tailgating behaviour were by far the most common, with few examples in between. 'Tailgaters' either had Range Rovers, wicker chairs and trestle tables weighed down with smoked salmon, haunches of venison and champagne, or Ford Cortinas with plastic garden furniture and tables made out of crates of beer. Whilst those in Range Rovers seemed almost perverse in their pursuit of home comfort, and had brought along silver cutlery and crystal glasses, the point for those in Cortinas seemed to be simplicity and relaxation.

Whilst those going into the enclosures were emphasising manners and convention by employing them entirely out of context, those who were not even going to enter the racecourse relaxed conventions, and set up barbecues as if they were in their own gardens. This latter group was reminiscent of the historian's image of the pre-enclosure atmosphere of the racecourse. The presence of a huge fair with rides, gaming booths, food stands, and all Gypsy Rose Lee's living relatives in caravans, further encouraged this comparison. The walk from the car park to the racecourse entrance was enlivened by women in head scarves selling lucky heather and carnations, and touts offering us spare tickets. These attractions ceased a respectable distance from the entrance to the racecourse, where men and women in smart uniforms punched holes in our badges and waved us through the metal detectors and bag search, into the midst of the official Derby entertainments.

Enclosure: inside:outside

Behaviour inside the gates of a racecourse differs in significant ways from that outside. The racecourse boundary marks the separation of the racing world from the outside world. It thus becomes clear why racing professionals such as trainers, to whom the racecourse is a display cabinet, dress as trainers whilst inside, even though they may wear wellingtons and waterproofs tied up with bailing twine whilst shovelling muck at home. Outside the racecourse, trainers are less well known than many other sporting people; however, once on the race-course they are often stars amongst knowing fans. Conversely, whilst trainers, journalists, professional gamblers and officials come to the racecourse to work, the majority of racegoers are intent on enjoying themselves, having left their workplace identity behind at the gate. Racing is a sport and also an industry; hence at the racecourse there are those earning a living and those trying to forget about just that by engaging in a frivolity.

Whilst behaviour inside the racecourse is different to that outside the race-course, it is the same between racecourses, perhaps reflecting a more general trend identified by the geographer Bale:

sports have emerged as highly rationalised representations of modernity which, as much as, (and arguably more than) any other form of culture, possess the potential to eliminate regional differences as a result of their rule-bound, ordered, enclosed and predictably segmented forms of landscape. (1994: 1)

The most obvious feature of the racing landscape is the perimeter wall, and the broadest distinction created by the racecourse is between those inside and those outside. This division is now taken for granted, in that everyone expects to pay in order to go racing, barring special promotions or a distant view from an overlooking hill. Entrance fees are, however, a relatively recent innovation, facilitated by the enclosure of racecourses, beginning with the park courses, at the end of the nineteenth century, as the sports historian Brailsford describes:

The ability to collect gate money was the final piece of the financial jigsaw. Once it was in place, by the end of the century, racing had become, in the words of its most perceptive historian, 'as much part of the economic as the social scene: it was an industry as well as a sport'. (1991: 59–60)

Before enclosure, race meetings were essentially local events, associated with annual holidays, and accompanied by all sorts of other distractions such as cockfights, prizefighting, sideshows and itinerant entertainers. Significantly, racing took place between all sorts of horses, not only thoroughbreds, as hacks, hunters and even ponies were drafted in to satisfy the demand for racing. The supply of horses was limited to those who could walk to the meeting, and so heats served to increase the number of races available as betting media.

The commercialisation of racecourses was facilitated by the advent of enclosure and the expansion of the railways as a means of transporting both horses and spectators. However, the railway alone would not be enough to provoke the mushrooming of racing's fortunes in the latter half of the nineteenth century, when prize money rose from £143,000 in 1839 to £495,000 in 1905 (Brailsford 1991: 60). Although racecourses made money from the tents and attractions that accompanied the racing itself, collection of tariffs and contributions before enclosure had been uncertain and dominated by physical confrontation. Enclosure provided huge opportunities both to ensure income from every spectator, and also to control the accompanying activities by bringing them within the walls of the racecourse. Sandown Park held the first enclosed meeting in April 1875. Those meetings that remained 'open' managed to do so on the grounds that: 'members and would-be members of high society felt a social obligation to put in an appearance at these meetings' (Vamplew 1988: 58). However, even conservative Newmarket had no alternative than to:

march with the times, to build stands, to make enclosures, to substitute the white rails of modern civilisation for the old-fashioned ropes and stakes of our forefathers. (The Earl of Suffolk quoted in Vamplew 1988: 58)

However, the mere fact of enclosure and expanded rail transport does not explain the increasing prize money, number of new meetings, horses in training and volume of bloodstock investment throughout the second half of the nineteenth century. People also had to possess both the money and the desire to go racing. According to Vamplew, racing was benefiting from a more general development on the back of the 70% rise in average real wages between 1850 and 1900:

The 1870s and 1880s are important decades in the history of commercialised popular recreation: they witnessed an expansion of the specialist music halls ... the rapid development of seaside holidays for the working class, the take-off of gate money soccer and of course the enclosed race meeting. (1976: 41)

In changing the nature of race meetings from free local carnival to paying and structured events drawing on a huge potential audience linked up by a railway network, enclosure changed the profile of racegoers. Ponies and hacks had by this time been replaced by English thoroughbreds, identified as such by their presence in the General Stud Book, established in 1791. Race meetings ceased to be gatherings of roughnecks enjoying the bawdy pursuits of drinking, gambling and beating up fraudulent bookmakers. Enclosed courses sought to attract new groups of people to whom racing had previously held little appeal. These groups were women and the working class. Sandown Park was again the trailblazer, racing on Saturdays and providing its male club members with badges for women. Although women went racing at Ascot, Goodwood and Newmarket, they spectated from the relative safety of carriages or private lawns. Saturday afternoon racing provided an opportunity for those who worked during the week to spend their wages racing at the weekend. Amateur officials were replaced by professionals, thus reducing the likelihood of an unpopular result prompting a riot, supplementary activities were restricted to those unlikely to provoke bad behaviour, and according to the turf historian Vamplew, 'segregation was also seen as a way of reducing trouble' (1976: 316).

Enclosure enabled the collection of entrance fees to provide prize money. Increasing prize money stimulated the bloodstock industry, encouraging competition between breeders and increasing the value of bloodstock, most of which remained in the ownership of private stables. However, racing itself had become a spectator sport, attracting large crowds who lacked any connection to the producers of racing. Segregation maintained the separation of the different groups at the racecourse. Trainers, owners and members entered the course through their own entrance, as they do today. Owners and trainers enjoyed their own stands and facilities, and retain the privilege of the owners' and trainers' bar at modern racecourses.

Within the inner circle

Although there are areas even fewer people are authorised to enter, for example the stewards' rooms and jockeys' dressing rooms, the paddock is a private zone in the middle of a public area. In order to be inside the paddock one must be associated with one of the horses in the race, or a race official. A sign on the paddock entrance draws attention to this fact.[6] Racegoers without a horse in the race line the perimeter fence of the paddock, leaning on the rail and evaluating the horses and, no doubt, the connections.

Horses enter the paddock half an hour before they are due to race, and it is their lad's responsibility to get them there on time. The horses are brushed and polished, their hooves are oiled and their manes and tails may be plaited. They wear bridles and rollers, and rugs if it is cold, often with their trainer's initials or sponsor's name on them. The horses are led around the pre-parade ring at a walk, always in a clockwise direction, so that the lad is on the outside. The horses warm up their muscles and the public are able to assess their choice before they place a bet. Horses' behaviour varies in the paddock, some are relatively relaxed, whilst some show signs of anxiety or excitement, either grinding their teeth or pulling hard on the rein. One of the horses I 'led up' was well known for his antics in the paddock, which included bucking and squealing as he jig-jogged round.[7] Each lad has a number attached to his or her arm and the horses wear number cloths for clear identification. As I walked round the paddock cheeky punters always asked me whether my horse had a chance, and, of course, I always said 'yes' with a conspiratorial wink.

The trainer

The trainer arrives with the saddle that he has collected from the weighing room. The saddle has been 'weighed out' with the jockey, so that the horse will be carrying the weight he has been allocated by the handicapper for that race. The trainer calls his charge into one of the saddling boxes on the outer perimeter of the paddock. The horse is backed in, its sheet and roller removed and replaced with its saddle and weight cloth. If it is cold, its sheet may be replaced along with its number cloth and roller. The trainer may squeeze a wet sponge into either side of the horse's mouth in order to moisten his throat. The lad leads the horse away and the trainer is joined by the owner in the middle of the paddock whilst the horse resumes its parade around the inner perimeter.

The paddock has been seen as a ritual arena which has survived in its original form whilst losing much of its significance. It was conventional in the few sociological considerations of horseracing to maintain that status decreased with increasing contact with the horse. Thus the owner was at the top of the hierarchy and hardly touched the horse, the trainer saddled it, the jockey rode it and the lad cleared up after it and inhabited the lowest rung of the ladder. Anthropologist Kate Fox has recently challenged this view:

The formal, official, public elements of racecourse etiquette continue to reassert these distinctions, but any reasonably astute observer of social behaviour will soon spot the shifting power-relations behind this facade. (1997: 16)

These two opposing interpretations of the paddock ritual are equally unhelpful, the first in that contact with the horse is a red herring, status in the paddock is determined by status outside the paddock. Kate Fox re-reads behaviour in the paddock as a 'vestigial' ritual in which the jockey is actually the centre of attention: 'the brightly painted warrior, who is holding court and receiving blessings for a few moments before sallying forth into battle' (1997: 16).[8] I think that a closer look at relationships between owner, trainer and jockey tells a different story.

Events in the paddock are repeated every time there is a race, at all of the different English racecourses, in a practically identical, hence codified form. Action in the paddock serves to reinforce the relations that exist between those taking part and those excluded. Outsiders to this ritual are excluded by the paddock fence, by the specialist knowledge which is apparently being transmitted be-tween actors, and by the specialist knowledge that really is necessary in order to negotiate the ritual itself (including the awareness that what is being transmitted is of very little importance). Behaviour in the paddock also serves to express and reinforce relations between insiders.

The optimum number of people involved with each horse in each performance of the paddock ritual is four, the trainer and lad, who have already been men-tioned, and the owner and jockey. I believe that any exposition of the paddock ritual should take seriously Schechner's observation that:

The great big difference between what a performance is to people inside from what it is to people outside conditions all the thinking about performance. These differences can be as great within a single culture as they are across cultural boundaries. (1990: 27)

In the discourse that emerges from the official racing sources, both of these sets of differences are denied.

The owner

The environment in which the main characters in the paddock find themselves is one of danger, excitement, risk and financial possibility, specific to that particu-lar race. The occasion of the race brings all of the features of racehorse owner-ship into sharper focus, and the owner is most identifiable as such in the paddock. The owner has no formal responsibilities in the paddock. Since the inception of public trainers at the end of the nineteenth century few owners have continued to take responsibility for issuing riding orders to the jockey, a task which has been transferred to the trainer. The question remains as to how the owner communi-cates his 'ownerness', and here Le Wita's analysis of the Parisian bourgeoisie is particularly helpful:

Let us dwell for a moment on the example of dress. Through it we can trace the formation and development of a true culture. The history of costume reveals how the bourgeoisie has repeatedly replaced the aristocracy's ostentatious distinguishing marks with marks that are more restrained, more discreet, though no less formidable in terms of symbolic effectiveness. (1994: 57)

Dress forms a necessary, but not sufficient element in the role of 'owner'. Winter suits are country rather than business, of natural colour and cloth, summer suits are lighter, often linen, the most significant features of both are their cut and accompanying accessories. Describing the cut of a suit in a way that hopes to transcend my own cultural mores is perhaps optimistic, and to say that a suit is well fitted begs all sorts of questions. Relying upon anecdotal experiences as a last resort I would say that these suits were of a sort that is recognised by others within racing society as the same as their own, which I know them to think of as well fitted and well cut. An element of this style that may be identified outside its own milieu is that these suits are classic rather than fashionable. Their price does not determine their value, and many inappropriate designer-label suits may be far more expensive. Their greater value to a racing person lies in their approximation to an ideal type of racehorse owner's suit. A new suit is not as desirable as a suit that seems older, comfortable yet bearing up well to the rigours of frequent visits to the races, possibly due to its high quality. Suits that look comfortable reproduce the most desired demeanour of the owner within.

Apart from dress, 'A person must know how to move in a closed world' (Le Wita 1994: 75). Because the owner has nothing to do in the paddock, he does nothing thoroughly. At most, he concentrates and may look at his horse with narrowed eyes. The most accomplished owners do not even look at their horse, because they are confident that everything is as it should be. They are serious, and exude an air of authority, as if they are performing a difficult and essential task with brilliant ease. In fact, whether they are there or not is a feature of the paddock ritual that affects only them. Owners choose a place to stand in the paddock and remain there until the bell rings and the jockeys enter the paddock and walk to join them.

The increasing number of syndicates, partnerships and women owners are gradually changing the constitution of the crowd in the paddock. However, they do not seem to be affecting its symbolic significance. The most 'horsy' women behave exactly as a man would, and are treated in the same way as a man would be. The class associations of a female member of the aristocracy 'compensate' for her gender, and this has always been the case for the number of women owners from this class. One member of this group to whom I spoke described her presence in the paddock as having an entirely practical purpose:

I go in solely to speak with my trainer, to speak with my jockey, and to look at the horse. It is necessary to have a space in which one may discuss things which are private and concern only those with runners in that race, and that is all the paddock is. It doesn't make me feel anything at all . . . Its purpose is entirely practical.

Other women to whom I spoke, who were relative newcomers to ownership, told me that they relished being in the paddock, and in adopting the behaviour of male owners:

It's quite a thrill, to stand and be looked at by people outside the ring. You feel a part of things that were closed off to you before you bought your horse. It's fun to think of all the other people who have horses with your trainer and to think that you have got a horse with him.

The new syndicate members to whom I spoke were visiting the paddock for the first time. One of these informants told me that she had felt an intense sense of discomfort to be 'on the inside, looking out, with everyone looking in on me'. To some extent, all of these experiences engage with the template of the archetypal male owner. Women who are well connected may be more adept at being male owners than some less well connected men. New women owners adopted male behaviour, and enjoyed the status this attracted, without challenging the basis of that status. The response of syndicate members arises from their awareness of the outsiders to the ritual, which the male owners take for granted, thereby naturalising the distinctions it symbolises.

The trainer shares many traits with the owner; however, as I was told repeatedly, being a trainer is a way of life rather than an occupation. Whilst the racehorse owner is just that by virtue of his other roles (aristocrat, bank manager, lottery winner etc.), the trainer's other roles seem secondary to, and often dependent upon, training, for example, smoker, drinker, socialiser, gambler, husband to woman from racing family, philanderer etc. After saddling the horse the trainer walks into the paddock with the owner. The two of them may both be carrying binoculars and their racecards, walking slowly and looking down at the ground talking under their breath, as if discussing a life-threatening secret. This discussion consists of a few unhurried words, probably concerning the ground or a rival, and will continue after they have come to a halt in the paddock. They will look up when the bell has rung and the jockey is approaching. The atmosphere is, again, serious. The trainer is engaging in impression management. He is paid to train a horse so that it will win races, and in the paddock the potential exists for him to be successful in this task. Therefore he is able to act as if this is exactly what will happen, and as if this is really what trainers do, with the unintended consequence that those who know better accuse them of pomposity, 'There are plenty of people who train horses who think that they are saving the world rather than preparing beasts to run round a field' (Edmondson, quoted in Sharpe 1996b: 4). As Sir Mark Prescott, one of the least pretentious of their number, admits, 'The most common reason for horses getting beaten is trainer error but, thank God, it is seldom reported' (quoted in Sharpe 1996b: 4).

The jockeys

When the jockeys enter the paddock they look around for the connections of their ride. They will be wearing the silks that are registered to that owner. As they approach the connections they touch the peak of their hat. The jockey is introduced to the owner by the trainer. The trainer and owner stand shoulder to shoulder and face the jockey, who rests one foot and then the other, and holds his hands behind his back. The jockey may smile, his conversation with the trainer will not be as secretive as that between owner and trainer. The jockey addresses both owner and trainer as 'sir', 'boss' or 'guv'nor'.

The final bell rings and the connections look for their horse. The horse keeps walking around the perimeter path as the trainer or assistant peels his rugs or roller off. The trainer then gives the jockey a 'leg up' by catching the jockey's bent left leg and lifting him slowly and seemingly effortlessly into the 'plate' as the horse keeps walking along, controlled by the lad. The trainer may say a few final words to the jockey before turning to walk to the stands with the owner in order to watch the race. The lad detaches his rein and holds onto the horse by his bridle, ready to release him onto the course. A race official enters the paddock and directs the runners out of the paddock, towards the track. Most jockeys are reluctant to be first out in case a horse 'plants' himself, that is refuses to move, requiring a lead. However, as the jockeys pretend to be unready to go, and say to the official, 'May I take a turn, sir?' the official gets annoyed and says that they may not. Races must run on time in order to ensure that they do not clash in the betting shops and courses that run late incur disapproval from the Jockey Club, the BHB and punters.

Jockeys tie a knot in their reins in the paddock, whilst control of the horse still rests with the lad. They gather the reins up during the walk to the track, and the horses begin to jog. The lad may run the last few paces to keep the horse's momentum going, again to avoid planting, and says 'good luck' as he lets go of the horse, relinquishing control to the jockey as the horse steps onto the track itself.

It is true that the status of the jockey has changed considerably since the end of the nineteenth century when servant boys were thrown up on horses. However, to say merely that their status has improved is to miss the point. Two examples serve to illustrate the ambivalent position of the jockey in contemporary racing society. The first of these examples is the 'steward's enquiry'. The stewards are the voluntary representatives of the Jockey Club at the racecourse, who serve to ensure that the rules of racing are observed. A steward's enquiry takes place when the stewards believe that a breach of the rules may have occurred in a race. The jockeys involved are called to the steward's room, where there are generally at least four televisions capable of showing a race from all of the different camera angles available. The stewards are guided in their decision to call an enquiry by the professional steward's secretary, who is also responsible for advising them on the rules of racing and the procedure to be followed when they are broken.

The jockeys stand in front of the panel of three seated stewards and are addressed by the chairman, whom they address as 'sir'. When I asked an apprentice jockey about the atmosphere in the room he told me that it reminded him of a headmaster's office, the jockey himself had felt 'like a naughty kid', and he continued, 'It's part of the job, you have to learn how to behave, how to bite your tongue if you know what I mean.'

In other professions the possibility of amateur observers disciplining professionals and imposing fines or suspensions seems unthinkable. It is rarely

questioned, of course, amongst racing society, because it is part of the arrangement they work so hard to maintain as 'natural'. The apprentice said that he
had been taught how to handle the enquiry at the British Racing School, the
basic technique being that of saying nothing but 'Yes, sir' and 'No, sir'. When I
visited the British Racing School and asked the instructors about this they told
me, 'Absolutely. Politeness is part of the right attitude.'

The second example, which draws attention to the status of jockeys within
racing society, is that of the Haydock riders' strike. On 16 October 1996, jockeys
refused to ride, and simply closed the door of the weighing room when called
to do so. They believed that conditions were unsafe, although the stewards had
held an inspection and decided that it was safe to race. The reactions of trainers
and owners to this state of affairs was mixed, but those who disapproved of
their actions voiced their opinion very strongly:

They're a bunch of misfits and should be forced to prove they have the necessary bottle
for the game . . . It's a joke. The jockeys can do what they want now. It's the tail wagging
the dog . . . This is a terrible day for racing . . . The jockeys have taken the mickey . . .
They are spoiled and pampered. (Trainer)

Any jockey who says he is not going to ride in a particular race because it would be
dangerous should not be a jockey – all races are dangerous. (Trainer)

I'm disappointed that the ringleaders have not been punished. My owners were very
angry, and I'm sure they will be disappointed by this verdict. (Trainer)

I am very surprised and bemused that the ringleaders have got away with no punishment.
Where does it end? (Dudley Moffatt, father of a young apprentice who wanted to ride,
quoted in Briggs and Lawrence 1997: 2)

The language employed, of 'punishment' and 'ringleaders', is that of school
discipline, reinforced by the idea that a breakdown in 'discipline' will lead to
anarchy. There were dissenting voices amongst a minority of trainers, including
Bill O'Gorman, who warned that, 'We should remember when we are rollicking
jockeys that it is a job where the ambulance follows you when you are working'
(quoted by Sharpe 1996a: 4). The relationship between jockeys and trainers is
illuminated by these reactions, and their belief that the jockeys' refusal to ride
represented a serious threat to the balance of power in racing demonstrates just
how that power is distributed.

The observation that the riders' strike constituted the 'tail wagging the dog'
reveals the connections' perception of the proper relationship between themselves and the jockeys. The strike was seen as a disaster by owners and trainers.
Their fears arose from the questioning of the order that they work so hard to
naturalise – jockeys and lads will do as they are told because that is the way
things are. That they did not at Haydock both undermines this order and also
raises the possibility that justification for the present order will be required

before it can be reinstated. In fact, the Jockey Club inquiry was extremely lenient, and only 'punished' Frankie Dettori. Dettori's punishment was perceived to have been incurred for his role as 'ringleader'. As the most successful and therefore most powerful jockey in the weighing room that day, he was seen as most culpable. Darren Moffat, the young apprentice who had wanted to continue riding, was hailed as a hero. Moffat had become a representative of the old order according to which jockeys obeyed the orders of their horse's connections, whilst Frankie represented a new, and potentially insidious, order, of jockey power.

The Haydock riders' strike is a remarkable example of the ability of a single day's racing to reproduce the naturalised order of the upper-class officials and producers of horseracing. The low-key Jockey Club inquiry reflected this ability. It was not necessary to reinforce order, because this was achieved the next day, when racing went ahead on three courses, according to the routine that had changed little over the past hundred years. A heavy-handed approach by the Jockey Club might have prompted a debate, whilst a slight rebuke merely indicated 'business as usual'. The strike was presented as of individual significance only, and the order that had re-established itself the next day was left unquestioned. In contrast to Kate Fox, I maintain that the jockeys express more than respect for tradition when they touch the peak of their hat as they enter the paddock. The status of jockeys as a group lags behind that of trainers due to entrenched historical factors, and their contemporary mutations.

Jockeys continue to serve apprenticeships.[9] In the nineteenth century, an apprenticeship referred to a period of time spent working for a trainer who had been placed in loco parentis by means of a contract signed by the parents of small boys, often found by scouts in Scotland and Ireland. Some of the taxi drivers in Newmarket can still remember picking up boys from the station who had labels fixed to their clothing giving the name of the trainer to whom they were to be delivered. Even the old school in Newmarket who express a fondness for 'the good old days' described these unfortunate boys as 'wretched', 'malnourished' and 'just scraps of things, some not more than twelve year old'. Many of these boys lived in stable hostels in dire poverty, working long hours under the threat of violence, miles from home. They were often treated with contempt by their employers. Trainer Atty Pearse is quoted as saying that boys are 'the very devil, the bugbear of a trainer, needing to be watched all the time' (quoted in Fitzgeorge-Parker 1968: 52). At the present time, apprentices continue to sign a contract with their trainer, who may give the young jockey rides in order to take advantage of his weight allowance and to give him experience so that he might improve. It seems that young boys are no longer 'pressganged' as was common in the past, but have often had some experience of riding racehorses, hunters or ponies. Many still arrive from Ireland, and most do not make it as jockeys and so become lads and work riders.

Apprentices are still referred to as 'boys'. In an apprentice race for example, I was told by a trainer, 'this horse wants a boy on it, because it doesn't like being told what to do by a jockey'. Even the horses are credited with the awareness that apprentices are less powerful than the professional jockeys they would like to become! Apprentices' rides are approved by their trainer, and their outside riding fees are withheld. The apprentice is paid 20% of these fees as 'pocket money'. It can be seen that jockeys who must come up through the ranks in order to make it as a professional must do so through the good grace of their guv'nor. Their careers are not in their own hands until they lose their weight allowance, and even then, trainers decide who rides their horses and so maintain the power in the relationship between jockey and trainer.

Conclusion

Everyone who goes racing colludes in order to create a liminal world. As one racegoer said to me when I explained my project: 'Don't spoil the dream will you?' Social relations infused with inequality are only one aspect of the racecourse, which is also an arena in which people are free to assume identities which they may be unable to adopt outside. The impression management of trainers, for example, is supremely attractive to those who have sufficient spare assets to buy racehorses. Those trainers who are considered to be 'characters' sustain the racing industry by attracting owners who wish to be part of a society that seems glamorous, secretive, exciting and successful, features a trainer must embody if he is to inspire confidence in his clients, just as the bookie, the star of the next chapter, must do in order to attract a wager.

The strong racecourse ethos of equality, and the mobility of the crowd, combined with the rapid turnover of money through the hands of bookies and punters, detract from the uncomfortable truth that the racecourse is really a map expressing hierarchical relationships between insiders and outsiders. These relationships are informed by the aristocratic history of horseracing, which was codified as a 'gentleman's sport' and has always valued exclusivity, as reflected in the form taken by the racecourse following enclosure. The temporary suspension of this hierarchy in the betting ring will be discussed in the next chapter. I shall suggest that a careful examination of behaviour in the ring reveals that the split between aristocrat and parvenu is reproduced in the role of professional and mug punter respectively.

NOTES

1 This is a stark characterisation of what is, of course, a far more complicated situation, but it is an opposition that is described by many people who work in racing or who attend race meetings.
2 During 1998 and 1999 charges were brought against a number of people in relation to the doping of racehorses. In all cases, the charges were dropped or there was found

to be no case to answer. However, the trainers of two horses who produced positive dope tests were fined under Jockey Club rules that require the trainer to take personal responsibility in such cases even if they were clearly not responsible (Griffiths and Yates 2000: 6, Masters and Green 2001: 4).

3 Horses entered into a race in order to run badly and thus be assigned a lighter weight or better odds for their next race are described as 'not off'. They may not be fully fit, they may be running on ground that doesn't suit, or over a distance that is either too far or too short. A lacklustre performance must not be poor enough to attract the attentions of the stewards however, as they may decide that the horse is guilty of being a 'non-trier', who will be suspended unless the trainer can explain its performance. Complicating this picture is the tendency of horses to run badly for absolutely no detectable reason, most often described as 'having an off day'.

4 Just as Hoggart's description of the eating habits of the English working class has dated, Bourdieu's description of a French working-class aversion to fish now seems unconvincingly static. However, the qualities attributed to the fish remain relevant – seafood makes for fussy, delicate eating.

5 The consumption of alcohol by racegoers is one of the major activities traditionally undertaken on course. Apart from the racing and betting, it is drinking that unites virtually all sections of racegoer. One must also add that drug use has always been apparent amongst a minority of racegoers, and appears to have become increasingly visible recently (see Green 2001).

6 Signs advise that, 'Only connections of horses in the present race may enter the paddock'. It is interesting that although no one monitors the entrance to the paddock, and in theory anyone could simply walk in, it is obvious that people do not. This is one of the ways in which the racing crowd is self-regulating.

7 If horses sweat excessively in the paddock it is usually seen as a sign that they have 'boiled over' and will not run well, although some horses run their best races exactly when they sweat up: another of the puzzles to be worked out before the money goes down.

8 Kate Fox's work on racing was funded by the British Horseracing Board.

9 The apprentice occupies a structural position within the racing industry that has changed enormously over the past century, and a study of the jockey's apprenticeship would warrant its own book. Here I just have space to describe a few of the features of the apprenticeship in order to address the point made by Fox.

5   Having a flutter

Introduction

Whether it's once a year on the Grand National, or every day in the local betting shop, 'having a flutter' is one of the most familiar aspects of racing to many British people. One of the most striking things about my fieldwork in betting shops and on racecourses was the intensity of winning reactions. I would chase triumphant air-punchers all over the racecourse to ask, 'How did that feel?', until I was no longer surprised to hear the response 'Yeahhhhhhh! Better than sex!' Betting is clearly a source of great excitement and pleasure for some, but can also be the downfall of others.

Rather than attempting to uncover the inherent properties of gambling[1] I shall discuss betting on horseracing (punting) as a practice which can fulfil a variety of purposes for the different constellations of people to whom it is significant. The particular contexts that I shall attempt to reconstruct are those of the betting shop and the betting ring. This chapter draws particularly upon fieldwork spent in the betting rings of a number of British racecourses, and in betting shops. I became a regular at two betting shops in Newmarket, where I enjoyed the nickname of 'Flaps', based (so I was told) on my arm movements during a race. I have never been a particularly successful punter, although I did virtually double my university grant on one memorable occasion at Huntingdon racecourse, and would have to admit that I am not immune to the excitement of the betting ring. I haven't had a bet since the summer of 2001 when I stood in the company of a man who lost $50,000 on a single race.[2]

Recent anthropological discussions of gambling typically emphasise its positive contribution to the smooth running of the society in question. Thus gambling can be a 'levelling mechanism' (Zimmer 1987, Mitchell 1988, Woodburn 1982), it can facilitate crossover between otherwise distinct spheres of exchange (Riches 1975), it can enable people to 'fall into patterns of sociability with each other' (Maclean 1984: 52), or it can provide a new means of asserting marriageability where traditional methods have been eroded (Zimmer 1987). Conversely, theological, psychological and sociological discussions of gambling, generally based upon data from Europe and America, emphasise its inherently anti-social qualities, specifically through the construction of the figure of the 'compulsive gambler' (Oldman 1978, Dickerson 1984, Thomas 1901). Gambling has under these circumstances been seen as a disease, as a sin, as pathological and as associated with organised crime. I shall argue that the study of punting as a form of gambling requires an awareness of the historical significance of horseracing in Britain, and in particular its class associations.[3]

The very act of betting on a horserace is based upon an opposition between punters and the producers of racing. When placing his bet the punter must believe that he has 'read' the race more accurately than the trainers who have entered the horses that he believes will not win. His financial involvement buys the punter a 'stake' in the outcome of a complicated and culturally loaded event. Few punters include breeding as a variable in their calculations,[4] concentrating instead upon 'going' (the state of the ground), 'form' and distance. In a number of ways, punters are opposed to the producers of racing, for reasons I shall explore in this chapter.

The current relationship between horseracing and betting

At the time of fieldwork, racing was funded by both a levy raised on the betting turnover of bookmakers, and also the profits from its own betting enterprise, the Tote. The Horserace Betting Levy Board (HBLB), established in 1963, distributed the Levy collected from punters by bookmakers as part of General Betting Duty (GBD). In 1998, GBD was paid on the stake or on winnings, at 9%, 6.5% of which went to the government and 1.75% to the HBLB. Bookmakers rounded up the deduction to 9% on all bets. The HBLB stated the following objective in its 1996 report:

The Board is charged with the duty of assessing and collecting the monetary contributions from bookmakers and the Horserace Totaliser Board, and with applying them for purposes conducive to any one or more of:
• the improvement of breeds of horses;
• the advancement or encouragement of veterinary science or veterinary education;
• the improvement of horseracing. (1996: 3)

The major outlay identified by the Board in 1998 was £28,910,096, which represented 45.4% of total prize money. Other contributors were the racecourse executives (16.4%), sponsors (20.8%) and owners (16.6%) (Wright 1999: 9). The punter thus occupied a central position in relation to the funding of racing, via a levy on all legal fixed-price betting, or through betting with the Tote, a poolbetting system, the profits of which go to racing.[5]

The racing calendar is thus, to a large extent, devised with the needs of the punter in mind. Punters prefer betting on handicaps and on races with as many runners as possible, whilst trainers, owners and the racing enthusiast may not have the same priorities. The Jockey Club has also introduced rules designed to safeguard the punters' interests. These include non-triers' rules that require trainers to explain any dramatic improvements in their horses or face a ban, with the aim that horses run to the best of their ability in every race. Jockeys must also ride to achieve the best possible placing and stiff penalties are imposed on jockeys who 'drop their hands' and lose a place in a finish.

'Punter power' sits uncomfortably with those who continue to imagine racing through the power relations which informed its early history. This struggle between punters and owners/trainers has frequently been expressed in terms of the sport:industry debate which is aired periodically in the racing newspapers and was a contentious issue during my fieldwork. Whilst some owners argue that they should not be expected to continue to invest in a loss-making enterprise:

[Some] may regard racing as a 'hobby', but racing is the country's sixth largest employer and that means the economic return for the racing product has to support an army of dependants.

others invoke sporting examples and emphasise that, for example, owning a yacht could never be subsidised but is something one does for the pleasure it provides, rather than for a financial return:

Seriously, anyone who goes into racehorse ownership expecting or needing to make financial sense of it is either nuts or badly advised. Of course prize money levels need urgent attention, but surely most owners are in the game for sport and fun and any money that comes back is a bonus.

In essence, the debate is whether wealthy individuals are still prepared to indulge in an expensive sport solely for pleasure, or whether the role of owner must be that of entrepreneur looking for a 'healthy return' on an investment.

The solution most regularly invoked to address the low levels of prize money in racing is that of an off-course Tote monopoly:

Australia, a society unhindered by obsolete mores and prejudices inbuilt over many centuries, has what countless experts have pointed out offers the solution to the modernisation of our sport. They have a system of bookmakers on track and only Tote off that guarantees the financial income, and the professionals at every level, to run an efficient sport which can compete with other forms of entertainment to its best possible advantage. (Underwood 1998: 4)

It is unthinkable that there would ever be an off-course Tote monopoly in Britain, because the traditions of bookmaking and racing professionals have developed separately.

The transition of racing from a sport to an industry, at least in its contemporary incarnation, is usually dated from the 1960s, influenced by the increased availability of air transport and the resulting internationalism. The transition is codified in 'The Report of the Duke of Norfolk's Committee on the Pattern of Racing', submitted to the Jockey Club in August 1965:

up to quite recently, the object of racing was a sport and the betterment of the thoroughbred. And many of the rules of racing today were framed to safeguard this animal through its racing career. Today the sport has turned into an industry, is looked upon almost entirely commercially and few of those who follow it think anything at all about the welfare of the horse. (quoted in Hill 1988: 186)

Significantly, the report predicted that without the protection of the English thoroughbred by the British government 'racing is liable to be debased to the level of roulette, and does not deserve to survive' (quoted in Hill 1988: 186).[6] A further instalment of this transition from sport to industry took place in the 1970s, following the oil crisis of 1972, when a massive amount of Middle Eastern investment flooded into British racing. The effect of this influx was a professionalisation of the industry and a growing nostalgia for the amateur 'sporting' past.

Traditionalist racing society prides itself on 'sport for sport's sake', explicitly comparing this higher pleasure with the base pursuit of profit through betting:

Betting isn't about sport, because only the result is important, not the means. Watch a chaser go round Aintree, all guts, bravery, courage. I want the horse to win because it deserves it. Punters only want the result and they want it to win so that they can collect. They miss what's beautiful and important about racing and only see what they can grab. They exploit racing. (Owner)

The antagonistic relationship between the betting fraternity and members of the racing establishment has led to the construction of opposing identities in terms of those features each side feels constitute their most significant differences:

Punters aren't part of this game – they are only interested in what racing can do for them without any effort. Real racing folk invest in racing by investing in the breed, and I don't just mean money. I mean blood, sweat and tears. (Breeder)

I think when you buy or breed a racehorse you have to leave your brain as a deposit. Racing wouldn't exist without betting. It's what it's for. They service our needs. (Punter)

This is an argument that reappears periodically in the pages of the racing press, and which cannot be resolved. However, the sources of the antagonism can be better understood by a consideration of the development of the two traditions of racing and betting.

The historical relationship between bookmaking and horseracing

Betting is the manure to which the enormous crop of horse-racing and racehorse breeding in this and other countries is to a large extent due.

(Black 1893: 349)

Many historical commentators accord Harry Ogden the distinction of 'father' of modern bookmaking (Chinn 1991: 40, Munting 1996: 89). Although betting has apparently accompanied horseracing since its inception, bookmaking is a relatively recent form of betting which was enabled by the increased number of runners in races throughout the eighteenth century, from the matches (two-horse races) of the preceding era to the sweepstakes (multiple-runner races) found today. Bets struck on matches were generally between the owners of the horses and their friends or other interested parties. Spectators were not encouraged at such affairs, those on foot, in particular, were effectively excluded by moving the race elsewhere, further away from prying eyes. Matches were usually bet upon 'at evens', that is, as if the horses were of equal ability. A gentleman could gain prestige by betting at evens with a horse he knew to be superior to his own.

The nature of horseracing changed fundamentally in the nineteenth century: At the beginning of the nineteenth century horse racing was basically a national sport carried out on a local level. Generally meetings were annual affairs intimately associated with local holidays . . . by the end of the century racing drew its spectators from far and wide, the carnival atmosphere had been dampened down, and the sport had become much more commercially oriented. (Vamplew 1988: 56)

There was a marked increase in the popularity of racing as a spectator sport, and in the attendance of race meetings, providing opportunities to raise gate money through the enclosure of the racecourse, first attempted at Sandown Park in April 1875 (Vamplew 1988: 57). The development of the railway further widened racing's potential audience (see Vamplew 1976). Although 'blacklegs' on Newmarket Heath would accept a bet from a gentleman on a particular horse in a race, throughout the eighteenth century there was no facility for all-comers to lay a bet on the horse of their choice.

With the expansion in spectator attendance, and the diversification of the gaming entrepreneurs into betting, an antagonistic association was born, which continues to inform the relationship between racing and bookmaking today.

Thus Newmarket and Epsom had ceased during the eighteenth century to be the exclusive preserves of the aristocracy and gentry, and had become also the hunting ground of optimists, crooks and upstarts who were in search of riches. (Blyth 1969: 39)

This time of upheaval, however, rather than breaking down the existing class-based divisions in racing, merely served to reinforce them as racing society dug in its heels in response to the onslaught.

Although bookmakers had sharks, adventurers and crooks as their predecessors, their trade is actually a very specific form of gambling, quite different from wagering. 'Making a book' on a race involves offering a 'price' (odds) on all of the horses in the race to anyone who wishes to challenge your judgement. These odds express the bookmaker's opinion as to which horse is most likely to win, second likeliest to win, and so on through the 'field'. These odds are displayed on course or in the betting shop, where 'punters' (those who bet) may 'take a price' (bet) on their 'fancy' (choice) if they feel that the horse has as great a chance of winning or better than that expressed by the book. Once punters begin to bet at these prices, the book becomes an instrument measuring the strength of support for each runner in the race.

The basic principles of bookmaking have endured since the eighteenth century. The relationship between bookmaking and British law, however, has been anything but constant. The form taken by horseracing effectively excluded anyone but racehorse owners from betting systematically until the eighteenth century. Before this time, legislation concentrated upon gaming in the form of cards or dice (Munting 1996: 10).[7] The title of Wray Vamplew's classic analysis of horseracing and the law, 'One for the rich and one for the poor' (1976), refers to the separation between those who had the facilities and resources to bet on credit and those who did not. The Bill of 1853, which banned bookmakers from operating in betting houses, exhibiting lists or advertising a willingness to take bets, turned on a distinction between those bookmakers who were prepared to bet with all-comers, the bookies, and those betting between individuals in men's betting clubs, particularly Tattersall's.

The 1853 Gaming Law 'made little difference to betting itself' (Munting 1996: 91), which flourished in the informal economy, in the era of the street bookie. A resurgence of the moral condemnation of gambling coincided with the Great Depression during which gambling was identified as the cause of alcoholism, poverty and moral regression. The National Anti-Gambling League (NAGL), and in particular campaigners such as B. Seebohm Rowntree, took up the banner from the Society for the Suppression of Vice (1802), the middle-class association that set out to 'stop Sabbath-breaking licentious publications and to campaign against private theatricals, fairs, brothels, dram houses, gaming houses and illegal lotteries' (Munting 1996: 21).

Gambling came to be described as an illness or an addiction. This vocabulary, the modern version of which is found in the figure of the 'compulsive gambler' and the language of Gamblers Anonymous, casts the gambler as subject to exterior forces, rather than as an agent of purposive action. His 'illness' can be cured by a gradual return to responsible decision-making through a series of activities that constitute his 'cure'. The figure of the 'compulsive gambler' reified by the NAGL in the early twentieth century, and still in existence in contemporary psychoanalytic material, is presented as a *defective* rather than a *deviant* individual, and by characterising gambling as a disease it is denied the status of a counter-ideology to the puritan work ethic, and reduced to an a-rational affliction.

In 1906 the Street Betting Act was passed, banning bookies and their runners, who operated on street corners and on factory floors. According to the Peppiatt Committee Report, this act was widely flouted, and police were either bribed or did not enforce the ban on betting. The committee reported in 1960, at which time credit and on-course betting were legal, whilst off-course betting was illegal, but flourishing. The class-based, paternalistic betting law reflected a tendency initiated in the earliest interactions between racehorse owner and blackleg, described by Jockey Club historian Robert Black in 1893, 'So long as it was between nobles it was a comparatively harmless pastime; but he felt that it was "sordid" for an aristocrat to bet with a commoner' (quoted by Chinn 1991: 38).

The Betting and Gaming Act of 1960 finally legalised ready-money betting shops. By 1963, 14,388 betting shops had been opened (Munting 1996: 98). The law regarding gambling remained paternalistic, however, with betting shops banned from having toilets, comfortable seats, refreshments or television until 1984. Their sepulchral air did not, however, prove unpopular with those who wished to bet. The lack of comfort in betting shops reinforced the association of gambling with the working class, and recent legislation permitting their improvement has been cited as responsible for the increase in betting amongst professionals.

The betting shop

Betting shops, despite being granted concessions, in 1986, to have comfortable seats and to sell soft drinks, remain something of an enigma in the era of the air-conditioned shopping mall and the sterile pub. The betting shop is one of the last bastions of the smoker, for example. Not smoking is frowned upon, whilst coughing or waving arms to clear the air is not tolerated. One of my favourite bookies in Newmarket was adjacent to a pub, and regulars brought in their pint from next door to sup on the agreement that they return the glass. Dogs were also always welcome in the shop, with or without owners. However, despite my fondness for betting shops, and the smelly charm of an afternoon spent watching racing in the company of familiar faces, I cannot report, as many sociologists appear to suggest, that betting shops service the needs of lower-class men to assert positive identities based on the successful interpretation of form and a financial investment in their own judgement.

Various studies have reported that, for working class males, the primary satisfaction from gambling is derived from the problem solving process involved. (Fisher 1993: 452)

Perhaps my gender and age excluded me from observing this sort of betting, but in my experience, and according to those I asked, a visit to the betting shop was 'part of my routine', spent in virtual silence, with little interaction between customers, minute stakes and little involvement. The more I spoke to fellow betting-shop habitués the more convinced I was that this was not 'Where the Action is' (Goffman 1969).

Goffman describes gambling as 'the prototype of action' (1969: 138), where action is defined as:

activities that are consequential, problematic, and undertaken for what is felt to be their own sake . . . The individual releases himself to the passing moment, wagering his future stake on what transpires precariously in the seconds to come. At such moments a special affective state is likely to be aroused, emerging transformed into excitement. (1969: 136–7)

For the majority of bets placed by the majority of people, this did not seem to be the case. For many punters, placing a bet seemed routinised, and devoid of intellectual involvement. Broad groups of people can be identified in relation to their betting behaviour in the shop. In the mornings, men and women come into the shop in order to lay a specific bet which they have decided upon at home. No time is spent gazing at the paper on the walls, and morning 'layers' tend to want to be in and out as quickly as possible. Men were often middle-aged or younger, and wore tracksuits, overalls or jeans, rather than suits. Men generally told me that they were either on their way to work or on a tea break. Their bets tended to be staked on a single horse.

Female customers were often middle-aged or older, wearing dresses and overcoats and carrying shopping bags. Most told me that they were in the middle of shopping, and that the betting shop was one of the shops they called in on most mornings. Quite often women placed the combination bets that had been suggested in the morning papers; for example, a permutation based on predicting the winners of all six races at a particular course. When I asked why they preferred to bet in this way I was told:

Well, it's just a bit of fun isn't it. You get better odds on combination bets, you see, so even though I only bet 10p a line, I could still get a really good return. I suppose its habit really, because I do worry that if I don't do it then I might miss out.

The other side of betting at long odds is obviously that the chances of the bet being successful are remote. The bets laid by women in the morning did not reflect any knowledge of racing or consideration of form, 'I wouldn't know one end of the thing from the other!', they were always described as 'just a habit', and seemed to have much more in common with premium bonds than hysterically cheering home a long-shot winner at a packed racecourse on a hot day in June. It seemed to me that the female morning punters had sapped betting of its intellectual component, its personal responsibility and its excitement. Placing their bet appeared to be approached as just another household chore, a form of investment rather than a risk-taking exercise. Accordingly, those few women who could recall ever having won any money told me that winnings were absorbed by the household budget, with no special purchases being made. In Newmarket, tips are a part of everyday life. Many of the women who came into the shop had a particular relative upon whom the rest of the family depended for a 'good word'. In keeping with this routinised arrangement, bets are placed without ceremony and winnings absorbed without fuss.

Live greyhound- and horseracing begins in the afternoon, along with the numbers draws which are succeeding in drawing custom away from the racing. Once racing begins, the older men who appear to spend the entire afternoon in the shop appear. The majority of afternoon regulars in each of the shops I visited regularly were old men, who had retired. Quite often they told me that they were widowers. These men were reticent about their betting. They looked at the papers on the walls, and may have had a daily paper of their own in addition. They frequently followed the advice of newspaper tipsters, but rather unsystematically. Deciding to place a bet was a casual undertaking, the name read from the screen or the paper, scrawled on a piece of paper and given with the couple of pounds stake to the cashier with little comment. Most remarks made to the cashier tended to be of the doom-laden variety, 'Here you go Peg, that's my last fiver. You may as well have that too.' I had hoped for passionate discussions of the merits of the handicapping system, distance and ground, trainer's form and jockey's abilities, but in fact I had to be satisfied with: 'I'm not sure why, I just fancy it.' These men tended to bet on every race, a singularly unsuccessful strategy, since some races are far easier to predict than others.[8] The strategy cemented my impression that for regulars, betting on horseracing had more to do with betting than with horseracing.

In between afternoon horseraces are greyhound races, which were instituted in their present form by the bookmakers, who owned the tracks and partly owned the broadcasting service (Satellite Information Service) which transmitted the commentary. Bookmakers Afternoon Greyhound Services (BAGS) began in 1967, in order to provide a betting medium between races, and to compensate when bad weather affected horseracing. Greyhound racing is universally sneered at by those who value horseracing for its own sake:

I can't imagine anything worse. Watching skinny dogs go round and round a featureless circuit chasing a mechanical hare, wearing coloured jackets like glorified flies on a wall. Greyhound racing has nothing whatsoever in common with horseracing; it's a lottery for deadheads who want to recycle their dole money. (Trainer)

Numbers betting, in various forms, is also available in betting shops, where there are live draws every afternoon. These draws offer better odds than the National Lottery, although with smaller jackpots. Numbers betting is incredibly popular, to the Horserace Betting Levy Board's chagrin. Speaking to regulars who placed bets on horseracing, greyhounds and numbers, it became clear that whilst there were those who focused on horseracing out of an affection for the horses themselves, there were also those who failed to see any significant difference between betting on horses, dogs or plastic balls, 'It doesn't make any difference what you bet on does it? As long as something wins!'

For a few punters in the betting shop the pleasure of betting does seem to reside in the intellectual stimulation of making a selection in a race based on knowledge of the intricacies of racing. The financial involvement is perhaps less significant to this punter than the satisfaction of being proved correct in his calculations, and perhaps to explain his train of thought to a few fellow bettors. However, discussions amongst such punters also commonly invoke the corruption they believe is rife in racing. I repeatedly came across the idea that the leading bookmakers employ a 'ray gun' that they use on the favourite over the last fence in order to prevent a big pay out.

When the favourite jumps the last in front, you'll have a bloke in the crowd looking at him with binoculars, and he'll activate the ray gun and bang, sort of shake up all of his nervous system and he falls. I've seen it with my own eyes! And one day they'll come unstuck because they'll hit the jockey and then there'll be hell to pay. But everyone knows that it's done, it's common knowledge. (Punter)

As Newman observed of such punters in London, success is celebrated:

Not as a tribute to the individual punter's excellence, but as a common triumph over the massed forces of the outside, over the superior external powers, a victory of 'Us' over 'Them'. (1968: 24)

The enormously powerful bookmakers are 'beaten', and their devious schemes overcome by the canny punter. In Newmarket, 'They' can also be identified more precisely, because, in behaving as though one knows more than the ranks of racing professionals who dominate the town, one may gain temporary as-cendancy over them. In Newmarket, in particular, this motivation was common to the lads of various types (sacked, retired, 'between yards') who spent their afternoons in the bookies, letting me know that they knew more about the chances of the horses in each race than any trainer in the town, 'They're all idiots!'

However, studies that cite intellectual motivations at the expense of more mundane explanations for betting behaviour also tend to focus on the experi-ences of winning punters, whose status is thereby improved.[9] Characterising betting as an empowering experience neglects the explanations of those punters who bet 'so that I'm out of the house', 'Because I always have' and, more precisely, those punters who lose. For these punters, I would suggest that the attraction of the betting shop lies not in its provision of opportunities for 'action', but in its isolation from reality, 'I come here for a bit of peace and quiet, and if I want a bet I might look at the paper or whatever.' In contrast to Goffman's division of the world:

On one side are the safe and silent places, the home, the well-regulated roles in business, industry and the professions; on the other are all those activities that generate expression, requiring the individual to lay himself on the line and place himself in jeopardy during a passing moment. (1969: 204–5) it seemed that many punters in betting shops find their lives outside the shop sufficiently stressful to lead to their identification of the shop itself as a sort of a sanctuary. The betting shop is often a passively social environment, rather than a hotbed of risk-taking and personal enhancement. This is an environment in which risk has been tamed, made to answer the bidding of men who want to be involved in something outside themselves but who also want to know when the wager will be resolved. In the betting shop risk is sufficiently contained by the television screens, company carpets and cashiers' uniforms: its subjects are two-dimensional. The sights, sounds, smells of the racecourse, so capable of making the blood rush, are entirely lacking from the experience. The same cannot be said of the betting ring.

The betting ring

Whilst fighting for air in a sea of people before the 2:05 at Yarmouth it occurred to me that the absence of the betting ring from anthropological literature was incredible. I was part of a crowd whose actions were determined by a row of men on upturned crates writing figures on a board bearing their ancestors' names, shouting slang which was relayed in incomprehensible sign language by a man in white gloves. The betting ring can be intimidating, it can be crowded, deserted, quiet (waiting for the result of an enquiry), or ear-drum burstingly noisy (when the favourite romps home in front). The ring is a male-dominated space, where women are tolerated rather than welcomed, and there is no room for the very old or the very young. The dialect and body language of the bookies and their customers, epitomised by the institutionalised sign language of 'tic-tac', make a visit to the betting ring a perplexing experience, but one which stimulates a desire to understand its conventions, and perhaps to become part of them.

My favourite bookmaker is an East End boy made good. He is middle-aged, portly, thinning on top, wears Pringle jumpers and slip-on shoes and a sheepskin coat when it is cold in the ring. He speaks quickly, and responds to questions before they are finished, replying with absolute confidence and a harsh wit. He has strong views about everything, 'I don't take bets from women and I don't do each way', 'That won't win, and anyone who says it will don't know what they're talkin' about!' He generally has either a wad of money in his hand or a batch of betting tickets, ready to distribute to punters who back with him because he is trusted and admired. He is loud and 'old fashioned' and admits himself to 'giving it the large one' occasionally, 'I s'pose I speak my mind, but you can take it or leave it can't ya!' He personifies the qualities a bookmaker appears to need in order to be successful, he is charismatic, confident and outspoken.

Bookmakers display their 'prices' (the odds they are prepared to offer on a horse) on colourful boards which give their name, and the name of the family member from whom they have inherited the 'pitch' (the right to bet at that racecourse).[10] The board also shows their home town, or town of origin, and may state the minimum stake accepted, or that the bookmaker accepts win-only bets. Below the board, suspended by one of its handles, is the standard issue bookmakers' money satchel, which may also bear the owner's name and family details. The bag hangs temptingly open, stuffed with rolled-up wads of notes.[11] Until recently, the bookmaker stood on a coloured crate that may also have been personalised. The equipment is referred to collectively as the bookie's 'joint' and, over the last year, has become standardised in the form of a plastic stand. Many bookmakers have two clerks, one to accept the bets, who stands to the left of the board, and one behind who calculates the liabilities and records each bet. The bookie himself hands out numbered tickets and adjusts the odds according to his own calculations or those of the clerk behind the board.

The betting market on course determines the 'starting price' (the price at which bets are settled), throughout the betting shops around the country. Whilst the weight of support for each horse on course is supposed to be reflected by its 'starting price', the major betting firms have a vested interest in attempting to make the price reflect off-course business also. This is where the tic-tac men come in. One of the functions of the tic-tac men, identified by their white gloves and windmilling arms, is to communicate wagers to the bookmakers in order to offset the weight of 'office money' communicated to them via the 'blower'. This information travels from the clearing house of the bookmaker, who calculates that at the current starting price the shop liability would be unacceptably large, to the 'blower tic-tac man', via the 'blower agent'. Professional punters often complain that 'office money' distorts the on-course market, although the bookmaker multiples deny that the practice is as extensive as the independent bookmakers and on-course professionals claim. However, the movement of money by the big bookmaking firms is communicated by tic-tacs in a secret code in contrast to the public signals used to transmit market information between bookmakers.

In constant communication with the tic-tacs are the rails bookmakers who deal in larger stakes than the ring bookmakers, and stand on the rail, between the Silver Ring and Tattersalls. Rails bookmakers have only recently been allowed to display their prices on boards, and they stand at ground level, 'shouting the odds', to be approached by those wishing to bet in large stakes. The rails bookmakers are often representatives of the major bookmaking firms, and their personal image is far more corporate and less individual than that of the ring bookie. Rails bookmakers wear long raincoats, smart suits and hats: no flat caps or battered trilbies as seen in the ring. Their demeanour is cool and self-contained, to match their turnout. The typical rails bookie is charming, well-spoken, intelligent and beautifully dressed. His bearing seems intended to suggest an honourable and trustworthy individual, or as an elderly racegoer put it: 'I'd trust him with the inheritance.' The point of honour amongst the rails bookies is that they will accommodate a bet no matter how large, and wish you all the best with it, as the following story concerning a mystery punter illustrates:

When Jigtime won at Ayr last month, the man had £12,000 to win £10,000 with Hills and [rails bookmaker] Ridley, smiling in the face of adversity, said yesterday, 'He also had £10,000 to win £3,330 with me when she won here previously. I don't know anything about him, but good luck to him!' (*Racing Post* 21 May 1998: 4)[12]

'Getting on' at the racecourse

Amongst racegoers, there are groups of people concerned solely with the enjoyment of a 'day out' at the races, 'I'd rather have a gin and tonic than a bet!', whilst there are those who told me that, for them, the racecourse was their office: 'It's a professional thing, Rebecca. When I'm on the racecourse I'm working' (Professional punter). Of course, the motivations for coming racing are not exhausted by business or pleasure; however, one of the most common forms of self-identification amongst racegoers was whether betting was their prime objective or merely a small part of an enjoyable day. Those who chose to bet 'just to have an interest in the race, you know, make it more exciting', and particularly women, often placed bets with the Tote, and explained this to me on the grounds that 'the ladies at the Tote are really helpful, they don't look down their noses at you like the bookies do'. The Tote has booths all around the course, often serviced by middle-aged women, who will explain bets and help inexperienced punters. Furthermore, punters queue for the Tote in an orderly fashion, whilst in the betting ring queuing is disorderly and women may find themselves pushed aside in the rush for a price.

The second major index capable of predicting whether a racegoer chooses to bet with the Tote or in the ring is that of experience. Women who are accustomed to the intensity of the ring are just as forceful in competing to take a price, that is to lay a bet quickly when a bookmaker momentarily advertises longer odds than his competitors. Inexperienced men also bet with the Tote, but generally with higher stakes than women, a feature of betting behaviour which is generally replicated in the ring. Men explained their higher stakes in the ring as a response to the 'minimum stake' requirement of the bookmakers, usually of £5. A bet of £2 is still known as a 'lady's bet', and will be avoided by the majority of men, who couldn't even contemplate betting in amounts less than the £5 they needed to stake in order to be 'taken on' by the bookmakers, 'I don't bet less than £5 because it's not worth your while betting anything less.' Asked why women apparently bet in £2 stakes this punter replied that, 'It's just to give them a bit of fun isn't it?', implying that, in his opinion, men and women had a bet for different reasons. The overwhelming majority of racegoers whom I asked had succumbed to the traditional distribution of stake money, but their interpretation of the significance of this contrast varied enormously, as one would expect. Some of the explanations of the larger stakes of men offered by women were as follows:

> They think that they're the big man, swaggering into the ring and putting down twenty quid, don't they [laughs]?
>
> I only need to put down a couple of pounds because I get all the entertainment I need from watching the men doing their Mafia act. As if they know anything about racing – my husband's a bank manager for God's sake!
>
> He knows more about it than me, I just have a bet to make it a bit more exciting.

Men explained their larger stakes as follows:

> It's the only way you can get a big return.
>
> Otherwise the bookies would think that you were a wimp.
>
> I'd rather bet less, but you feel a bit of a fool handing over £3.
>
> All men know more about racing than all women, love, fact of life.
>
> I'm luckier than my wife.

This variation should not detract from the existence of an ideology of masculinity based on successful risk-taking, and the possession of knowledge that makes this possible, which exists on the racecourse. Men avail themselves of this image for a variety of reasons, and with varying degrees of self-consciousness. Women see through this identity to various degrees and respond to it in ways which are a function of their off-course relationships with men. Individual explanations of the different stakes tendered by men and women clearly reflect more general ideas about gender; these ranged from women who saw through men to women who thought men more capable than women, and from men who laughed at their own foray into macho posturing to men who thought themselves inherently more capable than women.

Mugs

Amongst those racegoers who come primarily to bet on the racing it was difficult not to make the same distinction as is made in many betting manuals, between 'mugs' and 'professionals'. My experience of race meetings is that there are always groups of around eight to twelve men who spend a good deal of the day in the bar drinking and smoking. They place bets on all of the races, of amounts greater than £5, and they celebrate wins within the group with alcohol, and enjoy indulging in sexual banter. Singing, betting and drinking are only temporarily interrupted by altercations with other groups of men at the bar. Typically, a few words are exchanged whilst jockeying for position. Perhaps an individual is singled out as taking up a lot of room, or having especially sharp elbows. Whilst the groups 'square up' for a moment or two, it is left to the diplomat of each group to rush over and avert trouble, saying, 'Come on lads, no harm done, let's get a drink.'[13]

The subversion practised by these groups of men takes the form of contradicting the judgement of those racing professionals whom they identify as 'upper class'. The majority of the members of these groups would be described by my professional punter friends as 'mugs'. Describing non-professionals as 'mug' punters is driven by the professional gambler's self-image as the intellectual of the racecourse, as in this description by professional Alan Potts:

Every time I leave the racecourse at the end of a day's work, with a profit tucked into my zipped pocket, I offer a silent thank you to the mugs who make it possible – my fellow punters. Overall I regard the rest of the crowd with contempt, and use the term 'mug punter' as a collective noun in much the same dismissive way as I might say 'Arsenal supporters'. (1995: 16)

Whilst many mugs will choose to bet on favourites and second favourites, professional gamblers will often choose to oppose weak favourites with longer priced horses, since the strike rate needed to show a profit from longer priced horses is correspondingly lower than that needed to make a profit at evens or short odds, 'to me finding 10-1 winners at a rate of one in eight sounds much easier than finding even-money winners at a rate of two in three' (Potts 1995: 46).

'Mugs' were identified by professionals through their betting behaviour:

Mugs give in to the temptation to bet, even when they haven't thought the race through . . . Mugs bet for the thrill . . . They don't admit when they were wrong, they make excuses for themselves . . . Mugs go crazy when they win and they're suicidal when they lose. (Professional punter)

It was easy to dismiss my professional gambler friend's description of the mug as a fiction based upon the negation of behaviour becoming to a 'pro', but their predictions proved far more accurate than I had envisaged. An afternoon at the races for groups of twenty-something single men consists of a series of highs and lows, continuous drinking, a visit to the betting ring ('I wouldn't be seen dead betting with the Tote'), and a view of the race, usually on a monitor rather than in the flesh ('you can see more on the telly'). Watching a mug watch a race is a fascinating experience – confidence turns into uncertainty, into desperation and finally into disappointment. Mugs with a horse in contention in the closing stages of a race often ride a finish, eyes fixed on the screen, arms pumping backwards and forwards, accompanied, of course, by the battle cry: 'Go on my son!' When the winner crosses the line the successful punter invariably punches the air in triumph, shouting 'Yessss!' or perhaps 'You Beauty!'[14]

Mugs continually contradict the opinions of trainers and commentators. These racegoers most closely resemble the gamblers described by Zola in one of the few modern empirical studies of gambling, conducted in a bar in a large

New England city in the early 1960s. Zola describes how betting on horseracing in 'Hoff's' tavern gives the men an opportunity to assert a positive identity
which is denied to them outside the confines of the bar and its shared conventions, so that, 'gambling is more than a mode of communication. It creates a
bond between men – a bond which defines insiders and outsiders' (1967: 22).

However, on the racecourse, stratification extends to the betting community
no less than the professional racing community, and what unites some groups of
punters also serves to distinguish them from others. Mugs on course, and gamblers in Hoff's, unite against the bookmaker in ways that the professional would
find unseemly. Professionals see bookmakers as colleagues, and acknowledge
that they make their money, not from the bookmaker, but from the mug punters
who bet without skill or reflection. Bookmakers and professionals share more
than either has in common with the mug, but despite the apparent difference
being based upon betting for pleasure or business, the mug does not see his
betting as purely recreational. The mugs treat betting as a 'serious business',
and act accordingly. Mugs sit in the bar smoking and drinking with an intensity
which suggests that they are nervously awaiting results in which they have a
large stake, as they presumably imagine a professional would. They do not drink
for pleasure, but to express to the rest of the bar the extent of their financial
involvement in the race.

My experience of betting with professionals is that they come racing alone,
they may have a pint with their lunch whilst they go over the bets they have
prepared the previous evening, they watch the race from the stands or out in
the country with binoculars, and they must see the horse in the paddock and
down to the start before placing their bet. There is very little time for puffing,
drinking and looking anxiously at television monitors, and this would certainly
not be done in such a public place as the bar. The young men who dominate
the public areas of the racecourse, often drinking and smoking, are not the high
rollers, and the image they project is anathema to the professional, who, I would
suggest, they seek to emulate.

The mug's opposition to the bookmaker is complemented on the racecourse
by a condemnation of jockeys and trainers, even to the extent that a race may be
seen as 'fixed'. The mug's paradoxical belief that racing is fixed reflects his lack
of consistency that is the fault that most offends the professional punter, 'They
say that racing is fixed. Well if you think that and still bet then you really are a
mug' (Professional punter). Of course, corruption is just one part of the mug's
ideology, which can accommodate glaring inconsistencies when employed in
such an unsystematic fashion. Winning is thus explained in terms of knowledge
and inside information, whilst losing is explained in terms of corruption, bad
luck, or the misjudgement of the jockey or trainer. These explanations are often
accompanied by an exasperated mug declaring that: 'I knew it would get beat,
I said to you I fancied the winner didn't I?', because in the course of discussing

the race almost all of the runners will be mentioned and so at least one mug will have the opportunity to claim 'the one that got away'.

The professional

The professional gambler who gave me the best tips was a single, middle-aged, bespectacled, Renault driving, ex-computer troubleshooter. He is well known and highly respected, having written several popular betting manuals and contributed to a successful telephone tipping line. The time we have spent together has reinforced my impression that the professional gambler has assimilated many of the qualities admired by historians of this century in the 'sportsmen' of the eighteenth-century racing aristocracy, specifically in his construction of an identity in opposition to the mug punter and in the desired response to winning and losing:

A 'good sport' will take a 'sporting chance' with his money and will demonstrate his sportsmanship by showing neither regret at losing nor elation at winning his wagers. A 'poor sport' usually refuses to gamble at all. Or if he does so, his response to the outcome is unseemly. (Gorer 1955: 83)

Crockford soon discovered that his own temperament was well suited to gambling because he was bold without ever being rash, and systematic without being overcautious. (Blyth 1969: 51)

My informant takes great pride in the fact that it is impossible to tell whether he has won or lost by his reaction to the finish of a race. The more he emphasised the absence of a reaction, telling me that he had to put on a show of excitement for a television crew who had followed him for a day, the more I wondered what could possibly be behind this condemnation of expressive reactions to the result of a race. This 'underplaying' belongs to the same family of conventions as the 'poker face', and the self-effacing acceptance of awards with understated humility. However, although a poker face may have an instrumental value in the course of a poker game, celebrating a win obviously cannot affect that result.

The restraint showed by the professional serves to differentiate him from the amateurs surrounding him on the course. He distinguishes himself from social racegoers and mug punters by exhibiting control. He strips gambling of all its thrills and excitement in order to control the process itself. By reacting consistently to results whether winning or losing, the professional diffuses the power of the bet to control the punter. As he told me: 'I am not betting for the thrill, I am betting to make money. Mugs enjoy the thrill of the bet more than they do winning. I only know about winning.' This professional thought that the punters from whom he made a living willingly submitted to the excitement of the gamble itself, and his activities were opposed to this sensuous pleasure. In this way, betting is work, and an instrumental pleasure, not an end in itself.

By reproducing this discourse the professional aligns himself with the supply side of racing – the upper-class society with whom the mug is in constant competition.

Conclusion

The racecourse is 'Where the Action is' (Goffman 1969), whilst the same cannot be said of the betting shop. Betting on horseracing does not have the inherent ability to provide a medium for the enhancement of personal identities. However, the racecourse itself is a place capable of imbuing betting with significance as a result of its place in the imagination of racegoers, its stimulation of all of the senses, and the historical and contemporary relationship between racing and bookmaking. The characters of the racecourse, such as the tic-tac man, the bookie and the professional, not to mention the jockeys, the trainers, the horses, the turf, the silks, the open air, the toffs and the crooks, make betting on course a suitably complex and dramatic endeavour through which people may choose to express their knowledge and risk-taking capacity. Mugs express this ability by behaving as they imagine a professional punter would. Professionals rarely display their risk-taking, preferring to sap gambling of its uncertainty with a show of confidence and indifference that strips betting of its ability to move.

Betting in the ring with the bookies is far more involved than betting with the Tote. One of the arguments for retaining on-course bookmakers rather than allowing a Tote monopoly is that the bookmakers add character to the course, and that a racecourse without bookies would lack the excitement that encourages people to go racing in the first place. The encounter between punters and bookmakers on course is one of the sources of profound pleasure. The transaction is a *personal* matter of honour between the two, reinforced by the knowledge that gambling debts remain unrecoverable by the law. This responsibility is not conveyed by the Tote to the same degree, due to the structure of the different forms of betting, and the representatives of each betting medium. The Tote employs middle-aged women whose involvement in the transaction is to take your money and hand you your ticket and hopefully your winnings. You are putting money into a pool which will be won by a number of faceless, anonymous 'others' if you lose. If you win, you take the money staked, again by people unknown to you. The personal involvement of the men and women operating the Tote is limited to their desire to be perceived as fulfilling their role according to their terms of employment. Their sympathetic, smiling faces and familiar red jackets dilute the experience of betting as 'going to war'.

Placing a bet with a bookmaker is a highly personalised, highly competitive interaction. It is therefore unsurprising that a major axis of competition within the racing world lies between punter and bookmaker, despite the real competition on the racecourse being between punters. I have suggested that the bookie is in fact a scapegoat on two levels. The bookmaker deflects the uncomfortable truth that one mug's winnings are another mug's losses. This unites the mugs on course in a way that is consistent with an enjoyable and companionable day spent at the races. The bookie also stands in for the upper-class producers of racing when a punter predicts the outcome of a race, a prediction that depends upon highly prestigious knowledge in order to be successful. The punter thus achieves a temporary ascendancy over the producers of racing who are thought to be the exclusive keepers of this knowledge.

The professional gambler is generally a lone figure at the racecourse, the absence of company being testimony to his acknowledged competitive relationship with other punters, and hence to the different set of motivations he holds for going racing. Professional gamblers would not associate their behaviour with that of the casual punter; on the contrary, they see the casual punter as beneath them. Their symbiotic relationship is sustained via the bookmaker, and although professional gamblers are very clear about this, mugs vilify only the bookies whilst hailing the professional as 'one of us' (only successful). Professional gamblers are generally scathing about the mugs on whom they depend for their living, in the same way as racing professionals often condemn racing's consumers.

Betting off course in a betting shop is not part of a day out, and the atmosphere in which betting takes place could not be more different. For both men and women punters in the shops betting has become routinised, as a household chore for women and as an afternoon diversion for men. I have disputed the explanations of gambling that cite intellectual stimulation as a central motivation because they do not account for the overwhelmingly unsuccessful strategies adopted by punters. A bond does exist between betting-shop punters, in their opposition to losing, but this opposition does not appear to extend to the bookmaker as it once did. One explanation for this lies in the domination of the 'Big Three' bookmakers in providing betting outlets. Punters are confronted with an employee of a publicly quoted multinational, rather than a weasel of a bookie against whom they may 'pit their wits'. This argument was suggested to me by the contrast in atmospheres between small independent bookmakers, where the bookmaker himself takes your bet, and the chain bookmakers, where the cashier may know your name, but has no personal involvement with your bet. As in the contrast between the Tote and the bookie on course, chain betting shops can eliminate the tension between bookmakers and punters, as making a bet entails making a diffuse risk with an employee with whom the proverbial buck does not stop,

I must admit I'd rather bet with a proper bookie, because to be honest I've got so much in common with Dave [the manager], that I don't feel the same excitement as when I bet on course. (Betting-shop punter)

The betting shop has only a very short history, having come into existence in its present legal form in the 1960s. Whilst racehorses arrived on the racecourse before betting, they were preceded into the betting shop by gambling itself. This is evident in the betting behaviour of the two locations. Betting on course was described in relation to the overall experience of 'going racing':

It's part of it, isn't it? You have a drink, lay a bet, watch the race, cheer them home, then start again. It's great! (Middle-aged male racegoer)

It's a bit of fun! You pretend to know what you're doing, and if you win all the better! (Female racegoer)

Betting on course is a part of going racing and betting behaviour involves adopting whichever demeanour appeals, from bank managers who become Mafia men, to the woman who told me: 'I feel like Lady Muck!' Entering the racecourse marks a suspension of ordinary identities, and the potential for re-negotiating class differences, as described by a female racegoer:

When we get on the racecourse it's as if we all get on a cruise ship that doesn't go anywhere, but just floats about. Once you're on the ship you're the racing version of yourself, you can talk to anyone you like, because we're all being our racing selves![15]

The betting ring is potent, capable of creating a liminal zone in which iden-tities are fluid, dependent upon the result of a race. By making a bet the punter aligns himself with the connections of his chosen horse. His stake in the future of the race is embodied in his betting slip. He watches the race, not as a dentist, shift-worker, security guard or whatever else he may be, but according to the template of racehorse ownership that is etched onto the racecourse landscape and described in the previous chapter. Here there is a momentary individual freedom, which is pleasurable if inconsequential outside the course. Punters relish this freedom whilst many are aware of its superficiality, which does not seem to detract from its temporary intensity. Racegoers participate in a mas-querade, taking pleasure in the idea of being part of 'high society' without believing that anything has really changed. Betting is thus the veneer pasted over the fixed class structure of horseracing, the appearance of mobility that makes the structural inequality more palatable.

NOTES

1 In her examination of gambling in Western culture, sociologist Reith seeks to 'provide an analysis of the nature and experience of gambling in Western society; as something which is historically and culturally variable, and yet which nevertheless retains an essential character which transcends the specificity of individual games' (1999: 10). Reith gives a phenomenological explanation of gambling which focuses particularly upon the dream-like state of disassociation apparently experienced by each player: 'both gambling games and adventures can assume the properties of

dreams, a peculiarity which is caused by the occurrence of the adventure outwith the usual stream of life' (1999: 130). Reith's characterisation of gambling as centring upon experiences of excitement, vertigo, transcendence and repetition is compelling. However, she is aware that betting on horseracing offers an element of control inamicable to the games of pure chance that she is attempting to describe. Aspects of her analysis, including a belief in luck, charms, omens and reversed causality (punters are rarely happy betting on the outcome of recorded races) are relevant to my analysis, but the significance of betting lies, not in properties that may constitute quintessential 'gaming' behaviour, but in its sociohistorical importance.

2 In this chapter I shall concentrate upon legal bookmaking, although this man was betting with an unlicensed Kentucky bookmaker, and bets can be made with a surprising number of 'unofficial' sources in Newmarket.

3 Although sports betting is gaining in popularity, racing remains the mainstay of the British betting office, constituting an estimated 70% of business (HBLB 2001). Football and boxing are not funded by a levy system and so it is in the interests of bookmakers to encourage their customers to use these media at the expense of horseracing. The resilience of punting in the face of this competition requires an explanation.

4 Except in two-year-old races, where breeding is the only guide to horses who have had few if any runs. However, even in two-year-old races 'the market', that is the betting market, is believed to be a better indication of a horse's chances than its breeding. Where a two-year-old is fancied at home those 'in the know' will certainly try to 'get on'. Punters often follow these 'market movers' (horses who are supported in the betting market leading to their odds shortening), particularly if they come from a stable that has already had a number of two-year-old winners that season, or that is known for 'landing a touch' on its two-year-olds.

5 All this is set to change with the abolition of betting tax in the Labour Budget of March 2001. The Levy Board is to be scrapped in 2003, to be replaced by a funding deal for racing based on media rights, the nature of which is unclear at the time of writing. These changes have been made in response to developments in off-shore technology and the migration of betting offices from mainland Britain to, for example, Cyprus, in search of tax breaks. The role of the punter in the new global betting market will undoubtedly differ from that I have described in this chapter. It could fairly be said that this fieldwork took place at the end of an era. However, it is interesting to note that specifically 'British' aspects of the betting industry continue to act as an attraction to many overseas investors. Betting in the United Kingdom is highly respected and seen to be honest, unlike many newer gambling centres. According to Ed Pownall, public relations manager for online gambling company Bluesquare, 'It's easier to springboard overseas for us with a strong UK base. Take the Japanese, they love the idea of the Jockey Club' (Davis 2001: 12). The nature of transactions that make up the global £1 trillion betting turnover are outside the scope of the present study.

6 This is an extreme statement of the purist's vision of racing devoid of its sporting component, as there is no 'sport' in roulette. However, as pragmatic historian of racing politics Christopher Hill concedes: 'Fortunately, most owners and breeders have mixed motives, and as long as that continues, racing will still be enjoyable' (1988: 196).

7 The correspondence between the restriction of gaming and the interests of the ruling class has been documented by the historian Brenner (1990). Brenner argues that behind

the condemnation of gambling lurked a resistance to the idea that 'chance, rather than divine will or talent, can have a significant effect on the allocation and the reallocation of property' (1990: vii). Certainly, the idea of providence is more appealing to those who prosper, and least to those who struggle, whilst chance is an explanation well suited to failure.

8 Furthermore, betting on every race dramatically reduces the time available to look at the form of each horse.

9 I should add that punters in the bookies do not automatically accord higher status to a winner. In fact, in my experience, winning does not automatically lead to an improvement in status at all. A punter of low status in the betting shop pecking order who enjoys a win will not automatically be catapulted to the top of that order. Rather, a number of explanations that focus upon factors outside his control will be brought in to explain his good fortune. His success is attributed to luck rather than good judgement, and he remains at the bottom of the heap.

10 During the 1990s bookmakers were able to bid for pitches at auction, and so rather than being inherited, they are now 'bought' by the highest bidder. This has led to an influx of 'new boys' into the betting ring, many of whom come and go as their fortunes rise and wane. This system has also brought allegations of money laundering to the fore, as anyone with enough cash can buy a pitch, and with it the ability to put money through the books and in doing so effectively obliterate its source.

11 The unabashed presence of money at the racecourse is a refreshing corrective in the age of the credit card. Betting on course is still a cash business, and the quantity of notes in evidence is arresting. As Reith says, 'Despite the fact that gamblers do not play to win it, the presence of money in play is nevertheless important: it is vital to the game to be meaningful, as it is the medium through which participants register their involvement in a game' (1999: 146). Rolled up wads of cash dominate transactions all over the racecourse. Volume is important, and wallets are just too restrictive. No containment must be allowed to limit the growth of the money that, on the racecourse, possesses a fecundity of its own.

12 In a story typical of the racecourse, this 'lucky' punter was later jailed for stealing his original stake from his employer.

13 More sinister are the recent allegations of drug taking on the Rowley Mile Racecourse at Newmarket, where a hypodermic needle was found in the men's toilets and letters to the *Racing Post* complain that drugs were on sale from a cubicle (Green 2001).

14 In a very obvious way, these men are indulging in the kind of 'conspicuously unthrifty consumption' (1997: 69) observed by Stewart amongst the Rom brotherhood in Hungary. Amongst the Rom the meaning of gambling is to be found in opposition both to wage labour and to the household. And this is also the case amongst the mugs. By betting without reserve, the unity of their group is emphasised at the expense of more complicated, perhaps more onerous family ties. And of course, the whole Protestant work ethic that many of these men spend the majority of their lives upholding is thrown out the window with the first ripped up betting slip.

15 However, if this woman chose to attempt to enter the weighing room, the unsaddling enclosure, the paddock or the owners' and trainers' bar, she might find that this apparent suspension of off-course distinctions is fragile to say the least.

6   Going once, going twice . . .

Introduction

> The bloodstock market is founded on a central uncertainty. Nobody knows what a good racehorse is, or rather what exactly it is which enables one race-horse to run faster than another. Equally, nobody knows how to set about producing a superior racehorse, or how to select one from a mass of relatively similar yearlings. Every participant formulates his own ideas or theories in the knowledge that they will never guarantee success, nor will any two different theories necessarily be mutually exclusive. This uncertainty is hidden by the myths and rituals of the bloodstock world.
>
> (De Moubray 1987: xiv)

Before the rhythms of the auction lull the reader into a false sense of security, I should add to Jocelyn de Moubray's 'central uncertainty' the fact that racehorses on the whole make very poor investments. Only 40% of racehorses ever win a race. About 17% win two (Potts pers. comm.). In 1999 owners received, on average, 21% of their outlay from prize money (discounting purchase costs). Britain is thirty-ninth (sixth from bottom) in the international league table of world racing nations (Wright 2000: 6).[1] It is against this backdrop of negative equity that public auctions such as the 2000 annual three-day Houghton Sale at Tattersalls in Newmarket are able to net almost 33 million guineas, for 141 lots at an average price of 233,886 guineas per yearling.[2] Obviously, this behaviour requires an explanation.

In 1983 Sheikh Mohammed spent $10.2 million on a yearling that turned out to be too slow to run in a race. The winner of the 2000 Derby, Fusaichi Pegasus, changed hands at the end of his racing career for a reputed $60 million. Staggering figures such as these represent demand at the very top end of the bloodstock market, where some of the richest individuals in the world compete in order to possess the best bred yearlings of each generation, to ensure their place as players in the competitive worlds of racing and breeding. The most ex-pensive bloodstock is destined for the breeding shed, where the real money is to be made. The value of a stallion depends upon the covering fee he can command. Storm Cat, the most expensive stallion in the world in 2001, costs $400,000 (£277,000) per covering, about double that of his closest rival. If he produces 70 live foals in a season (a conservative estimate) he will earn his owner $28 million (£19.4 million). Potential profits from breeding dwarf those of prize money.[3]

Buyers of expensive yearlings justify their outlay on the grounds of breeding and appearance; however, my informants agreed that it 'becomes impossible to explain yearlings valued at over one or two million'. These yearlings are bought as potential stallions, in the hope that they might win a prestigious race and then go on to sire winners. In true racing style I was told that the chances of a particular horse achieving this were 7-1! In truth, yearlings are worth whatever an individual is willing to pay in order to prevent his competitor from stumbling upon a wonderhorse. These fascinating circumstances are the background to the drama that takes place in the sales ring.

The sales ring is the interface of the two main principles at work in racing society: risk and pedigree. It is in the sales ring that pedigree is expressed financially, and the risk of buying a young animal yet to achieve physical maturity is interpreted as an 'investment' according to its representation by a page in the sales catalogue detailing its breeding. The first section of this chapter briefly describes the passage of a yearling through the auction ring. This moment is the culmination of all of the efforts described in the next section of the chapter, which describes fieldwork spent preparing a yearling consignment for the 1997 sales. This description should communicate the importance of the appearance of knowledge. The scarcity of real knowledge in this arena is reinforced by my description of the yearling inspection, the means by which yearlings are physically assessed by bloodstock agents. I then describe the bloodstock agent who negotiates this arena with impression management, confidence and personality. In the final sections I describe other processes at work in the auction ring and explore the relationship between pedigree and ability.

Tattersalls auction ring

> Tournaments of value are complex periodic events that are removed in some culturally well-defined way from the routines of economic life. Participation in them is likely to be both a privilege of those in power and an instrument of status contests between them . . . Finally, what is at issue in such tournaments is not just status, rank, fame or reputation of actors, but the disposition of the central tokens of value in the society in question.
>
> (Appadurai 1986: 21)

The audience, who filled every available space in the packed amphitheatre, fell silent as the 'talking' yearling of the 1995 Houghton Sale entered the ring. Dark bay, white markings, an out-and-out Sadler's Wells, and a colt. Tattersalls was packed, everyone straining to catch a glimpse of the players who they expected to be involved in the bidding which would follow the Irish auctioneer's introduction of the colt:

Well now . . . (leans on podium, gavel in hand), (long pause).
What have we here? . . . (long pause)
(Stands up straight, speaking slowly and with great purpose) Ladies and gentlemen, he needs no introduction, here we have lot number 104 from Cheveley Park. A Sadler's Wells colt out of that prolific racemare Exclusive Order, dam of no less than eight winners of twenty-four races. And what winners they are, ladies and gentlemen. This is the full brother to none other than Sadler's Image and Dance a Dream, the half brother to Irish Order and Irish Wings. And doesn't he look the part? You really couldn't fault him, and just look at him walk. Ladies and gentlemen, what will you bid me for this unique opportunity? Who'll start me off? I'm not going to ask big money for him. Who'll give me a hundred thousand?

The timbre, intonation and grave pauses of the auctioneer's invocation produce an atmosphere of awe – a complete silence, pregnant with the overwhelming question: 'Who would dare to possess such a creature?' And suddenly, the silence is broken, the auctioneer has taken a bid, and another, and the duel commences. A whisper is raised in the crowd: 'Where is he?' Few have spotted either competitor. The price rises, toward the half million mark, where it sticks. The auctioneer entreats the underbidder to try another, 'I'd hate to see you lose him now, you've been with me all the way, try another, maybe one more will do it!' Movement in the crowd suggests that the vanquished opponent has beaten a retreat. Bidding raises the price from half a million to six hundred thousand, where the hammer falls. 'Going once, going twice . . . sold.' 'Thank you very much Mr Demi O'Byrne.' The audience erupts into gossip and speculation.

As I was looking for a yearling to follow at this time, I rejoiced inwardly at the thought of a six hundred thousand guinea sale-topping Sadler's Wells colt, who was already surpassing my expectations. Bought by the fascinating alliance of John Magnier, of Irish breeding venture Coolmore and millionaire Michael Tabor, quintessential East Ender made good through daring gambles, the yearling was put into training with champion trainer Michael Stoute, and, best of all, named Entrepreneur, after Tabor, a folk hero on the racecourse.

The sales

It was 4:50 in the morning. Outside it was raining. I was standing in a stable with a yearling who would later sell for 36,000 guineas. I felt the weight of the bridle in my hand and fought the rising feeling of panic in my stomach. The filly looked at me with mild interest and seemed docile enough. Once again, and not for the last time, I imagined that I was someone else, who was competent and experienced, walked confidently across the box, caught and bridled the filly and stood at the door of the box waiting for the call to 'pull out'. That was it. I was walking yearlings.[4]

'Walking yearlings' means partly just that. Yearlings must be 'walked' in order to build muscle and to burn off some of the energy which may otherwise explode whilst they are being inspected by a potential buyer. So, I found myself walking round and round an exercise ring with six other people, whom I had never met, each of us leading a yearling, in the dark in more than one way. After forty-five minutes we swapped these yearlings for five more, and walked for another forty-five minutes as it gradually grew light. Following this, the stud staff left myself and another temporary handler to 'do over' the yearlings whilst they went to breakfast. The learning curve of this particular segment of fieldwork was steep, and relied entirely on improvisation within the framework of the conventions and routines I had acquired during my experience with horses. Any spontaneous assistance from the other grooms was rare, although given freely if requested. Professing ignorance of a particular aspect of yearling management made the other grooms uncomfortable, but not impatient or cross.

The yearlings are experiencing a liminal phase in their cultural biography. They are about to embark on their careers as adult racehorses, having left their juvenile status behind on the stud farm. The process by which the yearlings leave one sphere and prepare to enter another involves familiar techniques of separation. The yearlings are separated from their mothers at weaning, and put out in fields at the edge of the stud so that their mothers cannot hear them and vice versa. They are turned out in same-sex groups and left 'roughed off' for the winter, during which time they receive minimal human contact and form close alliances with each other.

When it is time for yearlings to be prepared for the sales, they are brought in and confined, so that their diet and coats can be monitored. Excess hair is removed (rugs are fitted in order to deter the growth of a winter coat at all), their feet are trimmed and shod, they are fed on a controlled high protein diet, and they must learn to be groomed, to 'stand up', to be led, to wear a bridle and to 'walk'. At this point they do not have names, and are referred to as 'the Forzando filly', or 'the Zilzal', for example. In other words, they are referred to by their sire, who will have the most influence on their immediate future, at the sale. The yearlings are referred to in this way until they have been through the sales and found an owner who will name them. The yearlings are thus stripped of their identities as foals of a particular dam on weaning, and referred to as the yearling of a particular sire after weaning and during the sales. After the sales they become part of human society by being named by their owner.

The main business of the sale began at first light. The yearlings were all highly polished, paraffin water had been used to draw dust out of their coats, and Vaseline to shine their noses and eyes.[5] I had cleaned all of the bridles, the long leather lead-reins ('shanks') and polished the brass plates on the cheek straps which were engraved with the name of the stud. The stud groom had shown me how to 'stand up' a yearling, initially as a precaution 'in case we get really busy'. By the end of the sale I was responsible for showing and selling a filly in the ring, and had shown all of the other ten yearlings at various times. I changed my role in the operation by behaving sensibly, but also by exuding great confidence at all times. I realised that learning occurred not through exposition, but through observation and imitation. Confidence was the most valued personal quality, rather than any sort of 'willingness to learn' which merely revealed a lack of knowledge where the desired state was effortless competence. Learning not to learn too obviously enabled me to disguise my status as newcomer to a world of highly specialised knowledge.

The first interaction between potential buyers at the sales and the yearlings occurs in the yards that surround the sale ring. Although it is tempting to regard this as action on the periphery of the market, the first meeting between potential buyers and yearlings is often the most significant. The yearlings are brought to the yards several days early in order for buyers to have time to view them and evaluate them before they go into the ring. In other words, the relationship between the yearling and potential buyers is established before the lot enters the ring.[6] The agent will decide to bid for the individual on the basis of inspections made during the time before it is due to be sold. The time spent by the yearling in the ring does not change who will bid for it, but merely establishes who amongst those who want the yearling are prepared to pay the most for it. Or so it seems.

The yearling inspection

The yearling inspection is both standardised and repetitive. As grooms responsible for showing yearlings, we waited for viewers in the 'tack box', half a stable between yearling boxes which contains benches and all the horses' equipment such as rugs, tack and grooming kit. As people crossed the yards we tried to identify them. Most were bloodstock agents, although a few owners choose their own yearlings. This was a light-hearted but competitive pursuit, the stud groom thought it was important for us to know to whom we were showing. As potential buyers approached they greeted the stud groom, and looked in their catalogue to tell us which of the yearlings they were interested in viewing. We each hoped that the yearling we had chosen to show would be needed. Once we knew which yearlings were required two grooms dealt with each, one carrying a brush and tea towel, the other a clean bridle. Whilst one caught the yearling the other brushed straw from mane and tail, and ran the towel over the coat to remove any surface dust. 'My' filly was very popular, and I showed her approximately thirty times a day.

The stud groom opened my stable door to let me out when my turn came, according to the order requested by the viewer. I walked towards the viewer with the filly on my right, trying to make sure that all of her movements were purposeful and balanced, by not asking her to complete any sudden manoeuvres. The viewer took a look at the filly as we approached, and the quizzical stare, the quintessential pose of the bloodstock agent, was struck. My filly was small and always described as pretty, being a very solid bay, with large dark eyes. Quite often she prompted an acknowledgement such as, 'Hello filly'. The agent might then greet me, 'Good morning'. I would reply appropriately and 'stand the filly up', with her left side in front of the agent, and her legs placed squarely with my body in front of her. The agent would stand approximately ten feet away and stare intently at her. He might approach her and place his hand on her withers in order to gauge her size, possibly run a hand down her front left leg, or place his fist under her chin in order to check the size of her airway, he might just be content to stare. He would then move to the front, approximately six feet away, and I would move to her left side, out of his way. He would continue to stare at her front legs, for between ten seconds and a minute, then might look at her from the rear, though not always.[7] When at the front the agent might make a comment such as 'She's a bonny filly isn't she?' or ask a question such as 'Has she a good temper?' or 'Are you having a good sale?', 'Isn't it cold?', though many did not speak to me at all.

The first part of the inspection is ended by the agent saying, 'May I see her walk please.' I would reply, 'Certainly', and try to galvanise the filly into walk having just bullied her into standing still. A good walk is capable of transforming the impression of a yearling, and a 'good walker' will be forgiven a lot of technical faults. A good walker is described as 'athletic', 'free moving', 'powerful', 'racey'; a bad walker may simply be noted in the catalogue as 'ordinary', 'disappointing' or 'stiff'. The inspection walk follows a predetermined route, which pivots around the agent. The yearling is walked away from the agent, turned to the right, then walked back towards the agent, past him, turned right, back towards him, and halted with him in front, then 'stood up' again. The distances involved must be sufficient for the filly to get into her stride, and really to 'use herself', but not so far that the agent cannot see her or becomes impatient. Some of the yearlings had faults that benefited from being walked on a particular surface. Walking on the grass was generally more forgiving than on the gravel path. One colt was to be walked on the gravel because it sloped slightly in the direction that helped disguise his weaknesses. The end of the inspection is signalled by the agent saying 'thank you very much', he completes the notes in his catalogue and moves to the next yearling.

The yearling inspection is a form of connoisseurship, as described by art historian Brown, because it involves a judgement of quality placed beyond simple exposition:

attribution and authentication are not the whole of connoisseurship, which means to evaluate, and not merely classify. Having satisfactorily placed a work of art, the connoisseur may go on to assess its quality or intrinsic value. (1979: 11)

Throughout the inspection the concentration of the agent is intense, as reflected by his silence, and especially by his narrowed eyes. However, 'less is more' in these inspections. Although this may partly be due to the large number of yearlings to be viewed, I believe it is also part of the ideology which holds that spending too much time inspecting a yearling suggests uncertainty, or the absence of confidence, where the valued state is that of conviction on the grounds of comprehensive knowledge.

The bloodstock agent will discuss the yearlings he or she likes with the potential owner and decide which to have vetted. Vetting at Tattersalls is currently limited to non-invasive techniques, and includes checking eyes, heart and lungs, feeling legs and seeing the yearling walk to check it for soundness. The inspections I witnessed took under ten minutes. Once bought, most yearlings are wind tested, that is, exercised in a sand ring in order to test their breathing.[8] They can be returned to their vendor if they fail this test, unless the horse is described in the catalogue as, for example, 'having been heard to make a noise'. Similarly, buyers may return horses who wind-suck, crib bite or box walk, since these are nervous habits which must be acknowledged by vendors in the catalogue. The limitations on vetting in Britain are stricter than in the United States, where x-rays and endoscopic images are made available to buyers by vendors. This is one of the explanations given by Sheikh Mohammed for his preference to buy in Kentucky rather than Newmarket, and reflects the traditional emphasis placed upon the bloodstock agent's 'eye for a horse' by the British bloodstock industry.

The bloodstock agent

Events which precede the entry of yearlings into the ring are suggestive of the state of knowledge in the bloodstock trade. Most obviously, how closely does a fifty-yard walk and three turns relate to a race on a racecourse over a year later? What are the bloodstock agents looking for so intently? Why do yearlings have to stand in a particular position in order to be assessed? To use a human analogy, inspecting a yearling in the conventional way is the equivalent to asking adolescents to file past in walk, then stand in a particular position whilst an 'expert' predicts which of them will win the marathon and which of them the hundred metres at the Olympics.

The inspection generates the impression that the bloodstock agents, being experts in their field, assess each yearling according to an objective measure. The property that approximates most closely to what this could theoretically be is 'conformation', referred to as 'configuration' by Gray (1984). 'Conformation' refers to the structural qualities of the yearling, its skeletal and muscular construction. However, in my experience, assessments of conformation differ in at least three ways. Firstly, people's perception of a feature may differ, and secondly, their interpretation of that perception may differ. In other words, what is a fault to one agent may either not be seen as such by another or else not be thought of as a fault even when the feature is agreed upon. Thirdly, and perhaps most frequently, opinions differ as to which faults a yearling can 'get away with', i.e. faults which will be overcome, or grown out of before the yearling's career begins. These faults are particular to each stallion, hence a yearling by a particular stallion will be forgiven a certain fault whilst this same weakness may not be forgiven in the offspring of a different sire.

The perversity of the yearling inspection is only evident from an insider's point of view. Anyone observing who knows very little about racehorses could easily imagine that the agent is looking for something which can really be found, that is a yearling which will definitely make a fast racehorse in a year's time. Faced with the paucity of information that will help predict whether a yearling will prove talented, the agent has two options. Either he admits that this knowledge does not exist, and the fragility of the basis of his opinion, which remains just that, or he treats this knowledge as extremely *difficult to come by* but nevertheless discernible after a lot of squinting. Thus bloodstock agents enjoy the strange status of being experts on the unknowable.

The inspection is standardised and conducted by all agents within the same period of time, each professes to be looking for the same thing and all are granted access to each lot. Gray refers to the value based on an assessment of configuration of lambs by their shepherds as an 'instrumental value with objective meaning' (1984: 79). Gray's characterisation of lamb auctions on the Borders goes on to describe the confrontation of this objective value with 'limited world forms of cultural value with subjective meaning' (1984: 79), which may lead shepherds to reject economically viable bids on the basis that they do not reflect the shepherd's 'cultural evaluation' of his own lambs' value.

My thesis regarding the yearlings is that they do not and cannot have an objective value, nor is there any means of evaluation independent of the cultural mores specific to the bloodstock market. The conventions which surround the buying and selling of bloodstock seek to disguise this fact. Thus, the bloodstock agent does not withhold information which would enable anyone to choose the best racehorse from a group of yearlings, *he conceals the fact that this is unknowable*. The bloodstock industry can be described as a secretive society on the basis that it restricts information about information, which, if known, 'offers, so to speak, the possibility of a second world, alongside the manifest world' (Wolff 1950: 330). The question of whether bloodstock agents dupe their customers, or are themselves duped, remains.

The bloodstock market disguises the paucity of available information in a number of ways, most obviously through jargon, which must be mastered in order to identify the other disguises. The specialised language of the industry, itself a manifestation of secrecy, also achieves the more commonly observed function of excluding outsiders:

The use of jargon by a social group is one of the most potent means of inclusion and exclusion. It both expresses and encourages an esprit de corps, a form of bonding which is usually, though not universally, male. It is no accident that this form of language is so richly developed in total institutions, in which the inhabitants feel extremely distinct from the rest of the world. (Burke 1995: 14)

The specialist idiom of the bloodstock industry is both spoken and embodied. The spoken dialect is dominated by the names of horses in the form of pedigrees. The dialect is dominated by horses and their specific relationships, by the names of races, by the dates of famous victories, and by the human element who guide the horses through these achievements: trainers, jockeys and breeders. Thus a bloodstock agent looking at a yearling may say something like:

Has a brother with Michael Stoute, he says he'll run for him, I didn't like the colt by Kris, terrible backend, shocking wheels, and a dog on the track. Mind you, the family is definitely on the up since the Leger.

Fluency in racing dialect is the guarantor of knowledge in the racehorse auction. The favourite topic of the bloodstock industry is itself; the amount of gossip reflects the scale of this face-to-face community, which is often confined to a tiny geographical area at particular times during the annual cycle of sales, both in Britain and overseas. When I asked one agent about his views on the outside world he replied, 'Do you mean the sort of people who count ball-bearings in Bootle?'

Bloodstock agents also employ an embodied code that distinguishes them from outsiders. In particular, as mentioned previously, the bloodstock agent strikes an unmistakable stance when inspecting a yearling, legs slightly apart, catalogue hugged to the chest with fingers holding open relevant page, chin pushed back into the throat, and most importantly, eyes narrowed into a squint. The impression given is that the agent is studying and trying to take in a range of features which will tell him whether the yearling will be a winner.

The peculiar rationality of the bloodstock industry is thrown into relief by the stance of the bloodstock agent. Bloodstock agents behave as if they hold a blueprint that will identify winners. The idea that the good bloodstock agents possess a mental template which yearlings will emulate to greater or lesser degrees is founded in the ideology of the ability described as 'having an eye for a horse'. The brilliance of this ideology is that it is a talent, which often runs in families (as racing talents do), but which can never be taught or reduced to a list of necessary or sufficient physical or attitudinal features. Having an 'eye for a horse', or simply a 'good eye', is a trait particularly associated with the Irish, and is an entirely mystical notion, described in suitably nebulous terms. Whilst

Irish agents described this ability as relating to the overall look of the yearling, its attitude and expression: 'Does it look like a winner, Rebecca, do you know what I mean?' English agents were sceptical of this ability, preferring to refer to a 'good judge', but described the yearling's 'presence' as amongst its most important attributes, and advised me: 'Never buy without a hunch, Rebecca.' In other words, having a good 'eye' was described tautologously as being able to pick winners.

The bloodstock agent's emphasis upon visual skill completes the parallels with connoisseurship in art criticism:

the visual arts are, I repeat, a compromise between what we see and what we know ... knowing is now revelling in a victory, a 'knock-out' – a short one, let us hope, over seeing. (Berenson 1953: 14–5)

Berenson's preference for 'seeing' rather than relying upon historical study to contextualise a work of art is outside my own expertise, but the emphasis upon 'seeing' by bloodstock agents arouses my most cynical suspicions. 'Vision' is a mystically imbued sense, which implies the gift of prophecy to which bloodstock agents are, in effect, making a claim. Making the means by which a yearling appeals to a bloodstock agent a private matter, impossible to articulate, visible only to those with an 'eye', both sets this judgement outside criticism and also grants it magical authority:

I must add that Mr Berenson's procedure before a picture added to the effect of magic. He would come very close to it and tap its surface and then listen attentively, as if expecting some almost inaudible voice to reply ... to the lay eye, the whole performance looked rather like a conjuring trick, and aroused the suspicion of more laborious scholars. (Clark 1974: 138)

Whilst Berenson's methods created suspicion amongst his more 'laborious' colleagues, any bloodstock agent who uses a more 'hands on', physiological or technical inspection technique faces criticism as an impostor.

The bloodstock industry sustains its belief in the specialist knowledge of the bloodstock agent by treating evidence of their successes and failures in ways which reinforce their authority. When a bloodstock agent performs the ritual of the yearling inspection and buys what turns into a fast racehorse who wins an exciting and prestigious race at Ascot, the example will be remembered and used as proof of the agent's expertise, and of good practice generally. If the yearling should be a failure this is explained in terms of disappointment in the specific yearling rather than the agent's judgement. In other words, the agent was correct in his identification of potential, this particular yearling merely failed to live up to that promise. Buying a yearling who gets sold as a polo pony at four having never been on a racecourse is clearly far less memorable than buying the winner of the Derby.

Of course, one solution to all of this uncertainty is to buy horses of known ability, something that the wealthiest and shrewdest trainers and owners are doing more and more. However, the problem of when to buy remains. Many good two-year-olds fail to 'train on' (that is, reproduce their form), at three. A horse that has shown great ability at three is unlikely to be for sale since this is his classic year and his stallion credentials will be in place by this time. There is little incentive for his owners to sell and allow someone else to cash in on his breeding potential. The trick of buying older horses is to recognise potential that has gone untapped due to poor management of the horse. Some trainers are dab hands at this.

Inside the ring

The uneven distribution of knowledge, and the bloodstock agents' expertise in the unknowable is carried into the auction ring where it combines with still more complex information, misinformation, secrecy and mystification. A first glance at the auction in full swing in Tattersalls, combined with informants' explanations, gave the impression that prices were being set by 'competition', and that the auction ring itself represented a sort of three-dimensional mani-festation of the intersection between a supply and demand curve on a graph in an economics textbook.[9] I laboured under this illusion for days spent sitting in the audience, during a time that I now characterise as blissful ignorance. Once I had spent time walking yearlings myself, I discovered increasingly critical, and therefore productive, lines of inquiry.

I had attributed my inability to identify bidders to my inexperience and the bidders' subtlety. However, an informant at the sale suggested that this may not be the only possible explanation. He described the practice of 'ghost-bidding' whereby an auctioneer acknowledges an imaginary bid. My informant went on to add that this may take place when the vendor was a valued customer of the sales company, who would be embarassed if his product failed to secure a bid, or even a good price. Reserves placed on the yearlings mean that unless they reach a certain price they will be retained, in which case the yearling may not be 'on the market' throughout the bidding.

Even where bids could be identified, they did not necessarily represent 'demand' for the horse. Bloodstock agents estimated that approximately half of the yearlings at the Houghton sales were supported in the bidding by either their vendor, an agent bidding on his behalf, or a representative of his sire. A high pro-portion of these were thought to have been 'bought in', that is, bought by their ex-isting owner, directly or indirectly. At the Houghton sales bidding by the vendor is permitted, but, if it is identified by the other half of a duel, bidding will cease. Thus extreme secrecy surrounds just who is bidding, and on behalf of whom.[10]

Myths abound regarding coups made by agents in which they disguise their ownership of a yearling and persuade their client that it must be bought at any price. Agents have also been accused of arranging to bid against each other in order to swell their 5% fee, most recently in a High Court action against two bloodstock agents which has seen the payment of more than £51,000 in damages to a purchaser.[11] Agents compete for naive newcomers in order to buy them expensive yearlings, believing that no one has, strictly speaking, been swindled under these circumstances. Activity of this kind is not universally condemned. The bloodstock trade has a self-perception as thriving on the risk-taking, or even sharp practice of the 'entrepreneurs', the bloodstock agents, who play the game with a poker face, but who, more importantly, do so successfully, that is, profitably, and without being found out. They are winners, and racing loves winners.

The stallion manager also indulges in bidding without wanting to possess the lot in question. He 'bids up' his charges' offspring because where they would like to have knowledge of unknowable things, the bloodstock industry has, instead, statistics. The bloodstock industry is obsessed by statistics, in particular, figures regarding the median and average price fetched by a stallion's offspring. These figures are of extreme importance because they determine the stallion's covering fee for the next breeding season. A stallion may cover between twenty and three hundred mares a year, which gives some indication of the financial significance of his fee. In keeping with the ideology of complete knowledge upheld by the bloodstock agent, statistics are often treated as having an unproblematic relationship with reality. The result of this is that there are at least two markets in existence in the auction ring.

Not everyone bidding at the auction wishes to buy a horse to own and race. The most obvious exception is the agent, who has already been discussed. However, the most extreme exception is the 'pinhooker', who occupies a niche in the market between foals and yearlings. The pinhooker buys foals and sells them as yearlings the following year. He inhabits the commercial market for racehorses as a store of value, taking a gamble that he can sell the yearling for more than the cost of the foal and its upkeep.

Amongst the pinhookers, those who buy foals from first-season sires take the greatest risk. The driving force of the market in foals is that the real risk for the pinhooker is that he will have nothing to sell the next year, he buys in order to guarantee a 'slice of the action'. Foals are always a greater risk than yearlings, whether they are to be pinhooked or kept to race. There is a higher chance of a foal injuring himself in the time which must pass before he is able to race, and his physical appearance is only loosely related to the fully grown horse he will become two years later. Pinhookers are consequently the biggest risk takers at the auction. They are recognisable by their haggard expression and the cloud of cigarette smoke that hovers about them. Their gamble takes months to play itself out and their nerve must hold until the hammer falls.

The relationship between pedigree and ability

If the best bred racehorses were indeed the fastest racehorses then the auction would be less puzzling. However, a horse's pedigree does not determine its ability to any predictable degree. Breeding theories have proved incapable of identifying any more than a loose pattern for successful matings, and none of them offers any guarantees. The vagaries of reproduction ensure that even full siblings will not share the same genetic endowment. Furthermore, genetic endowment simply cannot have any straightforward relationship with a complex trait such as 'the ability to run fast', which depends upon the interplay of hundreds of disparate factors including physical and mental characteristics, none of which is insulated from environmental factors.

Even my most knowledgeable informant, who makes his living from pedigree analysis, told me that 'you may as well buy a lottery ticket as try to breed a classic winner'. My favourite of this expert's opinions, that 'the perfect horse is undoubtedly useless', confirms that the partial ideologies of breeding racehorses can comfortably accommodate even extreme paradoxes.

Similarly, selection on the basis of the yearling inspection seems flawed in that the relationship between conformation and ability is far from clear. Tony Morris, bloodstock correspondent to the *Racing Post*, has written a book about the stallions of the present era, which criticises almost all of them on the basis of conformation. 'Ahonoora's did not have the best fore-legs as yearlings, but they tended to harden into them as horsemen say' (1990: 26), 'Danzig was not unlucky, he was simply unsound' (1990: 59). His interpretation of the findings of his research is confined to a disillusionment with the modern thoroughbred. My interpretation of this book is that if all modern stallions have faults in their conformation, but are stallions because they have been the fastest horses of their generation, conformation does not determine ability. The book does not mean the same thing to Morris as it does to me.

The conclusion I draw from his research, that conformation does not correlate with racing ability, has potential repercussions that are successfully diffused by the widespread agreement in the industry that 'the thoroughbred is not as strong as it once was'. In other words, Morris' book is cited as evidence of a lost golden age. Discovering that all stallions have agreed-upon faults suggests to me that the yearling inspection is ruling out horses on the basis of an erroneous criterion, of 'correctness' which has only a weak correspondence with ability. Morris' conclusion, that the 'very top racehorses never ever get a horse as good as themselves', is similarly not pursued to its conclusion which would be that selecting stallions on the basis of performance is misguided. In the case of the bloodstock industry, the features which insulate the market from fundamental criticisms are the statistics which exhibit their own consistency. Thus, stallions who have the highest aggregate winnings from their offspring have the highest median yearling price, and consequently the highest covering fee.

The bloodstock industry describes itself in terms borrowed from neo-classical economics, and speaks of the 'distortions' of the market caused by 'bidding up' and the relative 'strength' or 'weakness' of various 'levels' of 'demand'. It does so, I would argue, for the same reasons as aggregate economists establish their model of the consumer:

First they establish an unquestionable moral foundation which implies that all economic mechanisms that supply goods to people are positive since people consist of unmet needs which goods requite. Second they imply that consumption is not influenced by factors such as advertising or emulation, or even other consumption choices, which might distort this process of rational self-interest. Third, they imply that no further inquiry is necessary into the actual practices of consumption since economics need only be concerned with aggregate demand. (Miller 1995: 13)

The Market model provides a description of the bloodstock auction that appears to contain its own explanation, rules and validity. It thereby makes any questions as to its true nature misplaced, the product of a misunderstanding.

Conclusion

Since I first sat in on a sale in 1996, Entrepreneur has completed all of the typical phases a good racehorse may experience, from being born to a famous sire and dam on a prestigious stud, to being a 600,000 guineas sale topper; from being trained by the champion trainer to winning the 2,000 Guineas, a Classic race. Much to my disappointment, not to mention financial embarrassment, Entrepreneur fell short of winning the Derby despite being an 'absolute certainty' according to the press. He was retired soon after the race, and has now taken up stud duties for Coolmore. Demi O'Byrne, the bloodstock agent who bought him, is quoted on his stallion advertisement as saying: 'Entrepreneur struck me from the moment I saw him at the Houghton Sale, he looked all speed – like a horse who would go like smoke.'

The significant feature of the bloodstock market, which creates many of the elements of risk described in this chapter, is the purchase of racehorses as yearlings, before their ability is established (before it is even established whether they will live long enough to race). Buying yearlings rather than older horses of known ability creates the uncertainty which can be a source of reward where a cheap yearling turns out to be a star, or disappointment when a sales topper is a dud.

In the absence of any knowledge of a horse's future ability or any means of accurately assessing its potential, the ideology of pedigree and the opinion of the bloodstock agent fill the breach. That the predictive capacity of both pedigree and the bloodstock agent are highly approximate is disguised by the appearance of expertise. A memory which recalls winners with greater ease than losers and a series of explanations of failure insulate the bloodstock agent from criticism.

The auction ring is presented as a 'market' by the bloodstock industry, in terms that analyse the statistics produced by a sale, and not the attitudes that produce those statistics. Knowledge of the means by which prices are established, including 'bidding up' and 'buying in', do not prevent bloodstock analysts from taking stallion statistics at face value, thereby perpetuating these mechanisms. It is for this reason that stallion statistics have become self-fulfilling, in turn shoring up the ideology of pedigree and creating the phenomenon whereby stallion choice is governed by 'fashion'.[12]

So how might one begin to account for this behaviour? The bloodstock auction is a performance, and the bloodstock agent is, in my opinion, the star turn. Undoubtedly some agents are more or less honest, better or worse judges of stock or more or less conscious of their role. But, as I was told again and again, they have to know how to play the game. Much like the bookmaker, the bloodstock agent facilitates the gamble, he is a crucial part of the scene. He's the middle man in a transaction that involves not just horseflesh and money, but also, and most importantly, status.

At virtually every elite auction held in the main centres of thoroughbred breeding, in England, France, Ireland and North America, certain horses capture the imagination of buyers. These individuals may embody particularly highly valued bloodlines or be outstanding to look at: the best will be a heady combination of the two. The 2000 Kentucky Derby winner Fusaichi Pegasus was one such yearling. The story of his sale to Japanese businessman Sekiguchi is illustrative of the principles at work at the auction:

'When I saw the colt', says Sekiguchi, 'he was acting himself – very inquisitive, rearing a little, a little wild. Those horses are the very intelligent ones.' That night his staff were called to his room. Sekiguchi was in his pyjamas. 'I want that horse' he told them, 'I don't care how much it costs.' The next day Satish Sanan, John Magnier and Michael Tabor formed an alliance to buy the Mr Prospector colt. Sekiguchi was not bowed. 'We were going limitless' he says. 'We were wearing red and ready for battle.' At $4 million Sekiguchi won the battle. (Ashforth 2000)

The story shows what is at stake in the auction ring. As Baudrillard states, 'the essential function of the auction is the institution of a community of the privileged who define themselves as such by agonistic speculation upon a restricted corpus of signs' (1981: 117). The thoroughbred auction offers an opportunity that cannot be reproduced by the art auction, and that is the potential to become associated with an animate creature and to establish a relationship with that creature whereby one can almost be said to come to embody the other, as is implicit in Sekiguchi's description of Fusaichi Pegasus' victory in the Derby:

When Fusaichi Pegasus won, it was very emotional. I felt that everyone there was celebrating for the new victor, my horse, Fusaichi Pegasus. It felt truly exceptional. And experiencing all the events that took place after the race, I felt that you need to become fit and tough to become the winner. I needed to catch my breath. I wished I could have infused Pegasus' power into my body. (Paulick 2000)

The behaviour of the horse in the ring, and later on the racecourse and at stud, encourages many successful owners to draw parallels between themselves and their successful equine purchases. A racehorse owner will emphasise the qualities in his horse he most admires in the people around him, and particularly in himself. Thus whilst both art and bloodstock auctions enable 'the destruction of economic value for the sake of another type of value' (Baudrillard 1981. 113), the nature of the thoroughbred auction can be said to be at least partly dependent upon the properties embodied by the object of exchange, the racehorse. The next chapter focuses upon a very different entrepreneur of the racing world, the racing lad.

NOTES

1 These dire statistics are the result of the costs involved in keeping a horse in training, an average of £16,000 a year. Britain is ninth in the international table of average prize money, but high training fees and maintenance costs send it rocketing downwards in the costs:prize-money ratio league table.
2 The Houghton sale offers yearlings only. Tattersalls conduct seven other sales during the year. As well as yearlings, horses in training, stallions, mares and foals are sold. Overall figures for 2000 were: 5224 lots offered, 4018 sold, for an aggregate of 137,299,230, at an average price of 34,171. All figures are in guineas. (See Tattersalls website, www.tattersalls.com for a selection of other facts and figures.)
3 Although domestic prize money is relatively poor, particularly at the middle and lower end of ability, races such as those of the Emirate World Series command fantastic prize money. The series consists of twelve of the most important races of the year, in ten countries on four continents, for total prize money of $26 million. The richest race in the world, the Dubai World Cup, with prize money of $6 million, is included in the series, along with the King George VI and Queen Elizabeth Diamond Stakes at Ascot, the Hong Kong Cup, the Japan Cup, the Breeders Cup Classic and the Arlington Million.
4 My opportunity to deal with yearlings came through playing polo, a source of contacts who consistently overestimated my ability and experience. The image of polo in racing society was of devil-may-care battle-hardened tough nuts, who jumped onto a new pony whenever their own fell beneath them, baying for the blood of the opposing team. This is only partially true. I was told to arrive at Tattersalls at five a.m. on the first morning of the sale.

5 Colts often benefited from a smear of Vicks on their nostrils, to disguise the tanta-
   lising smells of the fillies. Colts are often extremely powerful, and in the process of
   discovering their sexuality, which can make them highly unpredictable. A great deal
   of human energy is expended on keeping colts separate from fillies.

6 The most professional bloodstock agents may have been to see the yearlings at their
   stud farm before the sale, particularly if they think that their client may be interested
   in a particular individual on the grounds of its breeding.

7 Borneman has described the assessment of Arab and Quarter Horses in America as
   a form of body-part fetishism, 'nostrils, eyes and neck for the Arab, rear ends for the
   Quarter Horse' (1988: 39). In the case of the English thoroughbred, the legs, and
   the front legs in particular, are fetishised. The speed of the racehorse is derived from
   the relative length of its legs and therefore of its stride. However, it is not the length
   of the leg that is currently fetishised, but its straightness. As the length of the leg
   has increased, there has been an increase in the ratio of length to thickness of bone,
   making the racehorse a delicate creature at best. The front legs are particularly vulnerable, and bear the brunt of the horse's weight when racing downhill. And so
   bloodstock agents and trainers look for straight legs in which no uneven stresses or
   strains may be caused by the uneven distribution of weight. In practice, very few
   horses have straight legs, and lots of horses with incorrect conformation win races.
   However, straight legs are commercially desirable and this explains the fondness for
   corrective trimming and shoeing shown by yearling producers. Trimming the hooves
   of a young horse will lead to a change in the distribution of his body weight, and may
   lead to a 'correction' of a bent limb. In fact, most farriers will tell you that this is just
   as likely to introduce a different problem in its wake and that most young horses are
   best left alone, to 'grow into' their conformation.

8 Some people will still buy a horse that fails its wind test since yearlings often pick
   up bugs when at the sales, and are often under a great deal of stress, both factors
   which may cause a perfectly healthy horse to fail its test.

9 This is an image that has been applied to the auction by all sorts of people who
   should know better. As Geismar says, 'The process of auction has traditionally been
   described as a simple formalisation of price within a particular public space over
   a clearly delimited and public period of time: a fundamental index of the market'
   (2001: 25).

10 Some of the yearlings will be described as 'Property of a Gentleman' in the catalogue,
   perhaps the simplest disguise. However, if a horse is likely to be at all significant in
   terms of breeding and therefore price it is likely that established potential bidders
   will be able to find out who owns it. Of course this depends on being able to activate
   the right sorts of contacts.

11 The case of Pru's Profiles highlights a number of features of the bloodstock auction
   and its potential pitfalls for the inexperienced or unconnected. Paul Webber, then a
   bloodstock agent for the Curragh Bloodstock Agency, bought the then unnamed horse
   at Tattersalls Fairyhouse Sales in Ireland in 1994 for £8,400. He entered the horse for
   the Doncaster Sales and bought it on behalf of a client, Gary Heywood, for £29,400.
   Webber was bidding against Oliver Sherwood, a trainer and longstanding friend,
   from 14,000 guineas to the purchase price. Heywood maintains that at no time was
   he told that the horse belonged to Webber. The horse ran six times without success
   during 1995 and 1996. Henry Beeby, the Doncaster Sales Director, reproduced the

traditional idea of the auction when he said that, 'we maintain that the auction is the safest place to buy a horse because it is so open and everyone can see what is going on' (Green 1999: 6). The judge awarded £51,480 damages plus costs and interests against the Curragh Bloodstock Agency.

12 All stallions are 'well-bred' according to the fashion of the day. If a stallion's owners are sufficiently wealthy they will 'bid up' the price of his offspring, thus making the stallion seem successful. The stallion will attract more mares and enjoy a numerical advantage. The more expensive offspring will be sent to expensive trainers and given the best food, environment and medical attention, become successful and make their sire more successful, and so on. The stallion's breeding is regarded as superior, despite this being a financially led process.

7   One of the lads

Introduction

The dominant images of racing, generated by journalists, novelists and film makers, come from the racecourse. This chapter concentrates upon the more mundane social logic of the Newmarket training yard. It describes the central figure in this context, the racing lad. Whilst Wacquant sought out the amateur fighters of the training gym (1992, 1995a, b), a large portion of my fieldwork was spent amongst lads, whose structural position relative to professional jockeys is similar to that between amateur and professional fighters.[1] Being a lad in Newmarket does not just affect how the working day is spent, it is a role which affects the whole person, their physique, temporality, and perception of themselves and of others. In other words it can be seen as a particular habitus (Bourdieu 1984), where habitus is understood as the internalisation of tastes appropriate to a particular class, expressed through the medium of the body seen as so much physical capital.[2]

Both riding and boxing are skilled bodily crafts that provide a structure for experience in which linguistic explanations for action are excluded by the immediacy of physical involvement. By riding and boxing, myself and Wacquant engaged in 'edgework' (Lyng 1990: 863) that drove out the requirements of rational choice or normative theories of action, thus demanding an explanation in terms of a logic of practice. Both boxing and riding provide examples of skills in which 'successful practice normally excludes knowledge of its own logic' (Bourdieu 1977: 19). Describing my initiation into riding racehorses is thus a reconstruction of the lad's point of view that no lad would ever attempt. It seeks to convey the insights I gained when under pressure to fulfil my role in the yard whilst recognising that I had an agenda which made my position different from that of my colleagues.

This chapter begins with a description of the life of lads in Newmarket, and offers explanations for their involvement in a low-paid and dangerous industry which do not depend on the lack of ambition with which they are commonly characterised. The lads' lives will be made sense of in terms of their embodiment of the logic of racing, through which they become 'entrepreneurs in risky bodily performance' (1995a: 504), a description applied to boxers by Wacquant.

During my fieldwork, lads reproduced the story of their lives in racing according to their perception of me. Before I was accepted by them they told me of their poverty and their ill-treatment, and of the absence of alternatives to a hard life they would soon leave. I would suggest that these explanations serve to protect the lad. By reproducing the dominant ideology – that the lad is 'the lowest of the low' – they cannot provoke conflict with those more powerful than themselves. Valuing a lifestyle that is condemned by the higher classes is a risk which was only taken once the lads trusted me not to adopt an upper-class attitude towards them. Once I was able to ride alongside them, to take 'my own' horse racing and to fall asleep with them in the horsebox on the way home from the races, a more complicated story emerged. This chapter discusses the contrast between the 'public' and 'hidden' transcripts (Scott 1990: x) of the lad. The 'hidden' transcripts of the lads are the positive explanations of their choice to remain in racing.[3] The profession can only be made sense of by listening to those who have made the decision to ride, and by appreciating the considerable 'pay off' of a life spent in the background, playing second fiddle to a horse. Consequently, this chapter draws upon conversations with a number of the lads I encountered whilst working in Newmarket.

Being a lad in Newmarket

Newmarket High Street accommodates eight pubs and four nightclubs. Drinking in a pub in Newmarket is a sweaty, loud, airless and sometimes intimidating experience.[4] The most striking feature of the nightlife in Newmarket is the sheer number of people drinking every evening of the week. The average height and weight of the pub crowd was, predictably, considerably less than I had ever experienced. After a while it became obvious that people were not merely shorter and lighter, they were also weathered in specific ways that I came to understand after working myself. Individuals who, at a glance, seemed like fourteen-year-old boys of around four foot two, and six stone, gradually metamorphosed into little old men with gnarled hands, leathery weatherbeaten faces and bandy legs at a second look. Some faces were impossible to age, being apparently teenage, but attached to a sinuous body and huge rough hands. So who are these people?

Susan Gallier describes the variety of lads to be found in a Newmarket yard, and also gives a useful template for assessing the status of each of these different roles:

Within the stable yards, the trainer likes to rule his own kingdom. Under him are his head lad and travelling head lad, usually long-serving stable lads whom he has come to trust: the head lad takes charge during the trainer's absence . . . Travelling head lads supervise the horses when they are away racing . . . they are perhaps just a shade under the head lads in social standing. Very few aspire to heights above that of head lad or travelling head lad; to the trainers they remain staunchly employees. They still have to call the boss 'Guv'nor', and special privileges are few . . . Then there are the stable lads themselves, the drones in the beehive, toiling away for little recognition or reward. (1988: 32)[5]

Work begins between 5:30 and 6:30 a.m. For large portions of the year travel to and from work is thus in the dark. Some lads live in hostels in the stable grounds, and so fall out of bed and go straight to work. Tied accommodation and the high rents charged in Newmarket provided a common explanation of the choice to remain in racing. Few lads wished to face the double challenge of finding a new job as well as new accommodation for themselves and their families. As Sean told me, 'it isn't so bad for single lads, they just get a room somewhere, but I've got two kids and it's not that simple, so I'm stuck'.

Between three and five horses are mucked out before being ridden in three or four 'lots' that 'pull out' at intervals. Once the horses are 'dressed over' (groomed), 'let down' (untied) and their beds 'set fair' (tidy), the lads go home, at around noon. A small meal may be eaten, soup or a sandwich, crisps or chocolate, before taking a nap. 'Evening stables' during which the horses are fed again, mucked out and groomed, take place between 4:00 p.m. and 6:00 p.m. After this, the lads are free to go to the pub, usually eating a kebab, burger or portion of chips on the way home at closing time. Cheap food is available in the Clock Tower Cafe and the pubs that stay open during the day, advertising daily specials such as 'minestroney soup and roll' or 'minse and vegtibles in a Yorkshire pudding' (sic).

Lads are also responsible for taking 'their' horses racing, something that many of them look forward to. Trips abroad are particularly highly valued. Even when a yard has only one runner at a meeting it is likely that the lads will know someone else going to that course, or sharing the horse box. Quite often, the journey to the racecourse is spent sleeping, a luxury that is relished, and made especially enjoyable by the thought of some other mug mucking out the horses you have left behind. After reaching the course the horses are settled into their boxes and the lads go to the canteen to get a bite to eat. Racecourse canteens are highly variable, but the best ones are comfortable and warm and serve tasty, cheap food. Going into the canteen one can usually recognise a face or two, and this is a time for companionship and to catch up on gossip or play cards.

Some trips involve an overnight stay in a racecourse hostel and again these are variable sorts of places. In general, lads don't spend much time in their beds if they can help it and find a few friends and hit the town. After all, this is an easy day, one horse to feed in the morning, and not a lot else to do until the afternoon, and so the free time is enjoyed. Before the race the lad must prepare his horse and arrive in the paddock on time.[6] The lads watch the race, collect the horse, wash it down and then let it rest for an hour before beginning the journey home. The journey home is usually spent snoring loudly, sleeping off the excesses of the night before.

Being a lad involves much more than simply knowing how to handle race-horses. It is also about knowing how to behave. Much of the work done by lads is repetitive, and, as in the majority of workplaces, gossip is one of the means of alleviating boredom. Newmarket is a small place, and indiscretions are commonplace. Monday mornings often prompt a rehashing of all of the events of the weekend in gory detail. The number of pints, women, men or successful bets will all be exaggerated. In fact, the potential exists for bad behaviour on any night of the week, since many lads drink every evening. Drinking and the resulting bad timekeeping or violence was the only reason I ever came across for the sacking of lads.[7] Drinking and fighting also contributed to the constant circulation of relationships that I came across in my group of friends, which ensured a good supply of gossip.

As well as gossip, the yard tends to be an environment that engenders an atmosphere of constant flirtation. As Sophie told me, 'Every time you go to a new yard the lads try to get into your knickers. It can be fun! But it annoys the other girls. They soon pack it in if you don't lead them on.' Flirtation often takes the form of teasing, the primary occupation of many lads. Even within established teams, teasing continues, and lots of lads told me that it was a way of making the work more enjoyable, as I was told, 'It makes the day go faster doesn't it! I mean I've always been like it. I can't help myself if someone's got a new bloke or they've put their hair different or they've got new boots or they've come in late. Anything at all!' Newcomers are especially likely to endure the attentions of the other lads, as one teenager told me, 'They hate me. They won't speak to me except to tell me something I did wrong or ask me where I had my hair cut so they can send the boys round.'

The role of stable lad is now filled, in the majority of cases, by women.[8] I came across a number of male lads who were self-confessed chauvinists and witnessed many heated discussions between groups of men and women. These discussions usually focused upon riding ability. Chauvinist male lads told me that whilst men and women were equally capable of shifting muck, riding, the most prestigious part of the lad's job, was a male preserve. As Sean told me, 'Blokes are stronger for their weight than girls. And that's what you want. If you've got a big strong colt you want a lad on it. A girl can spoil it just like that.' Many female lads told me that they sometimes tolerated this sort of discrimination because it suited them. As Joanne told me, 'It's not just chauvinist pig stuff. Even though there's plenty of that. It's more . . . old fashioned than that. It's actually sometimes quite gallant! [laughs] Most of the things they don't want you to do you wouldn't want to do yourself!'

Female lads told me that they enjoyed certain advantages. They tend to get the easier horses to ride. They are slightly protected from the most physical jobs by male lads. And they tend to get along with trainers, who are usually men. If all the stories of affairs between lads and trainers in Newmarket were true it would be difficult to imagine that there was ever any time or energy left for training racehorses. Trainers do have affairs with their staff, and very occasionally they marry them. High profile cases occasionally reach the tabloid press, although the majority of affairs go unnoticed outside the town. However, female lads are not all wrapped in cotton wool, waiting for a chance to grab the attention of their powerful Guv'nor. As Sophie told me, 'We let certain things go, we don't argue about every sexist comment or whatever. And if we want a day off we might bat our eyelids at the Boss. But he knows as well as I do that I work harder than the lads and so I'm worth that day. I just make it nicer for him to give it me!'

'A skewed and malicious passion' (Wacquant 1995a: 523)

> The ring affords boxers a rare opportunity – the only one that many of them may ever enjoy – to shape to a degree their own destiny and accede to a socially recognised form of existence. This is why, in spite of all the pain, the suffering and the ruthless exploitation it entails, of which fighters are painfully cognisant, boxing can infuse their lives with a sense of value, excitement, and accomplishment.
>
> (Wacquant 1995a: 501)

Like the boxers who spoke with Wacquant, lads bemoan the low pay of their profession, the absence of promotional opportunities, the long hours and poor conditions, saying, 'It's a mugs game.' They often repeated that they would not like their children to go into 'the game', hoping that they might go into a more profitable and prestigious career. As Dick told me,

> I came into racing through my dad. He still rides. I think he's the oldest lad out there now. I started riding a few and tried as an apprentice, but I didn't make it. I ended up travelling horses but no real good ones. Got married. I don't know why I carry on. I can't imagine myself in a factory though. I mean trainers are all idiots and horses are mostly rubbish but if your mates are in racing then it's hard to leave. I'm trying to get a job as a groundsman because I fell off and hurt my back. I'd like my lad to be a lawyer or a doctor, but you just don't know. The other day I caught him riding a finish on the back of the settee when the racing was on telly and I gave him such a belt. But if he wants to try it I won't be able to stop him. What can you do?

Lads do not always devalue their career. Racing shares with boxing a variety of rewards which were identified to me by lads during conversations in which they felt either privileged or nostalgic enough to pity those who work in factories or service industries who 'don't know a trade' and therefore 'can't take pride in doing a job that only a few people understand'. In these conversations lads emphasised their independence, individuality, expertise, the good fortune of having had a lucrative horse or bet, and the fringe benefits which all of them seemed to have received at some point in one form or another. As Mick told me:

There's nothing like it. I mean it's hard and you can't be soft, but I've led up winners in France and that's hard to beat. And we know the horses best. Yeah. I can get on a horse and tell you everything about it. Just by sitting on it once. How far. What class. Which leg hurts. Anything like that. And I can tell you if it's a winner. It's a feel you get if you start to live off horses. I don't get a buzz off the crap any more, but ten crap horses are made worthwhile by one bit of class. Whoosh! You feel the difference like that! Then you get out your pocket book and make some money. That's why I do it!

Lads engage in a profession that grants a certain amount of autonomy. Individual responsibility for the horses in his care lies firstly with the lad, and only ultimately with his 'boss', the trainer. This control is most strikingly evident on the Heath, where the lads ride the horses and are unequivocally responsible for them. Whilst a boxer is responsible for himself, lads are responsible for themselves and their equine dependants. The lads' reaction to this responsibility is an example of the nonchalance that is so strongly cultivated in all of the tasks of the day, whether it be riding a hundred thousand guinea racehorse or drinking eight pints then driving home. Nonchalance is the desired state in Newmarket, whilst being seen to make an effort is discouraged. Amongst lads 'natural' ability was admired as proof of hereditary talent; however, making little effort also insulated the lads from the criticism that the menial role in which they found themselves reflected the limits of their potential. The role of the lad commands extremely low status in Newmarket, and one way of detracting from this association is to fulfil this role with minimal effort thereby implying that a lad could achieve a great deal more, given the opportunity.

When I first arrived in Newmarket I expected lines of well-groomed horses and riders in perfect unison, trotting neatly along the gallops. My first sight of riders on the Heath could not have been more different. Lads were swinging on their reins, slipping their feet out of their stirrups, pulling back to be next to their pals, pushing on to join friends at the front to share a cigarette, passing a can of Coke along the line, casually slapping the horses' necks with their whips, and generally enjoying the banter of the gallops. The air of extreme nonchalance assumed by the lads resembles that adopted by fairground assistants who wander past spinning machinery with yawning disinterest. By taking control of a racehorse on the Heath the lad exercises an element of control over the owner of that horse, momentarily reversing the relationship between the two in which the lad is apparently so structurally disadvantaged. All stable lads can tell you how much their horse was bought for at the sales and how much it has won in its career. It was never lost on me that although someone else owned the horse that I was riding, and had paid a great deal of money for that privilege, I assumed sole control of the animal on the gallops.

This control is the result of the mastery of techniques that are unique to the racing industry. The lads' presence on the Heath, in front of small audiences of journalists, owners, trainers and tourists, is an expression of this mastery, executed with the nonchalance of someone who obviously carries their ability lightly. Riding racehorses is conducted according to its own detailed set of rules that cannot be extrapolated from the technology alone, so must be learnt. For example, having saddled my horse for the first time, my trainer altered the order of the sheets under the saddle, tied my reins in a knot and brushed a couple of stray pieces of straw from his tail. He left me in the stable looking at the miniature saddle and tiny stirrups wondering how on earth I would ever get on the horse. I heard Patricia, the trainer's wife, shout from the next stable, 'You can climb in the manger with him.' Though I had no idea what to expect, rather than betray this ignorance I clambered into the manger and in a bizarre moment of complicity, the horse shimmied sideways towards me until I could jump from the manger onto his back. He and I were clearly collaborating in defining each other through our accumulated physical techniques.

As with boxing, the 'kinetic techniques' (Wacquant 1995a: 504) of riding racehorses offer opportunities for satisfaction through good practice. Having a 'good run' up the gallop involves being able to control the horse in order to fulfil the instructions given by the trainer, which may be to 'jump off at half speed, go up to join the lead horse at the turn, after two furlongs upsides let Mick come through behind you and kick on'. I anticipated that the nature of the riding experience itself would form part of the lads' justification for continuing to ride. Although lads did sometimes describe the thrill of being on a good horse, this was often valued instrumentally, as part of a cycle of permanent potentiality. The inherent pleasure of the experience which dominated my own attraction to riding racehorses was, for professional lads, also an expression of the potential rewards of the industry itself. The lads' motivation to stay in racing was described to me as essentially the same motivation as that of the owner or gambler. The chance of 'doing' a good horse motivated lads to continue for season after season, 'I'm finished, there's no money in this business unless you're rich or you've got a good horse.'

Of the three horses a lad cares for, once the ability of the oldest is established, the lad is given an untried yearling. Lads begin to rave about the new 'babies' as soon as they arrive in the yard: 'I've got a nice looking Prince Sabo I'm quite excited about, she's got a bit of speed alright.' It is significant that the ultimate accolade given to a two-year-old is that he or she 'could be anything'. The cycle in which lads are given untried yearlings at the beginning of each season (in the midst of winter when the job is at its least appealing) offers an incentive to continue couched in the idiom of risk that appeals most to those who are already fluent in the practice of horseracing.

This cycle of hope and disappointment was not described to me as based on optimism, but on a horror of giving up and in doing so missing out on a 'good horse'. Looking after a 'good horse' brings financial rewards, since its lad is given a disproportionate share of the stable's proportion of winnings. In addition, the association tends to generate respect for the individual on the grounds that he is a good lad, who (more significantly) 'got lucky'. I was told that Red Rum's lad made a living out of being just that, enjoying hospitality wherever he went amongst racing society, implying that his luck was seen as being contagious in the same way as that of a lucky charm. He was described as a 'human rabbit's foot'.

Lads are motivated by the chance of success that each new horse represents. Furthermore, they take pleasure, as do boxers, in being 'small entrepreneurs in risky bodily performance' (Wacquant 1995a: 20), revelling in the logic of an industry which is based on imperfect information and thus the successful negotiation of risk. At the same time, they recognise their exploitation and bemoan their hardships. They protest that 'racing is in your blood', and that it was 'impossible to walk away from the game, no matter how bad it gets'. Those who made the break would 'soon be back, because they don't know anything else'. As Gallier says:

Funny things, horses. Dirty, dangerous, greedy beasts, they get into your blood like a virus, and once you've got it, there's no cure. We all moan about them; most of us try to leave the game at some time or another, but it's hopeless. Within days you're fretting for the sight and sound and smell of them. (Gallier 1988: 9)

Learning the hard way

The individual learner is not gaining a discrete body of abstract knowledge which (s)he will then transport and reapply in later contexts. Instead (s)he acquires the skill to perform by actually engaging in the process, under the attenuated conditions of legitimate peripheral participation.

(Lave and Wenger 1991: 14)

The thought that riding racehorses was a quintessential example of legitimate peripheral participation did not occur to me until some time after my first gallop. My thoughts during this experience had revolved around death, repentance and the will to live. I had only met Bill, racehorse trainer, on one occasion before he rang to ask me whether I could cover for his stable lass, Sophie, whilst she went on holiday for ten days. The stud work I had done earlier in the year had involved dealing with mares, yearlings and foals, but not with 'horses in training', a category of bloodstock which drove fear into the hearts of all stud workers. Horses in training were characterised as overfed, unpredictable creatures. Those who chose to deal with them were deranged, whilst those who agreed to ride such creatures clearly had a death wish. In retrospect, by accepting this challenge I tacitly assumed that there was some such mechanism as legitimate peripheral participation, whereby, 'if learning is about increased access to performance, then the way to maximise learning is to perform, not to talk about it' (Lave and Wenger 1991: 22). It was only when I began to accumulate scars that I realised the extent to which my own body was implicated in this process.

Working days followed a routine, and I was expected to do all the chores in the yard from day one, although Bill managed to resist asking me to ride until the second day. Patricia and I would begin the day at 6 a.m., by putting four of the horses on the 'walker', a huge rotating cage separated into four sections, turned electrically, like a vast horizontal hamster wheel. This warmed up the horse's muscles, and took the edge off their morning exuberance, whilst Bill prepared the feed. Patricia and I would then muck out the boxes belonging to the horses on the walker, before changing the next four onto the walker and doing their boxes. Mick, who rode the fillies, arrived at 7:30, whilst Bill and Patricia would 'pull out' with the 'first lot' shortly afterwards, leaving me to finish the boxes. Following my recruitment to riding I would take my first ride out with Mick, and give him a lead around the sand ring. Bill, Patricia and I would then have breakfast of coffee and toast whilst Mick took out another filly. Bill, Patricia and I would then take out the final three horses around the sand. When each horse returned to the yard it was washed down with hot soapy water, particularly on its face, feet, legs and 'undercarriage'. Each horse was then led into the paddock for a 'bite' or 'pick' of grass, whilst drying. The horses were then brought back into their boxes, given a thorough brush, their feet picked out and oiled, their manes and tails 'dandied', and their sheets or day rugs put on, which is referred to as 'dressing'. The horses who are not in work were also put either on the walker or out into the paddock for twenty minutes to 'stretch their legs', and were also brushed or 'dressed over'.

This work was done by 12:00. After each morning I felt as if I had been run over by a tractor. Although mucking out was made slightly more difficult by having to keep up with superhuman Patricia, it was really the riding that exhausted me, and was quite unlike any other riding I had ever done. Although I have ridden since I was young, I hadn't ever ridden a thoroughbred in training. When he asked whether I could ride out Bill simply said that if I was capable of riding a polo pony that had once been a racehorse then I was perfectly capable of riding a non-ex-racehorse. Patricia tutted at Bill and took me to one side to say that I should only ride if I wanted to. Bill is very convincing. I rode the least valuable horse in the yard first, referred to by Bill as 'The Bastard', which didn't require much ethnographic sensitivity to interpret. Bill, Mick and I rode off out of the yard and for the first time I shortened my stirrups (jerks) and rode (as I thought) like Lester Piggott. I quickly let them down again when I realised that if I kept them short I would be exhausted by the time we got to the gallop we were going to use.

Bill had decided that we would do a twelve furlong (mile and a half) straight gallop on the turf inside the racecourse, called 'Back of the flat'. In retrospect, this was one of several examples of Bill's tendency towards baptism by fire. Horses are keener on grass than all-weather tracks, and on straight tracks than circuits. Typically, Bill had set me the stiffest task to begin with on the grounds that, 'if you could handle that then I knew that you could handle anything'. On the way to the gallop I had felt an unparalleled sense of elation to be riding across the Heath smiling and nodding to all the other lads. Quite a few things began to make sense. I felt a part of Newmarket in a new and exciting way, and yet I felt totally invisible, as if I had finally blended in with part of the way of life I was seeking to understand. Unfortunately, these feelings were soon overtaken by more pressing concerns of self-preservation.

Mick had told me to 'give him a yank in the gob as you jump off', to 'let him know who's boss', as if he was in any doubt. This horse has a reputation for setting his jaw and running away, although his saving grace is that he knows where to stop at the end of the gallops. I put my life in his hands and set off, giving his mouth a quick saw, as if that made the slightest difference. He took off and I had a sensation of flying. Bill had said that I would see a big mound at the end of the run and would thus know when to stop. All I could see was a vast expanse of grass with tiny markers either side of the strip we were supposed to gallop up apparently marking the way to infinity. We were going faster than I have ever been on a horse before (about 35 mph), the wind was catching my breath and making my eyes water so that I could hardly see, possibly a blessing. My legs were exhausted with supporting my own weight and setting against my horse's jaw. My arms were pulling desperately. My thoughts at the time were surprisingly clear, and almost removed. I established that this was by far the most frightening thing that I had ever done, also that it was the most physically demanding thing that I had ever done, also that I didn't ever want to do it again and must not be allowed to on any account. I pondered when the end would come, imagining that every molehill we flashed past was the huge mound that Bill had described. The mound was actually the side of a reservoir, and we ground to a stop once we reached it, as predicted.

By the time Mick and Bill caught up I had managed to sit up and to restrict my breathing to a mere gasp rather than the roar it had been initially. Bill casually enquired as to how I had found it, and out of my mouth came words like 'terrific' and 'incredible'. Bill looked so delighted that I overlooked my strange response, only realising on the walk back that for all of its horror my first trip up the gallops had been not just terrifying, but also one of the most brilliant experiences of my life. The primary satisfaction came from surviving, but this was mixed with the excitement generated by the experience itself, by the sensation of speed, the proximity of disaster, the loss of control. Before we had reached the yard these feelings had coalesced into a desperate ambition to be able to be good at something so testing.[9]

The natural

The idea that learning is achieved through performance is central to the philosophy of the training yard. Apprentices learn by LPP because in the yard horsemanship 'is bred, not taught'. According to Gallier:

Some of the newcomers can't even hope to make it as stable lads; they just don't take to the horses . . . These sorts of kids can't make a horse walk through a doorway, or stand still whilst being washed down. Horses will never behave well during exercise, either, for these people . . . These poor kids are never popular; the lads abuse them for their lack of skill, and trainers shout at them in exasperation. But horsemanship is a quality that is inborn, it cannot be taught. (1988: 83)

When I asked lads how their skills were learnt a common response was, 'You don't learn it, it should come naturally.' This sort of response is epitomised in the conversation below:

RC: How did you learn to ride?
Mick: I just sort of did it.
RC: Did anyone help you?
Mick: No, no one can, because you just do it or you don't.
RC: So who can do it and who can't?
Mick: It has to be in your blood.

Many lads told me of their racing ancestors in the same way as members of 'real' Newmarket families might. However, the attitude of lads to their own 'pedigrees' is ambivalent.

Whilst 'blood' was spoken of as the hereditary medium of talent, lads also offered an alternative explanation whereby talent could be assimilated by the individual from the environment. Lads maintained that racing was 'in the blood' without the commitment to this blood being inherited from ancestors. I was told that racing could 'get into your blood', that 'it sort of seeps into you', and that 'it gets under your skin'. The person in this case is perceived as permeable whilst the upper-class individual may seem closed, their destiny suggested by birth. Amongst lads, the fixity of the upper-class imperative whereby talent must be explained by an appeal to pedigree is replaced, at times, by explanations which imply a far more flexibly constituted person, perhaps suggestive of a more flexible class system, one of the 'hidden scripts' of the lad, as articulated by Dick:

I know a lad who was useless at first. I mean I thought that he would never hack it. I was just waiting to see him go home. And we weren't very nice to him because we didn't expect him to last. But he stuck it out. And he really started to get better. It was spending all his time in the yard. And he wanted it so bad. It sort of got a hold of him and made him into a lad. But he was never going to be like a natural.

If riding comes naturally then it can't be taught. In keeping with this, the amount of explicit guidance I was given throughout my time on the yard was pitiful, so how did I learn? Learning the ropes in a training yard includes experiences that seem to be common to many examples of apprenticeship. Firstly, as amongst Yucatec midwives, learning takes place without any obvious corresponding practice of teaching (Lave and Wenger 1991: 84). Secondly, the structural constraints of the division of labour determine the tasks undertaken by the apprentices, which are usually dirty or repetitive, as amongst apprentice meat-cutters in America (Lave and Wenger 1991: 76). Thirdly, as amongst Vai tailors, peripheral tasks are undertaken before the central techniques are attempted (Lave and Wenger 1991: 72). In the case of a racing apprenticeship, however, the defining features of the experience are determined by three factors; firstly, that a racehorse is a 'single-user tool', secondly that the unsuccessful practice of racehorse riding can result in serious injuries and even death, and thirdly that successful practice relies upon the embodiment of techniques which respond to stimuli without the intervening rationalising processes demanded by knowledge which is stored and transmitted as so much verbal information.

Just as the experiences of apprentice quartermasters in the American Navy were influenced by the design of instruments which did not facilitate joint operation (Lave and Wenger 1991: 73), riding a racehorse is a one-person-only task. It is therefore inevitable that the first gallop is made alone. Fellow lads all confirmed that the first experience of riding racehorses was untutored:

> He just threw me into the plate and off I went. You just get on with it don't you? They don't make pillion saddles you know. I didn't expect it to be as tough, I was shocked I suppose. But you get over it.

I asked both Bill and Mick for advice before I flew up the gallops for the first time. They didn't offer any help, humming and hawing and saying that 'you just have to learn for yourself, you'll see. It's impossible to explain, you just have to do it.' Bill's words as I shot off up the gallop were, 'Don't worry about anything, just enjoy yourself and get the feel of it.' As a jockey said to a television presenter recently when asked to explain what it feels like to ride a horse: 'It's very difficult to explain to a normal person.'

Once I had made my first run, advice was more forthcoming, partly because I began to ask the right questions, and partly because the advice could be presented as criticism of my own technique which did not depend upon any articulation of their own embodied practice. Lads were not happy to give abstract descriptions of riding racehorses, nor to generalise about the experience. They were more comfortable discussing particular horses, with the shared experience of racehorse riding as the unexplored, taken for granted context. These conversations would always take the form of, 'You know when the filly takes hold of the bit and twists her jaw like that?... Well...' The tips and advice I received were sought out. That the knowledge is difficult to articulate is not, however, the only explanation as to why this articulation is only very rarely even attempted.

My intention is not to suggest that the technique of riding a racehorse cannot be articulated, because to a large extent it can. The absence of teaching as such can be explained by two factors; first, discussing riding a racehorse is easier when both parties have even the most minimal shared experience, secondly, the status of the newcomer does not promote the easy sharing of knowledge. As the latest recruit to the yard, the newcomer is a threat to those above him to the extent that if he should prove talented he may 'make it' at the expense of an 'old-timer'. Thus, I was told that the newcomer must be 'thrown in at the deep end' to 'pay his dues like the rest of us'. The other experience common to many of the new recruits to whom I spoke was that, in keeping with their entry into a new and closed world, they were stripped of any status which would have contradicted their new structural position as 'lowest of the low'. They were given nicknames, which were generally not flattering, and teased about their awkwardness. I was teased about my elephantine physique and my big feet, other lads told me of being teased about spots and bad haircuts. The body is focused upon because successful racing practice involves control of the human and equine body. Where a body is 'out of control' it is a source of mockery.

There is thus a sense in which newcomers learn despite the efforts of those whom one might expect to teach them. They learn by accumulating experiences which are stored physically, but rarely articulated, and by the time they have acquired them, there is no incentive for them to pass them on to the newcomer to whom they have now become an 'old-timer'. Although it is difficult to describe how it feels to ride a racehorse, it is not impossible. The lack of teaching is partly due to the structural position of the newcomer; however, it is justified by an appeal to the idea of 'the natural'.

The British Racing School

The British Racing School is not universally respected by the trainers in Newmarket, some of whom dispute that the trade can be taught 'at a desk', thus encapsulating their perception of teaching as literate and riding as physical, the one irreducible to the other. The school takes groups of young people who are under nineteen years old, weigh less than nine stone and are physically fit. There are no other formal entry requirements, and the interview procedure rewards motivation and 'the right attitude'. By encouraging the 'right attitude', the BRS is teaching lads how to occupy their particular niche in the class system of racing. An array of behaviour is taught, including how to address the trainer, owner and steward. Deferential body language and a standardised appearance are also explicitly rewarded.

Courses last nine weeks, after which the apprentice lad is guaranteed work with a yard. Some of the recruits have not sat on a horse before they arrive at the school. The course begins with three weeks spent in an indoor arena. Those who have ridden before ride thoroughbreds whilst there are a few ponies for those without any previous experience. After riding twice a day for three weeks, the apprentices graduate to the sand ring, which they canter around. After doing this twice a day for three weeks they go on to the straight grass gallop for the last three weeks.

The apprentices at the school have to 'do' their own horses, so they must muck out and groom two horses whilst doing their share of chores such as sweeping and raking. Almost all of the lessons are 'practicals', taught in the stable or on the gallops. The elementary stages are taught more easily in the indoor arena, which provides a far safer environment for the riders than New-market Heath. Safer still is the Equisisor, a robotic horse that simulates the movements of a galloping horse. Once safe in these controlled environments where instructors can control the horse whilst the apprentice concentrates on developing a basic technique which is secure and balanced, the apprentices venture out. In order to overcome the problem of the horse being a single-user tool, the apprentices wear radio headsets, through which their instructors provide a constant stream of instruction. My visit to the school happily coincided with the first outing for a group of twelve, and watching their progress on a day that was extremely wet and windy was terrifying. One of the instructors noted my stunned expression and acknowledged that: 'It's something you never quite get used to.'

On the first trip outside the indoor arena for three weeks, the horses were understandably fresh. The young people riding them were excited and scared to be outside for the first time. The idea of the exercise was for one pair at a time to trot and then canter once around the inside of the enclosed sand ring. Whilst one or two pairs achieved this, the others got gradually faster and faster, until they were cornering like motorbikes, with their rider's feet almost scraping the floor. The pitiful cries of 'Whoa, steady boy, whoa' were whipped away by the wind as the horses shamelessly took advantage of their frozen, terrified passengers. Some people fell off, some horses simply failed to stop and did eleven circuits before their riders dropped to the floor with exhaustion, some were stopped by instructors waving their arms in their path, some took the instructors on, galloping past them. My favourite personal tragedy was the horse who got down and rolled in the mud whilst waiting for his turn to canter, covering his rider in mud in the process, he then took off around the circuit and whipped round when an instructor tried to get in his way, depositing his rider in the mud for a second time.

Although the scene was carnage, no one was hurt, and all the riders seemed quite happy. The experience raises questions as to whether cantering for the first time is made easier by instruction or not. I would have felt better had someone been speaking calmly to me during my own lightning progress up the gallop, but would I have been any more effective? I spent the entire day with the instructors, and took full advantage of their expertise, asking them for help with my own riding. They had lots of helpful suggestions, some articulated and some both articulated and demonstrated. They had theories of horse psychology, such as what made a horse pull, they advocated soft hands and a gentle voice, they held strong views on stirrup length and produced highly developed arguments on centres of balance. They had an entire vocabulary which had been lacking in my own 'apprenticeship', and they defended the practice of teaching what is usually only learnt.

The next time I rode out I used all of the techniques the instructors at the school had taught me. This was the best ride of my life. I was in control for a change, and I could explain why, according to my newly acquired theory. The problem is that on every occasion after that I tried to use my techniques and they failed, whilst my old 'don't know why I do it, but it feels as though it looks a bit like Mick does when he rides' also worked on some occasions and not others. I think that the problem lies in the presence of the other body in this experience, the racehorse. Not only do racehorses have characters, they also have moods. Their behaviour is unpredictable, and this accentuates the difficulties of teaching how to ride them by means other than experience.[10]

Even when I rode the same horse out every day, on the same route, the experience was never routinised. However, whilst each riding experience was unprecedented, the more riding I did the greater my confidence, because the more likely it was that I had a group of similar experiences to refer to before I decided how to react. Where there was no time to reflect, my body would automatically perform the action that had proved most successful in the past. In the absence of any prior experience my body would guess at whatever action seemed likely to aid self-preservation, guesswork made this the least successful category of actions. Lads concur that experience is a saviour, 'You'll get used to it', 'The more you do it the better you'll get.'[11]

Conclusion

Lads in Newmarket thrive on their membership of a small, close-knit community in which people are united by the business of racing. They believe that what they do is important, and between themselves they give credit to each other as experts. They cement relationships at work by teasing, and with a sense of humour that often highlights misfortune. Some of my informants described this as a cruel environment, but others were right to say that teasing was a means of paying attention to people in a way that was in keeping with the industry itself. Working as a lad is tough, and dangerous. It is competitive and badly paid. Teasing is one of the mechanisms by which this community of skilled people is pulled together.

Riding racehorses is an example of a skilled bodily practice in which theoretical contemplation is driven out by the immediacy of danger. The presence of two bodies of two different species further complicates the possibility of theorising the activity. Because riding a racehorse is almost always an unprecedented experience, the body is called upon to respond appropriately when there is no time for contemplation, just as a boxer must defend his body when his conscious facilities are compromised. However, these techniques are not entirely insulated from at least partial articulation, despite many of the learning experiences of novices such as myself being conducted as if they were. I would like to suggest that this articulation is not attempted by racing society for structural and political reasons.

The British Racing School provides examples of techniques whereby many of the difficulties of teaching can be overcome including simulators, indoor schools, quieter horses, radio headsets, enclosed sand rings, expert supervision and practical lessons. Newcomers in yards are often not taught because they represent a threat to their superiors who are the present guardians of knowledge, and were not taught by their superiors. The structural disadvantage of the newcomer to racing is justified by imagining knowledge as hereditary, a natural potential waiting to be realised through performance. I have argued that the reproduction of the hierarchy within racing may constitute an alternative explanation to the absence of overt tuition.

Not all lads lack ambition, nor can working in the industry be explained on the basis that they cannot do anything else. Tied accommodation and lack of financial stability discourage lads from seeking alternative employment and thereby uprooting their families. Furthermore, lads are retained by means of their insertion into the annual cycles of the industry which provide hope when disappointment threatens to overwhelm. An untried two-year-old was described to me as 'a free betting slip for the Derby' by one lad, explicitly establishing the link between gambling on a race and gambling on a life as a lad. A consistently hard life that brings with it a long shot of great reward is better than the certainty of a life seen as mundane. As Mick explained:

What am I going to earn in a factory or a shop? I'd know at the beginning of the week and that would be forever. In racing you never know, you might get lucky!

NOTES

1 I use the expression 'lad' and 'lads' to refer to the men and women who care for and ride racehorses in Newmarket. Female lads told me that they didn't like being referred to as 'lasses' or 'girls', alternative titles that are commonly used but which many of them found patronising.

2 On becoming a lad I lost weight, developed calluses on my hands, and got accustomed to wearing the same ragged clothes for weeks on end. Some people might add that I was often quite smelly after the morning's work. I accept the contention of Csordas, that, 'The kind of body to which we have become accustomed in scholarly and popular thought alike is typically assumed to be a fixed, material entity, subject to the empirical rules of biological science, existing prior to the mutability and flux of cultural change and diversity and characterised by unchangeable inner necessities. The new body that has begun to be identified can no longer be considered as a brute fact of nature' (1994: 1).

3 Lads engage in practices that might be described by anthropologists as 'resistance' (Scott 1990, Comaroff 1985). They complain, drag their feet, cut corners and ride badly. However, although to some lads these practices may constitute a form of protest, I would like to suggest that, amongst others, 'resistance' is practised because the dominant ideology demands it. Lads publicly decry their tied accommodation, lifestyle, skills and contribution, and conceal any more positive explanations to remain in racing. They register their resistance to their undervalued lifestyle in front of the upper class, whilst constructing an alternative ideology amongst themselves. This is not to suggest that the enjoyment of riding horses entirely compensates for their structural disadvantages. Rather, neither explanation is complete, and the decision to remain in racing remains a matter of individual circumstances.

4 My first foray into Newmarket nightlife proved a less than productive experience as the town had been under siege by the *Evening Standard* for several weeks, culminating in the publication of an article about heroin addiction entitled 'Small town poisoned by inner-city plague' (Adamson 1996: 12). The article highlighted the sixty registered heroin addicts, and estimated one hundred further unregistered users in Newmarket's population of twelve thousand adults. Alcohol and tobacco dominate recreational drug use in Newmarket. Alcohol has a role in all of the significant relationships in Newmarket; lads drink with each other, trainers drink with owners, successful punters drink their winnings with losers and racegoers slurp gin and tonics and champagne. Asked why Tony McCoy was presently the best jump jockey in the country, for example, Chester Barnes, a trainer's assistant, replied that: 'He doesn't drink and he's very dedicated', the order of that explanation being significant.

5 This is an extract from the only lad's autobiography of which I am aware. When I asked other lads to read it and to let me know what they thought of it they all felt that it gave an unrealistically rosy image of their life. Gallier's affection for horses overrides all her complaints, and the book is really a comical tribute to Newmarket. The last line 'However indignantly they deny the presence of such an unmanly emotion in their steely breasts, the truth must be that stable lads do it for love' (Gallier 1988: 176) was met with utter derision by one lad. 'Bollocks!' he sneered.

6 At one race meeting a fellow lad had started drinking before his race and carried on drinking when he should have stopped. He ran around the stables, chasing girls and shouting 'Come here you Beauty!!' like an extra from a Benny Hill Holiday Special. When it was time for his race someone got his horse ready and handed it to him, but he was utterly incapable of leading it around the paddock and kept falling over into the flowerbeds. His trainer was livid, and his box driver left him at Brighton racecourse. I never did find out how he made it back to Newmarket. In our yard, we still shout 'You Beauty!!' at each other in memory of this performance.

7 There is an extreme shortage of labour in Newmarket and the job market is highly flexible. Lads can, and do, walk in and out of jobs. Most lads are still extremely badly

paid, with the worst off taking home pay packets of £140 per week. The better yards enjoy extra income from betting and their share of prize money, the worst yards make do as best they can.

8 The ratio of male to female lads between 1991 and 1995 ranged from 1712:1395 to 1473:1202 (Racing Industry Statistical Bureau Statistics 1996: 210).

9 This ambition survived two deaths on the gallops in the time that I rode, and only faded slightly as my return to ordinary life approached. I began to be more careful on the grounds that it would be 'typical' to hurt myself just when I had almost 'got away with it'. Being 'more careful' spells disaster in a regime in which confidence, and the communication of that confidence to the horse, is paramount. My belief in a spiteful fate, and in luck perceived as a limited good (which must not be 'pushed') was a reflection of my total immersion in the social logic of racing. My loss of confidence arose from the awareness that I would soon remove myself from this context, thus acknowledging the existence of an alternative.

10 Some horses are easier rides than others. In general, even where a horse has a particular bad habit, such as pulling, it is better to ride such a known quantity than a horse who is unpredictable. Perhaps the most dreaded bad habit is whipping round. Yearlings in particular, who are narrow and difficult to grip on to, can deposit riders with great ease. They spot something potentially dangerous in the middle distance (often imagined) and start suddenly, before whipping around and dropping their heads at the same time. Racehorses are extremely agile. They can jump vertically upwards, and land facing in the opposite direction. They can rear and buck standing still and on the move. Some continue these tricks whilst galloping. They may fly leap – jump into the air with their front legs before following up with a terrific buck behind, swerve from side to side (called 'plunging'), or simply run, out of control and with their heads in the air, in the wrong direction.

11 Riding racehorses is really a confidence trick. The most effective way of doing it is to convince the horse that you are totally uninterested in any prank it might care to pull because you are invincible, and it will either gain confidence if it is nervous, or give up trying to terrify you if it is mean.

8   Doing it for Daddy

Introduction

In this chapter I shall concentrate upon the relationship between racehorses and humans that obtains in contemporary Newmarket. This relationship takes the form of an intersubjectivity whereby gains or losses in status of the racehorse accrue to those with whom it is associated. This relationship is relevant to all aspects of racing, as it facilitates the cross-over of ideas of pedigree from horses to humans. Although I shall draw specifically upon fieldwork conducted on a stud during the spring of 1997, the analysis in this chapter is informed by all of my fieldwork.[1] The first section describes the personalisation of racehorses as it occurs on the thoroughbred stud. In this environment, racehorses are granted traits more commonly attributed to humans. This personalisation is significant because it is carried over into their relationships with humans, such that the discourse of personalities in Newmarket includes both humans and animals.

Contextualising this chapter is Clutton-Brock's contention that: 'a domestic animal is a cultural artefact of human society' (1994: 28), and its enquiry is centred around asking what the racehorse reveals about the human society by which it is defined. Lévi-Strauss separated racehorses from human society, saying that they:

> do not form part of human society either as subjects or objects . . . they are products of human industry and they are born and live as isolated individuals juxtaposed in stud farms devised for their own sake . . . They constitute the desocialised condition of existence of a private society. (1966: 122)

In fact, my fieldwork suggested that racehorses are both subjects and objects in particular contexts, they are not solely the product of human industry, though the breeding industry might like to imagine this to be the case, and they are certainly not entirely de-socialised. In the context of the stud, for example, the horses are 'family', and managing their interaction is about managing the quirks of family members who can be both loyal and recalcitrant.

Lévi-Strauss argued that racehorse names were a reflection of their anti-social status, whilst this chapter will suggest that the naming of racehorses reflects their dual status as subjects and objects to different configurations within their

124

environment. Many racehorses' names are derivative of their breeding, being combinations of their sire's and dam's names such as 'out of Gulf Bird by Majority Blue – Blue Persian', or the comic 'out of Bachelor Pad by Pleasuring – Bobbitt'. The registered name reflects the individual's place in the General Stud Book, where horses are at their most objectified, as conduits, temporarily embodying one of the possible combinations in the overall flow of 'noble blood'. However, these names are almost always complemented by a stable name, which is often human, as when Hawaiian Dot becomes 'Wyatt', or inspired by some personal quirk, such as the smelly foal nicknamed 'Kipper'.

Formal names are complemented by highly personalised names that draw the horse strongly into its human environment, if not when it is racing so much as when it is cared for in the stables before and after racing. Racehorses are thus both personalised and objectified according to the perspective from which they are described, and the context in which they find themselves.[2] In keeping with this dual identity, horses' personalities are said to change when at the races, where they become excitable and unpredictable, or more specifically: 'He's terrible when he goes racing, he just won't listen to me . . . even though he's good as gold at home.'

The implied existence of communication between horse and human and the introduction of images of domesticity through the identification of the training stable as a mutual 'home' are an example of the general tendency towards the personalisation of horses in Newmarket. At the races, however, when he is likely to be evaluated according to the written record of his breeding and form, the horse is presented as denying his communion with his handler. Neither attitude dominates either context entirely, thus it would be inaccurate to identify a split between 'home' and 'work'. At the racecourse, lads will seek to communicate with horses, and the death of a horse on the track is, for its lad, one of the worst things imaginable, being compared to 'losing a family member'. At home, horses may be treated as objects when, for example, they are being weighed, or having their blood analysed by vets, who do not know their names or their characters.

In the context of the stud, locus of the physical reproduction of the English thoroughbred, it is particularly interesting to examine ideas pertinent to gender and procreation. Virility will be identified as the supreme male value attributed to the stallion (and by implication to the stallion man), whilst the association of femininity with nurturing will be revealed by an examination of the treatment of the 'foster' mare. The following chapter will suggest that ideas of heredity implicit in the activities and opinions of the stud worker are systematised in the ideology of pedigree that informs ideas of relatedness in both humans and horses in Newmarket. This ideology, which draws upon notions of 'blood' in order to explain heredity, will be examined in more detail in the following chapter. The two chapters should combine to suggest that the selective breeding of horses can only be made sense of in terms of the pedigrees of humans in Newmarket.

Human–animal relations

Without wishing to sound sexist, the only point I would like to add to the debate concerns gender. Colts tend to be bigger and stronger than fillies and even with a 5lb allowance, Cape Verdi might not appreciate being on the receiving end of the competitive aggression of a big field of colts. Perhaps she has the speed and temperament to rise above it and win. Perhaps not – and she might suffer badly from the experience.

(Kennedy 1998: 8)

This letter from the *Racing Post* epitomises the tendency to apply human categories, properties and emotions to horses. It refers to the decision made by Sheikh Mohammed to run the filly, Cape Verdi, in the Derby, a race usually contested by colts, the Oaks being the equivalent Blue Ribbon event for fillies. The final foreboding sentence of the letter prompts the reader to imagine just what fate might befall Cape Verdi at the hands of the colts. The writer explicitly blurs the distinction between humans and horses in saying that he does not wish to sound 'sexist', which does not make sense unless one imagines that it is possible to talk about gender issues in relation to horses, expressing opinions which may in turn be construed as 'sexist' rather than merely 'about horses'. The letter illustrates that in attributing human properties to horses we reveal our perceptions of the nature of those properties and, by implication, of what it means to be human.

Horses acquire human traits, and in the same moment humans are discussed in terms of properties and ideas of relatedness that are only fully worked out amongst privileged animal species, for example:

Fergal Lynch, the nineteen-year-old apprentice from Londonderry... has all the right credentials to, as they say, 'make it'. A member of a keen racing family, his two brothers race-rode and one of them, Cathal, now has a growing string under his care in Atlantic City. ('Audax' 1996: 31)

My father was a trainer, and his father before him. My grandfather was a real stayer, a real dour man, all heart and enough about him to bring up a family. My dad was a different sort of brave, but he still had it in him, and so have I. I can spot a good horse a mile off and you won't beat me in a close finish. (Trainer)

The relationship that obtains between humans and horses in Newmarket determines that those properties admired in well-bred humans are attributed to well-bred horses and vice versa.

Horses constitute a 'privileged species' (Thomas 1983: 100) in the English imagination, and have most commonly been associated with nobility, disdain for authority, loyalty and freedom.[3] The physical treatment of horses has not always reflected this privileged status, and Thomas tells us that neglect and cruelty were still rife in the sixteenth and seventeenth centuries:

One morning in 1581 Sir Thomas Wroth counted 2,100 horses travelling between Shoreditch and Enfield; but another observer added that within the next seven years 2,000 of them would be dead in some ditch through overwork. (1983: 101)

Attitudes appear to have changed during the eighteenth century, when Thomas notes the

increased sensitivity of eighteenth century passers-by to the cruel treatment of horses in the street or the mounting volume of protest against the traditional practices of docking the animal's tail or cropping its ears or tying up its head to make it look more imposing. (1983: 190)

The intellectual conditions which resulted in the formation of, for example, the Royal Society for the Prevention of Cruelty to Animals in 1824, are thought by Thomas to have resulted primarily from increased industrialisation and the consequent separation of animals from the means of production. I would suggest, however, that the continual murmur of disapproval prompted by the mistreatment of horses arose from their permanently ambiguous relation to production. Horses were undoubtedly beasts of burden of critical importance; however, they have also always been creatures capable of offering opportunities for excitement which are essentially lacking in, say, a cow. The horse offers a means of travelling through space at speeds only approached by the car, and the association with freedom exploited by car advertisers applies equally well to the horse, an idea shared by numerous horse cultures, including, for example, the Rom studied by Stewart in Hungary:

As Zeléno put it to me: 'You can't ride cows. Horses go like this (and he made a graceful gesture with his hand); they make one's good mood (voja); they know how to move. You can't bridle up a cow. Nor can you sing about cows. It's only in Hungarian songs that you find them singing about cows!' (1997: 143)[4]

The horse is a particularly rewarding animal to attempt to control due to his feckless nature. He will always retain sufficient independence to make a worthwhile adversary in a struggle of wills. Horses, unlike dogs, will do something a hundred times and on the hundred and first occasion behave as if the situation is totally unprecedented, usually employing their favoured response to novelty, of running away. The horse's nervous energy has usually been interpreted as 'spirit', his dimwittedness as bravery, for example, in the writing of journalist Laura Thompson who attributes to Lamtarra, winner of the 1996 Derby, a 'Quest for Greatness'. The seriousness with which Thompson describes Lamtarra 'toying' with the horses he beats is an example of the anthropomorphism that dominates this genre. The attribution of human traits to horses is by no means exclusive to racing journalists or Newmarket residents, as Stewart's study of the Rom makes clear, 'Comments about the intelligence and good sense of horses were so common that I gave up noting them' (1997: 144). I was repeatedly told that the horses in Newmarket were morally superior to the human population: 'Newmarket's alright – it's just the people I can't stand!'

The anthropomorphism of a society such as Newmarket contradicts the category distinction continually identified by theorists as central to the modern perception of the relationship between humans and animals. I would suggest that the generalisation that 'modern' or 'Western' societies make a category distinction between humans and animals obscures a far more complex relationship. Much anthropological literature contrasts the oppositional view of 'modern' 'Western' society with the 'continuum' view of less developed societies as, for example, in the work of Ingold, 'What we distinguish as humanity and nature merge, for them, into a single field of relationships' (1994: 18), or Lévi-Strauss:

The total apprehension of men and animals as sentient beings, in which identification consists, both governs and precedes the consciousness of oppositions between, firstly, logical properties conceived as integral parts of the human field, and then, within the field itself, between 'human' and 'non-human'. (1966: 101–2)

The limitations of this framework of analysis lie in its identification of two (predictably) *opposing* views that merely rediscover a further oppositional relationship between 'us' and 'them'. This process has been identified by Latour as 'The Great Divide' (1993), the asymmetry which precludes comparison of 'primitive' with 'modern' societies. In blurring these distinctions, my fieldwork obviously supports Latour's contention that 'We have never been modern'. In Newmarket, animals are sometimes used to 'stand for' humans, whilst they are sometimes distanced from humans as a subordinate species in a hierarchical relationship with man. As Tambiah's work in Thailand confirms, the relationship between humans and animals in a society cannot be generalised:

I submit that the villagers' relation to the animal world shows a similar complexity which expresses neither a sense of affinity with animals alone nor a clear-cut distinction and separation from them, but rather a co-existence of both attitudes in varying intensities which create a perpetual tension. (1969: 455)

Tambiah urges that when considering the attitudes a society exhibits towards animals, it is imperative to ask 'why the animals chosen are so appropriate in that context to objectify human sentiments and ideas' (1969: 457). The homology between animal categories and social organisation identified by Lévi-Strauss (1966), Leach (1972) and Douglas (1957) suggests that those animals that occupy the interstices of these systems are those which are 'good to think'

(Lévi-Strauss 1963: 89). Leach identifies the horse as just such a 'marginal case', identifying the English taboo on eating horse-meat as reflecting the horse's status as 'sacred and supernatural creatures surrounded by feelings that are ambiguously those of awe and horror' (1972: 32). This interpretation neglects both vertical and synchronic considerations. The horse possesses an aristocratic history, which unfolds symbiotically with its class association. In Newmarket, where 'everything is horse', the role of the racehorse in both idealising and envisaging alternatives to the pertaining social logic of racing society is predictably central, its class associations intact, as might have been anticipated from Löfgren's insistence that:

'thinking with animals' in the cultural complexities of Western societies needs to be related to the historical processes of class formation and conflict, cultural hegemony and resistance, as well as to discussions of the material experiences behind the production, reproduction, and change of such cognitive systems over time. (1985: 213)

Whether one believes that a horse can be loyal or brave, is secondary to the observation that, in Newmarket, horses are both, and also naughty, funny, wicked and spiteful. They are at times 'people just like us' and at others 'man's noblest creation'. It is the tension between these two positions that enables horses in Newmarket to be such flexible resources for thinking about relations between humans and between humans and nature.

Studwork

I spent the spring of 1997 working as a stud hand in a village outside Newmarket. The rhythms of this village are entirely dictated by the stud work in which a large number of the residents are involved, and many of the houses are tied to particular studs. Traffic is mainly horseboxes or bicycles, and a visit to the shop at lunchtime means joining a steady stream of booted and anoraked stud hands buying papers and cheese rolls.

Working on a stud has in itself been described to me as contributing to the maintenance of the 'great family', that is the breed of the English racehorse. It soon became clear that, as in every family, some of the mares on the stud were loved elderly aunts whilst others were black sheep. The function of mares on the stud is solely that of reproduction. They are no longer ridden and once 'let down' from peak fitness after their racing careers, their bodies change from that of the sleek racehorse to the swinging bellied mare.

A day on the stud began at 7:30, when all the five outdoor staff met in the top yard. Idle chat on the way to the 'foaling yard' generally included a discussion of what I had eaten for supper the previous evening, since my vegetarian diet was a constant source of fascination. The morning rounds began in the foaling yard with the 'heavies' – the name given to the mares who were about to foal.

We looked at their 'bag' to see whether they had begun to 'wax' on their teats, which would suggest that foaling was imminent. Mares very rarely foal during the day and we would invariably put all these mares out into their paddock for the day.

After we had put the 'heavies' in their paddock, we all squeezed into a tiny van with a variety of dogs and drove the short distance down to the main yard. John the stud hand fetched the 'teaser' from his box. If I once knew the 'teaser's' name, it must have been mentioned so rarely that I have now forgotten it. My sympathy for the 'teaser' lasted until he bit my elbow whereupon he became as invisible to me as he was to the rest of the staff. He was as much a machine as I have known a horse to become, and was treated no differently to a lawnmower, the other piece of equipment with which I became most familiar during this time.

I was corrected for referring to the 'teaser' as a stallion. Although he is 'entire', he was not referred to as a stallion as he does not 'cover' mares on a regular basis, or rather covering is not his primary function. His primary function is to establish whether the mares are 'in season', i.e. whether they are receptive to mating, which indicates that they are ready to be sent away to be covered. The teaser was put in a box with a 'trying board' between him and the mare who was led into the next box. The mares were fetched individually, and the stud manager, Hugh, and stud groom, Brian, watched their reaction as stud hands Rachel, Norman and myself led them through. The mares kicked the boards if they were either not in season or in foal. If they were in season their reaction would vary from merely tolerating the 'teaser' to throwing themselves against the board, squatting and peeing and 'winking' at him with their vagina. Most of the reactions required some interpretation by Brian and Hugh, who were familiar with the mares and with the signs they showed at particular times of their cycle. Mares who misbehaved at the board were firmly reprimanded with a tug on their rope, or on the bit of a Chifney, a handling bit that gives more control to the handler.

Once the mares had been 'teased' the horses in the main yard were put out into their paddocks. When leading a mare and foal the foal is held on the right and must be pushed through doorways and gates in front of the mare so that she does not trample it. Foals are held with two fingers under their chin on the headcollars ('hats') that they have worn since their first or second day. Because foals are unpredictable and strong it is advisable to have a person walking behind pushing the foal along in case it chooses to 'go into reverse'. Norman and Rachel generally teamed up in this way, whilst I helped and was helped by everyone. When Norman followed Rachel with a foal John and Brian wondered aloud whether he was following the foal or Rachel. Brian handled the foals gently, but firmly, he spoke to them all the time, and laughed at them when they were naughty. Norman was more forceful, and sometimes shouted at them or disciplined them. Brian's explanation for this was that Norman had 'lost his bottle'.

All of the staff used terms such as 'Mummy' when returning a foal to a mare, and Brian called all of the foals 'Foaly' or by their nicknames. Nicknames were applied to most of the horses, and were mainly a reference to their real name in the case of mares, for foals a reference to their sire (e.g. 'Little Lion' by Lion Cavern, or 'Barry' by Barathea), or a reference to their personality or appearance (e.g. 'Kipper', who was smelly, or 'Chopper' who always tried to bite, or 'Donkey' who looked like a donkey when he was a foal). In other words, the individuality of the horses was highlighted through their nickname, and considerable time was spent discussing the right choice of name according to the 'personality' of each horse.

Once the main yard had been put out we took the van to the lower yearling yards to put out the colts and fillies, in what was the most terrifying part of the day. The only predictable yearling behaviour was that they were all 'gobby', that is they continually tried to bite your arms, legs and face. Otherwise they were totally unpredictable and incredibly strong. We would leave the stables in co-ordinated waves, because if a yearling felt that it was being left behind it would pull away to give chase to its companions. Sometimes they would just 'have their backs up', particularly when it was windy which I really dreaded. Once we got inside the field we all turned and faced the yearling with our backs against the hedge for protection, and the person who had shut the gate behind us shouted 'Okay!' We would let go at the same time, in the hope that none of us would be trampled or dragged off. The yearlings who came into the field first would often get impatient whilst waiting and rear up on their back legs over our heads, trying to get their leg over the line to get away. Brian laughed, Norman shouted and yanked on the line and I put my hands over my head and let go, although the knowledge that these animals were to be sold for hundreds of thousands of pounds in six months' time gave me an exceptionally strong grip at times.

Once the yearlings had been turned out I breathed a sigh of relief and we returned to the main yard where Hugh and Brian discussed any arrangements for mares to go away for 'servicing' during the day or for mares or mares and foals arriving to board. Brian and I then went up to the foaling yard whilst John went down to the yearling yard, Rachel and Norman remained in the main yard. Brian and I mucked out the boxes every other day and 'picked up' the droppings on the intervening days. Finally, we swept the yard and put their feed in their mangers. Brian was convinced that the horses should be treated 'as you would like to be treated yourself' and in his opinion if I wouldn't eat or drink from a trough myself then it needed cleaning. When the boxes were ready we shut top and bottom doors. At 10 a.m. we had 'breakfast'. Everyone else went to their respective houses whilst I sat in the 'rest room', to read back copies of sales catalogues, which documented the sales of the yearlings born on the stud in previous years.

From 10:30 until 12:45 I helped in the main yard and, if there was time, began mowing, strimming or sweeping. The main yard contained thirty boxes, all of which were mucked out and 'set' i.e. refilled with straw. I usually got the job of cleaning mangers and water drinkers, whilst Norman and Rachel mucked out onto the muck trailer and Tony followed, 'setting fair', that is, laying a bed of straw. I was also allowed to sweep the road and to rake the grass in the main yard to remove stray pieces of straw by hand. The stud is rigorously maintained. All of the lawns have their own particular pattern of straight lines and geometrical shapes mown into them, and straw is not allowed to build up or fly about around the buildings or on the grass. An obsession with orderliness, attention to detail and precision informed almost all of the activities of the stud hands. I would suggest that this obsession arises from the same impulse which motivates the mapping and manipulation of thoroughbred pedigrees, the impulse to control the environment, and to predict the outcome of 'natural' processes such as reproduction. The stud farm is an environment in which nature is defined by 'nature-like' features such as lawns and flowerbeds, which caricature rather than reproduce any notion of nature as independent of human control. In this environment, horses live inside, grass is grown in straight lines and the muck associated with horses is hidden.

Lunch was taken at 12:45 until 2:00, during which everyone again disappeared into their own houses. After lunch there was occasionally a mare to take to be covered, but otherwise the afternoon was spent mowing, strimming or sweeping in order to maintain the immaculate state of the stud grounds. I became well known for my ability to mow in a straight line which was ill-advised, since there was a never ending supply of grass. John and Tony both helped me with my mowing, giving me tips regarding overlap and the importance of frequent emptying of the clippings trap. Tony also made me promise not to put my hand in the mower to unblock it, but rather always to use a stick. Norman saw me using a stick and said that I was being silly, and to demonstrate stuck his hand inside the mower and said 'See, it won't hurt you.' I thought that I might die of boredom. Norman and Tony's strong opinions about matters such as lawnmowers got them through the day.

The breeding shed: doing it for Daddy

On several occasions I was allowed to take a mare to be covered, which was a real privilege. On the first occasion, Brian had noticed that I gave my apple core to a particular mare each day after lunch. He said that I had obviously 'taken' to her, and allowed me to take her for covering. The idea that I had formed a relationship with the mare as an individual fell easily within Brian's interpretation of dealing with horses. He thought that she would be happier to go to the stallion with me because she had obviously 'taken to me' too. When I asked Brian about particular horses he was initially bashful saying that he had no preferences except for those animals which were easy to deal with, stayed free from injury and illness and went for a good price at the end of it. After a while, however, Brian admitted that he had favourites amongst the older mares, because they had been 'together' for quite some time, and he had got to know all their 'little ways'.

Brian particularly liked a quirky mare, and delighted in her unpredictable nature. Brian explained that he enjoyed the knowledge that he could deal safely with her having invested a great deal of time in his relationship with her. He told me that 'the more individual they are the better I take to them, but don't tell my wife!' I pondered what this could possibly mean, other than that Brian either thought that his relationships with mares constituted an infidelity to his wife, or that I shouldn't tell her as she might imagine that he would prefer her to be 'difficult'. In either case the cross-over between ideas about horses and people is significant, and Brian often described his relationship with 'his' mares according to the template of marriage.

Taking mares to be covered was a huge responsibility, not only because they were very valuable but also because I was made to feel that I was acting as a catalyst in the vast chain of thoroughbred pedigree. The first time I took a mare I was very nervous. The lorry arrived, and it was a short journey down the road to a neighbouring stud. We waited in the box for ages and the mare became rather agitated, trying to see out and calling to other horses. She took no notice of me apart from the odd distracted bite of my arm. It was easy to imagine some truth in the box driver's claim that 'the old mare knows where she is'. Eventually, the 'stallion men' let me out of the box where I was standing holding her, and took her from me. To my surprise, they ushered me in to watch which is standard practice to ensure that the covering is witnessed. This witnessing is not the final guarantor of paternity, however, since it still enables substitute horses ('ringers') to be used. In addition, stud managers must provide a sample of blood from each foal, which is tested by Weatherbys in order to establish parentage absolutely.

Three men were in the covering barn. One held the mare using a twitch (tourniquet) on her nose, one put felt boots on her back feet, took a swab from her vagina and bandaged her tail. Another man held the stallion, on a shank (a long chain and leather rein). The man holding the mare commented that 'he's very quiet' whereupon the stallion started screeching and we all laughed. The spare man then said 'Come on then, Donkey Dick', and the stallion mounted the mare, who stood quietly. The spare man held a 'belly bar' between the stallion's stomach and the mare's back. The covering was over within a minute. The boots were then undone and the mare flicked them off and was handed back to me. She seemed alert and excited. We climbed back into the lorry, came home, and I led her out of the lorry to her paddock. As I walked across the yard, she coughed, and a jet of fluid came flying out of her vagina into the path of Hugh who had been following us. He shouted at the mare, 'Keep your legs shut you stupid bitch, that cost seven and a half grand!'

On another trip I told the box driver that the stallion had been very quiet and he laughed and said that anyone would be on 'four jumps a day'. The implication was that the stallion in question had low fertility and was having 'empty' mares returned to him to be re-covered. Low fertility in stallions is dreaded by their managers, but particularly by the 'stallion men' who are the grooms who have sole charge of a stallion. Their very nomenclature suggests the fusing of human and animal, such that a stallion man conjures up images of a centaur, rather than a small grumpy man in a brown coat. These men wear long coats with their stallion's name on their back. They are often the only person who has any contact with that stallion, and develop strong bonds with their charges. These men are the most extreme example of the individuality and personalisation of horses in Newmarket since they come to be identified with, or even to personify, their horse.

Heated discussions of fertility rates in the pub are an integral part of the season, and criticism of a stallion in front of his man may lead to the exchange of blows, as one man said to me: 'You can criticise my wife, but leave the horse out of it.' Implicit in the criticism of the horse is criticism of 'his' man, thus casting aspersions on the horse's sexual prowess also brands his man impotent. In a society in which potency is supremely valued by men, a lack of virility is amongst the worst insults available. The stallion may also provide a substitute for the man's virility, where this is lacking. The stallion man who encourages his charge during coverings with cries of 'Do it for Daddy!' is perhaps the most respected stallion man in Newmarket, his outburst is explained on the grounds that, 'Well, of course, Bob has no kids of his own.' Identification with their stallions is competitive amongst these men, whose pastimes include measuring their horse's testicles, symbol of potency, in order to brag about their size in the pub. Basking in the glory of the stallion, the apex of the thoroughbred pedigree, these men become 'studs' by association.

After mowing patterns for most of the afternoon, preparations would begin for the vet's afternoon visit. The teasing box housed a set of horse stocks, which held mares still during their internal examination. I generally got the job of holding the tail out of the way. On my first day the vet 'stitched' two mares whilst I held the tail. Mares who have had several foals tend to have a dropped uterus that can suck in air and cause infection. In order to stop air getting in the vet injects a local anaesthetic, makes a slit either side of the vagina and stitches it together. This was a test for me, and made me cringe. Norman laughed at my expression and said that he hoped I liked my steak rare. As in the training yard, I was continually teased in this way, being the lowest of the low on the stud, but also occasionally indulged and protected as when Norman shared his home-made pea wine with me as we scrubbed water troughs in the rain.

The vet used ultrasound in order to detect pregnancies and on my last day at the stud he found a set of twins, and used the head of the scanner to burst one of the fertilised eggs, explaining that twins would usually be aborted rather than going full term. I teased the vet about his choice, and suggested that he might have just popped a champion. He failed to find much humour in this thought, and creased his brow in annoyance. He explained that he had chosen the most 'symmetrical, well shaped, healthy looking egg', thus guaranteeing that he had left the 'fittest' to survive. I quickly smothered my laughter with a cough when I realised that he was being entirely serious.

Where a mare is slow to cycle, she is given hormones in order to bring her into season, whilst infections which may prevent fertilisation are flushed out with saline drenches. The vet thought that under 'natural' conditions the thoroughbred would be an alternate year breeder, and told me that the selective breeding programme based upon the desire for speed had resulted in a variety of genital deformities, and weaknesses in foals. The vet came every day and saw between three and ten mares. The work was routine, except for a case of joint ill and an x-ray of a yearling's leg, during which he was doped. Once the vet had finished we brought in the rest of the mares and foals. The day finished at 4:30, when I would exercise polo ponies in return for the privilege of having spent another day sweeping, mowing and holding tails. The rest of the staff refused to have anything to do with the ponies and laughed at me for my involvement with the 'second class citizens' (their expression). Polo ponies are a 'type' rather than a breed, and are granted no respect at all by the racing community.

The odd couple

The experience of working at the stud was characterised by long periods of boredom interspersed with brief moments of excitement and almost profundity. The language used on the stud was fascinating, but soon taken for granted. A mare is 'empty' before she is 'covered' or 'jumped' by a sire. She may then 'take' and become a 'heavy' with a 'bag' and in time have her foal, becoming a 'mum' in the process. Her foal must learn to wear a 'hat' (headcollar) on its second day. If she is yet to have her first foal she is a 'maiden', whilst others may be at the end of their breeding careers and so join the 'barreners'. The jargon betrays essential features of the stud. The mare is 'empty', not because of any ignorance of the reproductive organs of the horse, but because of the ideology of procreation that obtains throughout the industry, which will be discussed in the next chapter. The consistent personalisation of ties between humans and particular horses blurred the category distinction made between humans and horses on the stud. The use of categories usually restricted to humans, such as 'maiden', 'mummy', 'baby', 'hat', etc., reflects the propensity of those who work on studs to imagine their lives through horses and horses' lives through their own. One episode at the stud exemplified this propensity.

During my stay at the stud a foal was rejected by her dam, and so became an 'orphan'. Hugh had hired two 'foster mares', and had had no success with either of them. The trade in foster mares can be grim. At best, a thoroughbred mare who has lost her own foal can be given an orphan. However, supply rarely meets demand, and a number of ponies may find themselves shunted around the country to perform the function of wet nurse to thoroughbred foals. We had one of these ponies on the stud, and people perpetually referred to her as 'him'. When I asked about this Brian responded that he referred to 'it' as 'he' or 'it' because it lacked any maternal instincts and added in an incredulous tone: 'It tried to kill the foal!' The pony was of an entirely different physical type to the rest of the mares, being a heavy carthorse sort, which may have contributed to her nebulous status.

Whilst this mare was treated as of indeterminate gender, the spontaneous adoption of the foal by another mare enabled her to achieve 'superfemininity'. This mare had her own foal, and was stabled in the box next to the orphan and we noticed that she called to her when she was taken out to be fed, and when she returned. We gingerly introduced the three and the mare accepted the foal, ostensibly treating her in the same way as she treated her own foal. The three were an object of amusement for the stud, and were collectively referred to as 'the odd couple'. The foal was called 'Herbetina', a feminised version of Herbert, an affectionate term for naughty foals who had redeeming features. Everyone was very fond of the mare, she was regarded as a model mare, because her maternal instincts were strong and indiscriminate. The foal was liked as it was cheeky enough to drink from her, as well as being fed by us.

The stud is the locus of the physical reproduction of horses who have places in pedigrees known to the bloodstock industry. Activities on the stud thus reflect the ideas of procreation and gender built into the pedigree method of relating racehorses. On the stud, horses are also personalised and individualised, granted human traits and drawn into relationships which operate according to the template of human interactions, thus encouraging metonymic thinking in which horses can be made to 'stand for' humans and vice versa.

Conclusion

This chapter concentrated upon those contexts in which horses are personalised or individualised in seemingly human terms. I shall now introduce a context in which the power of the analogy between human and horse depends on a separation of the two such that the English thoroughbred racehorse is cast as 'man's noblest creation'. The sameness of humans and horses asserted by many of their day-to-day interactions in Newmarket is complemented by a hierarchical relationship between them in which man is the god-like master of all he surveys. In this role, breeders of thoroughbred racehorses have appropriated the power of 'God' or 'Nature' and selectively bred to their own design. Racehorses in this context are the objects of their all-powerful human creators. Where the protracted genealogy of 'man' has been lost, the thoroughbred's is intact, its aristocratic properties recorded and thus maintained, perhaps even concentrated as suggested by Beer:

blood succession becomes a means of stemming the tide of time – replication is emphasised and change is accommodated – the dead king is replaced by a live king whose blood succession ensures that no radical alteration has taken place. Each produces 'after his kind'. In kingship the aspect of *restoration* is intensified, and succession becomes not a means of change but a way of standing still. (1983: 32)

It is no coincidence that one of the champion racehorses of 1997 was called 'King of Kings'.

The defining feature of the English thoroughbred is that all its present-day stock can be traced to three male progenitors imported to England in the eighteenth century. The genesis of the breed is recorded in the General Stud Book (GSB), which has recorded births and deaths amongst the thoroughbred population since 1791. Since that time, the breed has operated a closed book breeding programme, to the extent that 'over 80% of the population's gene pool derives from thirty-one known ancestors from this early period' (Mahon 1980: 22). In order to be eligible for entry into the GSB a horse must trace all lines of its pedigree to horses already registered in the GSB or in another recognised international stud book.[5] The boundaries of the breed are fiercely policed by, for example, the obligatory blood testing of every foal in order to guarantee paternity and maternity. There are no other criteria by which a horse can qualify as a thoroughbred and any thoughts that a thoroughbred may 'become' such by means other than birth are nonsensical. The pedigree of the English thoroughbred is thus fixed.

The pedigree theory that informs ideas of relatedness between thoroughbred racehorses contains an implicit notion of man as controlling nature, an impulse made visible in the maintenance of the stud. However, the co-existing attitude that denies any boundary between humans and horses facilitates the projection of this means of ordering the world from horses onto humans. This projection could equally be described in reverse, from the English aristocracy of the eighteenth century onto their racehorses. Both directions are fundamentally constitutive of the intersubjectivity observed within racing society.

The persuasiveness of this technique depends upon the separation of nature and culture, such that cultural mores may be justified by an appeal to their natural analogues. The multiple meanings of 'nature' in thoroughbred breeding are thus evident. 'Nature' can be both man made (the thoroughbred), and also the culturally immune standard by which artifice should be judged. It can therefore be both dominated and treated as an ultimate authority. Humans and horses can thus be both the same and different, according to human purposes. The following chapter will discuss the ideology of pedigree in more detail. It will pursue the idea that the relationship between horses and humans in Newmarket facilitates an extended dialogue in which opinions about humans are expressed as opinions about horses.

NOTES

1 The relationship between lads and their horses is also relevant. In particular, distinctions between colts and fillies are maintained by male lads and explained by human analogy. Some lads encourage colts to 'act like men', by treating them roughly and encouraging aggressive behaviour. I was told off for petting a colt because it would 'make him soft'. Fillies, on the other hand, should be 'gentled' because they respond better to a soft word, 'just like you Gorgeous!' I haven't ever seen a female lad 'toughening up' a colt; however, their explanations of coltish behaviour are similarly anthropomorphic, 'Typical bloke!' Some trainers and owners also profess to the kind of relationship with their horses that I am trying to evoke, and spend hours describing their personalities in minute detail. Sheikh Mohammed, for example, after losing his champion horse Dubai Millennium to grass sickness in 2001, told the BBC that it was like 'Losing a member of the family'.

2 One punter friend described the difference between his perception of horses and my own as follows, 'You see a soft nose and a friend to be taken care of. I see a handicap mark and a pedigree.' Punters often objectify horses. However, certain horses like Desert Orchid and Red Rum become 'personalities' in the betting shop as well as in their own yards.

3 Since its domestication in the Ukraine 9000 years ago, the horse has fulfilled many roles, but it began its association with man as a tool of war, belonging first to the Hittites, the Mitanni, the Kassites and the Aryans. As Budiansky states, 'It was as a terrifying and unprecedented weapon of war . . . that the horse made its entrance at the gates of the civilised world' (1997: 63). Furthermore, 'The connection of horses to wealth and aristocracy is as ancient as the connection of horses to warfare' (1997: 71). Chariot horses were a huge expense for the elite warrior class who kept them, and so Budiansky argues that, 'The unavoidable expense of horses made them something only the richest members of society could afford; given the nearly universal belief that wealth equalled nobility, and given what Piggott calls, the "ever latent anthropomorphism of antiquity", the association with nobility made the horse itself a Noble Animal' (1997: 73).

4 In his epic, *Role of the Horse in Man's Culture*, Harold Barclay permits himself a single generalisation drawn from his assembled data, 'People who have employed the horse have invariably held it in high regard, primarily because out of the relationship between man and horse has come an admiration by men of certain qualities of the horse, and what may be termed a "centaur effect". That is, the control of the horse, particularly in riding, enhances the feeling of power, freedom, and mobility. There is

the exhilaration derived from working with and from being part of a powerful, supple living force. Thus the horse is recognised as a very unique kind of animal deserving of special treatment and concern' (1980: xi).

5 The one exception to this rule is that of the 'vehicle', the name given to a horse that is the eighth cross from a non-thoroughbred. A thoroughbred crossed with a vehicle will qualify as a thoroughbred, despite the fact that the vehicle may not. I could only find one example of such a stallion, called Clantime, who was a popular sprinter in the 1980s and died in 1997. Obviously there is little incentive to cross your thoroughbred mare with a non-thoroughbred stallion and the produce would generally mark the end of a family line as stallion managers do not like their charges to cover non-thoroughbreds (considered a drop in class!). In volume 43 of the GSB two mares are shown as vehicles with only seven proven crosses, one has the eight consecutive crosses necessary for promotion to 'thoroughbred' (out of thirty thousand mares).

9   Blood will tell

Introduction

At the beginning of the last century the genealogical method was thought to be a neutral tool of exposition, enabling the mapping of kinship data from 'primitive' societies by anthropologists. As Rivers wrote in 1910, 'The genealogical method makes it possible to investigate abstract problems on a purely concrete basis' (1968: 107). The idea that the methodological tools imported by the anthropologist might influence the image of 'primitive' society thereby produced was yet to be formulated, and there is a sense in which constructing genealogies remains legitimate anthropological business.

However, some anthropologists have come to realise that the genealogical method contains specifically English cultural resources that make its relationship to the 'raw' data it purports to represent anything but unproblematic. Teaching this method to Portuguese students, for example, led Bouquet to conclude that, 'pedigree thinking was so important to English middle-class intellectuals that it was absorbed in the processes of making knowledge about other peoples' (1993: 219). Bouquet has uncovered the 'pedigree thinking' behind the genealogical method, using the *Tales of Beatrix Potter* as an example of a cultural product that was contemporary with Rivers' work, and showing that the two contained the same ideological resources. Bouquet believes that the connotations of English animal breeding and pedigree were assimilated by the genealogical method and that, 'These connotations include the control of procreation through keeping written records that enable the careful channelling of "blood" as a key to nobility' (1993: 189).

Racing society in Newmarket provides a contemporary example of this historical phenomenon, and shows how ideas of relatedness look when they are based upon 'pedigree thinking'. The relevant ideas are most fully worked out in theories of thoroughbred breeding, and in the literary forms these practices give rise to. In this chapter I shall describe the standard thoroughbred pedigree as it appears in British sales catalogues. Implicit notions of procreation, heredity and gender, all of which betray a particular conception of 'nature' and its relation to humanity, will be exposed.

140

The thoroughbred racehorse has proved a particularly rich resource for modelling the preoccupations of the societies to which it has been significant; as Russell notes, 'The parallels between on the one hand, the human obsession with title, hereditary position and social caste, and, on the other, animal pedigrees, are too obvious to need emphasis' (1986: 19). The tendency to project traits valued by human society onto the horse can even be detected in contemporary anthropology. Atwood Lawrence emphasises the 'sensitivity' of the horse, and its capacity for 'fine tuned communication' (1985: 197), in what can be seen as a response to the conventional distinction between animals and humans based upon the possession of language. The reaction is a tacit acceptance of this animal–human distinction because it seeks to establish a factor that unites both sides, rather than identifying its cultural and historical specificity and thereby diffusing its claims. Like eighteenth-century horse owners and modern thoroughbred breeders, Atwood Lawrence is indulging in thinking made possible by the freedom of the horse from the roles which curtail the ability of other animals to stand for humans.

Racehorses are not agricultural workers, servants or food sources, and are thus a striking example of Appadurai's 'luxury goods', constituting 'incarnated signs', the function of which is entirely political (1986: 38). The motivation to control their husbandry was ideological rather than practical, and as Ritvo has argued, 'Discourse about animals in eighteenth and nineteenth century England also expressed many human concerns linked only tenuously to the natural world' (1987: 3). The same might be said of contemporary Newmarket.[1]

The history of racehorse pedigrees

The General Studbook (GSB) was the first record of any breed of any species, and predated the compulsory recording of human births and deaths by more than forty-six years (Morris 1997: 10). The first edition was the work of energetic amateur William Sidney Towers, and his record was accepted as comprehensive and accurate enough to encourage thoroughbred breeders that it was in their interests to attempt to gain entry to the book for their stock. This was not the first record of racehorse pedigree, but it was the most extensive yet, and its aims were at odds with those of the scraps it replaced.

Following the Restoration, racing developed at an enormous rate, and prize money mushroomed. It seems that one of the motivations behind the recording of pedigrees was the need to verify the ages of horses entered for races restricted to particular age groups. Higher stakes had made the falsification of pedigrees and the entry of 'ringers' in races for which they were not qualified a common practice, and Towers' explicit aim was to 'rescue the turf from the increasing evil of false and inaccurate pedigrees' (Towers quoted in Willett

1991: 19). Towers does not seem to have had any explicit intention to pre-serve a 'pure' breed, and the word 'thoroughbred' did not appear in the original Stud Book.

Racehorse pedigrees recorded before the Stud Book reflected a different idea of heredity from that which was to dominate once the thoroughbred had become a distinct breed, with sufficient pools of stallions and mares to enable the breed to be closed to outside 'blood'. In the sixteenth century, racehorses were failed hunters. By the mid-eighteenth century the thoroughbred dominated the racecourse, as it does today. During this time, racing had changed funda-mentally, from races of up to eight miles contested by mature horses carrying up to twelve stone, to the sprinting style of young horses at light weights with which we are now familiar. Breeding practices had also changed, from a belief that the best racehorses were cross breeds of Oriental stallions with native mares to the closed breed of the modern English thoroughbred.

Prior to the eighteenth century it was believed that the qualities of Oriental stallions were environmentally determined, such that absence from their coun-try of origin would lead to their diminution. Furthermore, their ability to pass on these qualities was believed to be limited to a single generation. Thus selec-tively bred specialist racehorses were originally cross breeds, whose 'pedigrees' recorded only their type, to ensure that they were crossed appropriately. When the importation of stallions became prohibitively expensive in the seventeenth century, a group of breeders attempted to preserve the pure-bred Oriental type for themselves, and in doing so established the thoroughbred (Russell 1986: 99). Selection was not on the basis of racing ability, and the Oriental type was un-suited by the endurance races of the seventeenth and early eighteenth centuries. The thoroughbred's dominance depended upon a change in the style of racing which was to occur during the eighteenth century.

By recording thoroughbred pedigrees, breeders had created a new form of wealth; as Ritvo states, 'these catalogues concretised a rather abstract compo-nent of the value of the animals listed within them' (1995: 421), the ability of some horses to reproduce their most valued traits in their offspring. Pedigrees thus became a means by which value was elicited from animals by their hu-man keepers. There is some evidence that the apparently revolutionary ideas of Robert Bakewell, the most important of the eighteenth-century British stock-breeders and agricultural improvers, were influenced by developments within thoroughbred breeding (Ritvo 1995, Russell 1986). Bakewell transferred the idea that the most important qualities of an animal were hereditary from prestige animals such as racehorses and greyhounds to farm animals, and in doing so cre-ated such thoroughbred analogues as the Dishley sheep. Racehorses, however, with their noble associations and exhilarating potential for sport and mobility, remain the pedigreed animal par excellence.

Nature vs nurture

The racehorse's ability is mediated by the trainer with whom it is placed. The status of the trainer thus reflects the extent to which environment and training regime are thought to influence ability. I found that in Newmarket, the consensus was that a trainer cannot instil talent in a horse, but he may inhibit its expression. The horse possesses a finite amount of talent, the trainer can only aid or hinder the extent to which the horse fulfils this potential. Even the most brilliant trainer is not seen as creating talent, rather he may be paid the ultimate accolade: 'He hasn't fucked up too many', an opinion this bloodstock analyst echoes:

Trainers and jockeys cannot 'teach' a thoroughbred to have guts, perseverance or the will to win. All they can do is strive to bring out the best competitive qualities inherited by an animal from its parents by using their professional skill on the training track, in scientific nutrition and use of modern veterinary knowledge and in general stable routine. (du Bourg 1980: 200)

The resilience of such pedigree thinking in the racing industry cannot be explained on the basis of the results it achieves, since, as breeders reluctantly admit:

The only certainty of pedigrees is that they will confound you. No animal species is better documented than the Thoroughbred, yet, after two centuries of controlled racing and breeding, the laws of reproduction decree that luck will always be a major factor. (Rac 1990: 40)

Whilst this breeder urges caution in predicting the outcome of a particular covering, studies of horse genetics go further, in questioning the effectiveness of selective breeding itself. The geneticist Bowling, for example, argues that, 'So little is known about the genetics of desirable traits, it is premature to suggest that any general technique of structuring pedigrees consistently produces either better or worse stock' (1996: 140). The lack of any dramatic improvement in race times through the modern era of thoroughbred racing has been used by some as evidence that the breed has reached the limits of useful selection (Hill 1988: 678).

The idea that a racehorse's pedigree determines its ability is, however, remarkably resilient and insulated from criticism by a number of conventions. Pedigrees are employed in a piecemeal fashion, with little effort made to maintain consistency, or to pursue the contradictions to which they unfailingly give rise. For example, in discussing the 'story of Anabaa', a precocious sprinter, and winner of the July Cup at Newmarket in 1996, Peter Willett, a 'Bloodstock expert', writing in *Horse and Hound*, stated that: 'The specialist speed of Balbonella and the speed which Anabaa has inherited could not have been anticipated from her pedigree' (1996: 27). Despite this, Willett goes on to suggest that the colt may well stay a mile on the basis that his great grand dam, great grand sire, and great great grand dam were 'stayers' (horses more suited to racing over longer distances).

Pedigree is further protected by the absence of a single measure of performance thus making racehorses' abilities a matter of opinion. The 'racecourse test' creates potential for disagreements between experts that is (at least) twofold. They may disagree about the ability of the horse in question, or they may disagree about any one of its ancestors. The most common factors brought in to discussions of the relative merits of racehorses are: interrupted preparation for a race, poor opposition, jockey or trainer error, race conditions (weather, going, interference), injury and bad luck. Thus, for example, poor opposition may lead to a horse being overrated or injury may prevent a horse from fulfilling his or her potential. So the quality of a racehorse's pedigree may be disputed on the grounds that its own or its ancestors' abilities were misrepresented. As a result, where a horse's pedigree does not coincide with its racecourse performance any number of mitigating factors can be invoked to explain this mismatch.[2]

Where experts really struggle to explain the presence of a sprinter in a family of stayers, for example, the individual is cast as 'the exception that proves the rule'. 'Individuals' such as 'Soba', the incredibly fast filly who came from an undistinguished family and bred undistinguished offspring, was described as a 'freak' by my informants. My argument is, then, that pedigree as an explanation of ability is actually an explanatory mechanism, applied retrospectively and to subjective assessments of such nebulous qualities as 'class', 'heart' and 'guts'.

Ideas of heredity in racehorse breeding

The first works on horsemanship to make reference to breeding theories began to appear in England in the late sixteenth century, and, as the historian Edwards has described, they were by, and for, the upper class:

[These works] had a profound effect upon the consciousness of the upper classes, and if the influence of the Crown is not immediately discernible, it surely is no coincidence that three of the four earliest authors on horsemanship emerged out of the circle of gentlemen pensioners. (1988: 43)

Specifically thoroughbred breeding theories continued to be produced by breeders themselves, with less cross-over with the veterinary or biological sciences than might be expected. The theories they generated, which involved in-breeding, out-crossing, line breeding and dosage systems, have all been undermined by their failure to produce consistent results.[3] What remains is a jumble of ideas, unsystematically applied and therefore remarkably resilient.

The pedigree thinking that informs the contemporary breeding of thoroughbred racehorses relies upon a biometrical theory of genetics which states that the proportion of genes in the overall genome of an offspring will be half of each parent, quarter of each grandparent and so on, as Rae states confidently, 'It is a law of genetics that the foal will inherit 50% of its genes from the sire and 50% from the dam, and no amount of agonising over the covering will change that' (1990: 4). This is an identical idea to that which Wolfram has identified behind anthropological notions of consanguinity:

Parental 'bloods' were supposed to mix in the progeny so that the heredity of a child was a solution, or an alloy of equal parts of the parental heredities. The heredity of a person was thought to be an alloy in which the heredity of each of its four grandparents were represented by one quarter, of each of eight great grandparents by one eighth etc. (Dobzhansky quoted by Wolfram 1987: 13)

The conventions by which thoroughbred pedigrees are interpreted reflect the biometric theory of genetics and also confirm the significance of 'blood' as the substance of heredity. Relatedness between thoroughbreds is expressed both in human family terms and also in terms of blood. Thus foals by the same dam and sire will be full siblings. Foals by the same dam but different sires will be half siblings. Foals by the same sire are not identified as half siblings because stallions produce too many foals each year for this to be considered a meaningful description of their relationship.

Aside from relations modelled on human families, foals may also be, for example, 'own sisters in blood' by virtue of their dams having been full sisters, as illustrated below.

185 (WITH VAT)

A CHESNUT FILLY
(first foal)
Foaled
April 5th, 1996

Bluebird (USA)

Scammony (IRE)
(1991)

Storm Bird (CAN)

Ivory Dawn (USA)

Persian Bold

Polyester Girl

Northern Dancer
South Ocean (CAN)
Sir Ivor
Dusky Evening (USA)
Bold Lad (IRE)
Relkarunner
Ridan (USA)
Garrucha

Own sister in blood to **LAKE CONISTON (IRE)**.
E.B.F. nominated.

Extract from catalogue entry for Lot 185, 1997 Houghton Sales. Reproduced by permission of Tattersalls Ltd.

Foals may also be, for example, 'Three-parts brothers in blood', as Molesnes and the bay colt below.

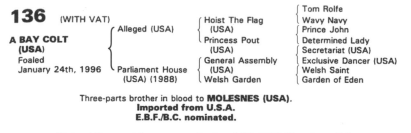

Extract from catalogue entry for Lot 136, 1997 Houghton Sales.
Reproduced by permission of Tattersalls Ltd.

Many other calculations can be made according to which all sorts of fractional relationships in blood can be claimed. The limit to these tends to be in the third generation, after which the catalogue records such innocuous claims as 'bred on similar lines to...', in order to claim a famous relative. The substance of heredity can thus be separated from the individuals who serve as its vehicles.

Breeders have also begun to engage with ideas of heredity based explicitly upon genetic endowment. Many of the early twentieth-century breeding manuals appear to suggest that the role of the breeder is to breed selectively until a 'fast' gene is isolated and made homozygous to the English thoroughbred. Whilst I was in Newmarket, for example, the work of the Professor of Equine Reproduction at Cambridge was the subject of a great deal of discussion. I was continually told that he had identified the 'speed' gene, which facilitated a more efficient breakdown of lactic acid in the muscles of the racehorse.

Ideas of genetic inheritance in racehorses in contemporary Newmarket depend upon the notion of preformation, which maintains that genes are insulated from environmental influences. They also reflect the influence of the one-gene–one-trait model of Mendelian genetics rediscovered at the beginning of the twentieth century. As one racehorse breeder admits, 'Mendelism and Mendel haunt horsemen, like Banquo's ghost to Macbeth, to the point of utter senselessness' (Varola 1974: 2). The idea that an ability to run fast is a trait that could be determined by a single gene remains strong in Newmarket. For example, I was told by a breeder that 'this foal's dad had ability and so we're hoping he will too, but it's a fifty:fifty chance isn't it?'

Recent work within biology has undermined the separation between genes and the environment that pedigree thinking depends upon, creating an epigenetic approach which acknowledges the two-way traffic between genes and the sociocultural milieu inhabited by the organism in question:

environmental regimes influence the physiology of the organism, and these organismic influences leave physiological traces that may also be passed on, as hormonal/nutritional status, maternal effects, and sometimes, as alterations in the genes themselves. (Ho pers. comm.)

More simply, the influence of environmental factors may have been mistaken for evidence of heredity. As Bowling has shown, 'When family members share an environment the effects of non-genetic factors may mimic the appearance of an inherited trait' (1996: 141). In Newmarket, evidence of the influence of nature is 'seen' with far greater alacrity than that of 'nurture'.

Representing pedigrees – the sales catalogue

The impact of the literary form taken by pedigree is a feature highlighted by Bouquet who notes that the 'emphasis on the written [and graphic] record [acts] as the guarantee alongside biology of control over procreation' (1993: 187). In this section I shall introduce the theory of procreation and heredity which lies behind the pedigree ideology specific to racehorses and show how these theories inform their representation. Whilst Bouquet concentrates upon scientific and Biblical precedents to the genealogical method, I would like to add thoroughbred pedigrees to the repertoire of graphic forms which reveal complex ideas about procreation, and therefore kinship, gender and class.

The structure of the catalogue page determines the quantity and nature of information offered to the buyer by the vendor. The catalogues are so repetitive that envisaging alternatives and thinking about what they would mean becomes virtually impossible. When asked about the format of the catalogue, bloodstock agents were of the opinion that they shared this format because 'that's the way it is'. My subsequent suggestion that the format was a convention was dismissed, and the explanation restressed: 'it *isn't* just the way its done, it's the way it *is*'.

The catalogue page devotes a disproportionate amount of space to the dam (female) line, also referred to as the bottom line, or tail line. This was explained to me on the grounds that the dam line is the weakness which must be shored up by being associated with successful relatives. Although a large proportion of racemares go on to have careers at stud, very few colts go on to have careers as stallions having retired from racing. Thus, whilst a stallion's quality is made evident by his very presence at stud, mares are at stud by default, simply on the grounds that they are female and too old or slow to race. Selection of racehorses is thus sharply skewed, stallions are intensively selected on the basis of their pedigree and racecourse performances, whilst mares are often 'given a chance'. Geneticist Bowling reports that, '94% of colts and 48% of fillies do not contribute genes to the next generation' (1996: 127). The characterisation of the racehorse as the quintessentially selectively bred domestic animal is thus only partially true, because it is only male racehorses who are 'selected'.

THURSDAY 2ND OCTOBER 1997

YEARLING, from Cheveley Park Stud

Will stand at Park Paddocks, Highflyer Paddock F, Box 73

349 (WITH VAT)

A BAY COLT
Foaled
April 16th, 1996

	Sadler's Wells (USA)	Northern Dancer	Nearctic
			Natalma
		Fairy Bridge (USA)	Bold Reason (USA)
			Special (USA)
	Exclusive Order (USA) (1979)	Exclusive Native (USA)	Raise A Native
			Exclusive
		Bonavista	Dead Ahead
			Ribotina (ITY)

Own brother to **ENTREPRENEUR (GB)**, **SADLER'S IMAGE (IRE)**
and **DANCE A DREAM (GB)**.
E.B.F./B.C. nominated.

1st Dam
EXCLUSIVE ORDER (USA), **won** 4 races at 2 and 3 years in France, 755,000 fr.
including Prix Maurice de Gheest, Deauville, **Gr.2**, Prix de la Porte Maillot,
Longchamp, **Gr.3** and Prix du Calvados, Deauville, **Gr.3**, placed second in Prix de la
Grotte, Longchamp, **Gr.3** and Prix de Seine-et-Oise, M'-Laffitte, **Gr.3** and fourth in
Prix de la Salamandre, Longchamp, **Gr.1** and Prix Jacques le Marois, Deauville, **Gr.1**;
dam of **eight winners** from 9 runners and 10 foals of racing age-
    ENTREPRENEUR (GB) (1994 c. by Sadler's Wells (USA)), won 3 races at 2 and 3
        years, 1997 and £189,827 including Pertemps 2000 Guineas, Newmarket, **Gr.1**
        and placed fourth in Vodafone Derby Stakes, Epsom, **Gr.1**.
    IRISH ORDER (USA) (1986 f. by Irish River (FR)), won 2 races at 2 years in France,
        275,750 fr. including Prix de L'Obelisque, Longchamp, **L.**, placed once viz
        second in Prix de la Grotte, Longchamp, **Gr.3**; dam of 2 winners viz-
        IRISH WINGS (IRE) (c. by In The Wings), 3 races including Golden Gate
            Handicap, Golden Gate, **Gr.3** and Prix du Lion-d'Angers, M'-Laffitte, **L.**,
            placed second in Inglewood Handicap, Hollywood Park, **Gr.3**.
        Cour de France (FR) (f. by Sadler's Wells (USA)), 1 race in France and
            128,000 fr., placed second in Prix La Camargo, Saint-Cloud, **L.**
    SADLER'S IMAGE (IRE) (1991 c. by Sadler's Wells (USA)), won 4 races at 3 years
        and £49,794 including Chester Stakes, Chester, **L.**, Racing Post Godolphin
        Stakes, Newmarket, **L.** and placed second in Quantel Aston Park Stakes,
        Newbury, **L.** and third in Dalham Chester Vase, Chester, **Gr.3**.
    DANCE A DREAM (GB) (1992 f. by Sadler's Wells (USA)), 4th top rated 3yr old
        filly in England in 1995, won 2 races at 2 and 3 years and £92,294 including
        Cheshire Oaks, Chester, **L.**, placed second in Vodafone Oaks, Epsom, **Gr.1** and
        third in Heath Court Hotel Fred Archer Stakes, Newmarket, **L.**
    Maitre A Bord (USA) (1985 c. by Riverman (USA)), won 3 races in France, placed
        third in Prix de Boulogne, Longchamp, **L.** and Prix Sir Gallahad, Saint-Cloud, **L.**
    Mizaaya (GB) (1989 c. by Riverman (USA)), won 3 races at 3 years and £51,602,
        placed 6 times including second in Leicestershire Stakes, Leicester, **L.**
    Dancing Surpass (IRE) (1990 c. by Dancing Brave (USA)), won 5 races at 3 and
        4 years in Japan, £364,804, second in Meguro Kinen, Tokyo, Jpn-**Gr.2**, Sankei
        Osaka Hai, Kyoto, Jpn-**Gr.2**, Takamatsunomiya Hai, Chukyo, Jpn-**Gr.2**, Centaur
        Stakes, Chukyo, Jpn-**Gr.2**.
    EXCLUSIVE VIRTUE (USA) (1988 f. by Shadeed (USA)), 1 race at 2 years, £10,617.
    Exclusive (GB) (1995 f. by Polar Falcon (USA)), retained in training.

2nd Dam
Bonavista, **won** 3 races in U.S.A., second in Scarlet Carnation Stakes, Thistledown;
dam of **nine winners** from 13 runners and 16 foals of racing age including-
    ATHENIA (USA) (f. by Mr Prospector (USA)), won 3 races at home and in U.S.A.
        including Illini Princess Stakes, Hawthorne **R.**; dam of winners.
        ATHENIA GREEN, won San Francisco Handicap, Bay Meadows, **Gr.3**.
        Kiandra (USA), unraced; dam of **STRAIGHTAWAY (USA)**, won Florence S., **L.**
    Teddy's Courage (USA) (c. by Exclusive Native (USA)), won 6 races in U.S.A.,
        placed second in Hawthorne Gold Cup Handicap, Hawthorne, **Gr.2**; sire.
    Historically (USA) (c. by Raise A Native), won 6 races in U.S.A. and $121,214,
        placed fourth in Arlington Washington Futurity, Arlington Park, **Gr.1**; sire.
    CAT LUCK (USA), won 1 race in U.S.A.; dam of winners.
        RESTLESS CAT (USA), winner in U.S.A.; dam of **FORTUNATE MOMENT
        (USA)**, won American Derby, Arlington Park, **Gr.1**; sire in U.S.A.

Extract from Tattersalls Sales Catalogue, 1997 Houghton Sales. A highly
desirable pedigree showing plenty of 'black type', denoting the winners of
high-class races.
Reproduced by permission of Tattersalls Ltd.

Thoroughbred pedigrees are 'read' from left to right. They also possess a shorthand whereby they may be summarised by either their 'top' or 'bottom' line. The top line charts the sire and sires of sires, the bottom line the dam and dams of dams. The top line is said to represent the 'strength' of the pedigree, the bottom line the 'weakness'. Of course, it is possible to have a weak top line or a strong bottom line, but these are relative to the overall top:bottom bias. The most common shorthand for summarising a pedigree is that of mentioning the sire and the dam's sire. Thus, for example, Zafonic, who is by Gone West, out of Zaizafon, who is by The Minstrel, will be described as: 'Zafonic (Gone West, The Minstrel)'. Everyday discussions of yearlings similarly refer to, for example, 'a Sadler's Wells colt out of a Danzig mare'.

The proportion of the catalogue assigned to the dam line and the idea that the dam line is the 'weakness' in a pedigree relate to ideas regarding racehorse fertility and procreation. The relevant image of procreation is that the stallion will bring a substantial but finite amount of talent to the mating. If most of this talent must be 'used up' in trying to bring the mare up to the standard of the stallion, then very little will be left to pass on to the foal itself. The mare is thus 'empty' before being covered. The mare always represents a deficit, relative to the stallion, who is complete.

This image can be extended to apply to the entire catalogue that becomes a map representing the annual distribution of blood embodied by the yearling crop. 'Blood' is thus presented as a limited substance, distributed according to an equation that balances the amount of talent brought by the stallion against that used up by the mare in their production of a foal. In this way, there are no real additions to the English Thoroughbred, just novel combinations of blood, relative to each successive generation.

The image of the thoroughbred racehorse perpetuated by its breeders supports the contention of Yanagisako and Delaney that origin stories are 'a prime locus for a society's notion of itself' (1995: 2). Thomas' characterisation of the three founding stallions of the English thoroughbred as 'a kind of equine Adam, Noah or William the Conqueror' (1983: 59), fails to mention the most significant feature of the story: the omission of its female protagonists. The patriarchal stallion myth, expressed in the dogma of prepotency and sire dominance, is supported by the most *visible* ancestors of the racehorse being male, and can be deduced from the structure of the catalogue page.

Since only the male ancestors of this species are visible, the original blood is gendered, and thus diluted when combined with female blood in order to create a foal:

the existence of three initial progenitors, and their continuation by not more than one progenitor each and three progenitors in all, far from being a matter of course which every student of the Thoroughbred has always taken for granted as one of the curiosities of history, is instead a dramatic punctuation of the essence of the Thoroughbred as an elite animal destined to be influenced at every stage by an amazingly small number of individuals. (Varola 1974: 7)

The representation of male and female racehorses in the catalogue can thus be explained. The inherent weakness of the dam line is protested against by the presence of illustrious relations in the catalogue, and the small number of stallions at stud serve as highly concentrated sources of the limited quantity of 'noble blood'.

Assessment of the thoroughbred at each of the most significant stages of its career – at the sales, on the track and at stud – reflects the disproportionate influence with which the stallion is credited. Breeders and pundits discussing a two-year-old will predict its ability in relation to its sire: 'Like all Sadler's Wells, he'll appreciate getting his toe in' (horses by Sadler's Wells are thought to run faster on softer ground), 'He's by Ela Mana Mou, so he should get the trip' (Ela Mana Mou is thought to be 'an influence for stamina'), 'He's just got geed up in the paddock, like a lot of Diesis do' (Diesis is thought to pass on a nervous disposition). At first glance, racing society could almost be mistaken for a society in which maternity was denied or went unnoticed.

The skewed structure of thoroughbred selection reveals a form of mono-geneticism similar to that identified by Delaney in relation to Turkey, where 'The male is said to plant the seed and the woman is said to be like a field' (1986: 496). In Newmarket, as elsewhere, 'paternity is not the semantic equiv-alent of maternity' (Delaney 1986: 495), because the sire's contribution is qualitatively superior to that of the mare. Perhaps the most explicit statement of this version of the sire's contribution is to be found in the work of Italian thoroughbred breeder Frederick Tesio. Tesio, the 'Wizard of Dormello', was an authority referred to by several informants in Newmarket. His theories were many, and had consistent themes, for example, 'the mare is like a sack which gives back what has been put into it' (Tesio 1958: 10):

The female is by nature weaker. The purpose of her existence is the state of pregnancy. As soon as she becomes pregnant the nervous – almost neurotic – symptoms of virginity disappear . . . The hereditary influence of the male is superior both in quantity and in quality to the hereditary influence of the female. (Tesio 1958: 10)[4]

Thoroughbred breeders are therefore able to combine monogeneticism and biometric genetics because though the foal is said to be '50% its sire and 50% its dam' the contribution made by each is complementary but different in kind. The stallion is thus seen as contributing those traits that are most valued by racing society, physical conformation and those mystical qualities that affect racing ability: 'presence', 'courage' or 'heart'. The mare's contributions are often either temperamental or mundane.[5]

I was often told that good racemares rarely made good broodmares. On the stud, for example, Tony the stud hand told me the story of a famous racemare who was 'no good' at stud: 'She was a right bitch, she wasn't having any of it. She thought that she was a stallion. I s'pose that's why she was so good. She was used to beating colts and she didn't want to be a mother.' The good racemare is an anomaly because she excels in a male-dominated sphere. Tony attributed her difficulty at stud to her own gender confusion. As the previous chapter established, femininity on the stud correlates with ideas of fertility, mothering and nurturing.

Phenotypic fetishism

Hocks are the main joint on a horse's back legs, sort of knees in reverse. Looking at hocks illustrates that the yearling's catalogue entry determines more than its price, it also determines the faults it can be forgiven, and those that it cannot, summed up in the phrase that, 'there are hocks and there are hocks'. When examining a yearling by the stallion 'Kris', for example, I noted its weak hocks in my catalogue. My detection of this fault should give some indication of its severity. I also looked at the Sadler's Wells full brother to Entrepreneur, and couldn't fault him. When I discussed the day's work with a team of agents, I mentioned the Kris colt and they became enthusiastic. The phrase 'Krisish hocks' was bandied about. I asked about the significance of this and was told that Kris also had bad hocks, and if the yearling had his hocks it was likely that he had Kris' good features too, such as his courage and overall soundness. When I mentioned the Sadler's Wells colt I was met with the unanimous cry of 'weak hocks!', end of discussion.

It is desirable that a yearling should resemble its sire because this is taken as evidence that the yearling has also inherited its sire's racing ability. As in the example used, this ideology extends to the faults of the stallions, which are excused and even valued in their progeny. The reproduction of traits, however apparently trivial, is seized upon as evidence of the sire's influence, for example, the manager of Cheveley Park Stud was very excited about the full brother to Entrepreneur on the grounds that he had more white on his face, and so resembled Sadler's Wells, his sire, even more closely than his full brother, the winner of the 1997 Guineas.

This fetish for phenotypic resemblance does not extend beyond the offspring of a particular sire. Thus, a racehorse would never be identified as a 'dead ringer for Batshoof' for example, unless it is by that sire. It is not the appearance of the yearling that is being praised, as illustrated by the ideology applying to faults and irrelevancies. The resemblance is desirable because it is treated as evidence of the sharing of something far more significant: ability, but equally importantly it is evidence of heredity itself. The mating has been a success because the stallion has successfully overcome the mare's weaknesses with enough quality to spare; this excess quality has been inherited by the foal, as made explicit by this breeder:

the qualities of both stallion and mare should be complementary to one another and the aim should be to choose a stallion who will counteract any shortcomings in his mate. (Napier 1975: 17)

Pedigree determines price

'All a pedigree tells you is how much a yearling is going to cost' (Bloodstock agent). In making this statement, this agent fractures the ideology that governs his trade, at the same time as acknowledging its power. The significance of the statement is its implicit denial of the guiding axiom of the bloodstock industry, that pedigree determines ability. If pedigree *only* determines price, then it cannot also determine ability. However, this bloodstock agent also predicts that the bloodstock market, constituted by himself and his colleagues, will value the yearling according to its pedigree.

The statement thus has two separate implications, firstly that the price of a yearling is determined by its pedigree and secondly that its ability is not. This poses the question: what are bloodstock agents paying for? The answer lies partly in the structure of the market for yearlings, who are sold before their ability is established, when all that is really known about them is their breeding. However, these are obviously not the reasons that would be given by the majority of members of the bloodstock industry, who would contradict the idea and maintain that pedigree is the single most significant determinant of ability in a yearling. Explaining this conviction depends partly on understanding the self-perpetuating mechanisms which govern the prices of yearlings and partly on understanding the compulsion of ideas about 'blood' and heredity.

The means by which yearling prices are established are circular and therefore difficult to describe. However, I shall only explain them briefly since they have been mentioned in chapter six and I only want to treat them as the epiphenomenon of the ideology of pedigree that is my concern. Ability on the racecourse is the only criterion of success for mature racehorses, thus when a horse wins a big race agents will begin to buy offspring of its sire. The sire's manager may then put up the nomination fee, i.e. the cost of the mating. The stallion will then attract better quality mares, and the yearlings will be more expensive at the sales. The yearlings will go to better trainers than their less fashionable contemporaries, and may be successes or failures. Shoring up this cycle is the tendency of expensive stallions to cover large numbers of mares, up to three hundred a year, whilst less fashionable sires may not 'fill their book' of fifty mares; an element of the 'numbers game' thus enters into the equation whereby a fashionable stallion has a greater number of chances of success.

The effect of these cycles is that a few stallions dominate their era, because they enjoy support at the expense of their competitors, the more successful they are the more they are supported and so on. The dominance of particular stallions is interpreted by the bloodstock industry as evidence of 'prepotency', the belief that certain stallions are able to 'stamp' their offspring who then bear a strong resemblance to their sire. It is a continually restated horseracing 'fact' that a very small number of stallions dominate their era before an heir is made apparent a couple of generations later. The few horses who do seem to have had a greater than expected influence over their adjacent generations are termed 'prepotent' by pedigree enthusiasts. The notion of prepotency can be found in British breeding manuals until the 1930s:

The belief is still widespread that the good judge of livestock can recognise the prepotent animal from its phenotype. The assumed indicators are masculinity in the male and femininity in the female. (Winters 1939: 143)

This observation is flanked by two plates, of a particularly fat stallion, and a mare with her mane and tail in plaits and ribbons. Breeders told me that in order for a stallion to be successful at stud he 'must look masculine'. Of course, masculinity was not reducible to a list of necessary and sufficient conditions, and often depended upon entirely subjective notions such as 'presence', or 'arrogance', impossible to verify or falsify. As well as giving rise to the expression of images of masculinity and femininity, the ideology of the 'potentate', referring to the monarch's potential 'kingliness' or nobility, can be detected in the notion of prepotency:

The heightened power to shape progeny was called 'prepotency'. It was, of course, essentially comparative. That is, it offered a way to discriminate among breeds as well as between pedigreed and nonpedigreed animals. It could therefore, be used as a measure or conformation of breed quality, especially since it could be tested in practice. The workings of prepotency seemed often simply to confirm the value of unsullied descent – to exemplify the rule by which 'the most in-bred parent generally influences the offspring to the greatest extent'. (Ritvo 1997: 115)

The notion of prepotency clearly complements the bloodstock industry's ideas of heredity.

From eighteenth-century Irish ostlers to the cloning of Cigar

During fieldwork, my Irish surname continually provoked my reinvention as a descendant of Irish ostlers of around the eighteenth century. My own ignorance of this heritage was taken as evidence of the intensity and antiquity of my ancestors' involvement with horses, 'it must go back a long way to have remained dormant for so long and yet to come out so strongly in you', I was told.

This was the only possible explanation for my 'passion' for horses. Similarly, when Bill the trainer asked me the nature of my father's involvement with horses, I knew that my honest response would not be accepted. I told him that my father detested horses, being of the opinion that one end bites, the other kicks and in between is uncomfortable. Sure enough, this met with further inquiries: surely he had some involvement, however minor? After I had denied this several times, Bill compromised and asked me a hypothetical question: 'What sort of horses would your father be involved with *if* he had an interest in horses?' He sat back looking smug and I was forced to imagine the unlikely image of my father in jodhpurs. I plumped for showjumping rather than racing out of malice, and Bill seemed satisfied. I was not at all surprised by Bill's periodical comments regarding 'my father – the showjumper', although I was slightly thrown when he asked me whether my father was interested in a 'super jumping mare', before I remembered the background to such an inquiry.

The pedigree theory that informs ideas of relatedness amongst horses applies equally to those about humans:

The notion of reckoning descent through either the male line or the female line, as a criterion for group membership, is an outgrowth of the basic notion of selective breeding. This is quite explicit with animals but camouflaged as 'descent reckoning' when applied by anthropologists to human groups. (Bouquet 1993: 192)

There is no such camouflaging in Newmarket, where people move seamlessly from talking about horses to humans, and from breeding to kinship. This idea is particularly visible in discussions of new reproductive possibilities in Newmarket.

Artificial insemination (AI)

AI is hardly a 'new' reproductive technology:

The first reported use of AI, though not documented, was in 1300 by some Arabian horse breeders. Rival chieftains reportedly stole stallion semen from one another to breed their own mares. (Bearden and Fuquay 2000: 151)[6]

AI provided one of the most potent means by which agriculture became industrialised, and is now a taken for granted technique used by the vast majority of industrialised nations in the production of pork and, in particular, beef (see Bearden and Fuquay 2000). Many horse breeders have also embraced AI as a means of reducing disease, increasing the rate of genetic progress of their stock, and allowing the international movement of semen (see Wallin, Kidd and Clarke 1995). However, opposition from within the racing industry towards the technique remains strong. The Chairman of the National Stud, Peter Player, recently responded to a government report that suggested that the stud should widen its remit by saying:

As long as I'm chairman, there will be no unacceptable veterinary research, in any form, carried out at the stud – in other words, practices contrary to those allowed in the worldwide breeding of thoroughbreds. Those that spring to mind include artificial insemination, embryo transfers, cloning and, particularly, genetic engineering. No Dolly the sheep. You couldn't possibly have any of that going on alongside the stud being open to the general public and acting as a shop window for our industry. We're thoroughbred through and through, and should stick rigidly to that principle. We must not mix oil and water. (quoted in Smurthwaite 2000)

AI is currently banned by the rules of the International Stud Book, which state that:

A horse is not qualified to be entered for start in any race unless it and its sire and dam are each the produce of a natural service or covering, and unless a natural gestation took place in, and the delivery was from, the body of the mare in which the horse was conceived. (*Ruff's Guide to the Turf* 1996: 124)

The majority of people to whom I spoke were against AI, on the grounds either that it was 'unnatural' or that it would prompt the diminution of the thoroughbred gene pool; although a few thought that acceptance of AI was long overdue.

The most sustained opposition to AI that I experienced came from a thoroughbred breeder who had recently retired from riding in amateur races at the age of seventy-three. She had extremely clear views, believing that a connection between the mare and stallion was a physiological necessity for a healthy foal:

The semen used for pigs in Holland has become diseased and the farms in this country are using bulls again for a 'top up'. My mares in season will try to get to the teaser because they know where he is, even though we put the foal in the box first! How is a mare's instinct to be covered going to be satisfied? By the vet and some semen in a false vagina? The best winners I have ever bred have been by sires whose legs really pump away like pistons during copulation – I'm sure that some transfer of energy is capable of improving the chances of getting a good energetic foal. What will fulfil that criteria in AI? I'm very worried about it.

She also told me the story of the conception of a great racehorse that was the result of two horses 'falling in love':

It was when the horses were walked everywhere before the horsebox, and the stallion was being led along the road, and passed a mare on her way to something else, I mean, she wasn't even going to this horse. And they looked at each other and that was it. They overcame their handlers and made love on the Cambridge Road.

Similarly, a stud groom on a tour of the Equine Fertility Unit, which is currently championing the cause of AI, responded angrily to the suggestion:

The mare needs to feel the weight of the stallion on her back, and for the energy of the covering to go into her. Using a test tube won't produce the same effects and you can't fool these old mares. They know what's natural.

These ideas echo the work of Tesio and his followers. In fact, the foal bred on the Cambridge Road belonged to Tesio and was called Signorinetta. Tesio's explanation for her undoubted talent extends the same reproductive themes:

in the case of Signorinetta, it is not unlikely that the issue was affected by the circumstances of the unplanned encounter between her parents. The arrows of an equine cupid roused the sexual urge to a maximum of tension which endowed the resulting individual with exceptional energy . . . this result is never achieved with artificial insemination because the parents are cheated of their pleasurable spasm with its violent nervous release. (1958: 93)

Star of Naples, full-sister to Signorinetta, and the produce of a planned mating, proved untalented, the produce of a lacklustre covering due, according to Tesio, to the embarrassment of the dam and sire following their previous exploits.

Bob McCreery, chairman of a group commissioned by the Thoroughbred Breeders Association to investigate the potential impact of AI, remains bemused:

I have never known why AI provokes such controversy. To people who know about breeding and animal husbandry it is not so shocking . . . It would be a great change and that is upsetting to some people. (quoted by Hislop 1997: 17)

It seems that McCreery does not realise how shocking AI is to those who believe that horses fall in love, or how ineffective it seems to those who believe that the 'heat' and 'weight' of intercourse is necessary for conception to occur. Opposition to AI is intense because of the centrality of the idea of procreation to all other aspects of imagining connections between horses, as it is amongst people, 'everything that surrounds the act(s) of procreation bears on how people represent the meaning of being related to one another' (Strathern 1993: 16).

A related objection to AI lies in the belief that it would prompt the depletion of the gene pool:

Hamish Anderson, Weatherby's stud book director . . . said: 'One of the concerns is what AI might do to the gene pool. Going back twenty-five generations takes us right back to square one, the days of the Byerley Turk, by which time there are about 66 million ancestors to a single mating.' With proper, and costly, research under its belt, Weatherby's should be able to predict what would happen, if, as is feared, no more than ten per cent of the stallion population survives the unnatural selection imposed by AI. (Smurthwaite 1997a: 17)

By referring to the 'unnatural selection of AI' this journalist appears to imply that the selective breeding of the racehorse is actually 'natural'. Selective breeding, which used to be the opposite of natural selection, has now become 'natural selection' relative to that which would be facilitated by AI. I would suggest that this response to AI is partly based on a fear of blood being out of control.

The theory of pedigree rests upon the ability of breeders to maintain the 'purity' of the breed by witnessing coverings and blood typing foals. The depletion of the gene pool constitutes a loss of blood, offending those who see themselves as custodians of noble blood, responsible for determining its distribution. This loss is often imagined through stories in which blood crosses international boundaries and is thereby lost to a malign foreign influence:

In 1978, many breeders were thought to be in dread of AI because of the overriding fear that it would be wildly abused. According to the Duke [of Devonshire], 'fanciful stories' arose about vials of frozen semen being shipped around the world at will, making for priceless bargaining chips allowing an elite band of stallions to cover hundreds of mares at the expense of others. The impact on the gene pool would be unimaginable. If only the stories were true. (Smurthwaite 1997b: 7)

The blood of the stallions no longer in demand would be lost, and could not be regained. These are stories about loss, and also loss of control, in which blood would no longer be mapped or limited, and so, being unrecorded, would lose its capacity to explain ability. AI also prompts a confrontation with the limits of desirable inbreeding, prompting the use of imagery associated with incest, thus sperm becomes 'diseased', 'hybrid vigour' is lost, and monsters result, as the stud groom told me: 'You start messing about with nature and you get Frankenstein don't you?'

The loss of blood is also the theme of the 'stallion drain', another major concern of the bloodstock industry. The terms in which it is described again reflect the threat that export constitutes to the national identity of English blood by resonating with xenophobia, as in this extract from an article in the *Guardian*:

It is hard to see in these Japanese incursions much more than mere acquisitiveness, a desire to possess comparable with the desire to buy great works of art, many of which now languish unseen in the Tokyo bank vaults. At the Houghton Sales in Newmarket last week, I have rarely seen people look more bored than the phalanx of Japanese who sat around the auction ring dressed in perfect English county clothes but carrying cameras rather than binoculars. Like the art works, the horses that go to Japan are disappearing into a black hole ... we see no more than the occasional foal by Generous who returns to run in Britain, bringing with him a wealth of memories and a terrible sense of loss. (Thompson 1996: 6)

Put even more starkly, I was told: 'What on earth would the Japanese do with an English thoroughbred? They may dress as Englishmen but they don't have horses in their blood.' It seems that, as in the eighteenth century when the blood of a thoroughbred reflected positively on that of his aristocratic owner, it is necessary to be of the right blood oneself in order to be favoured by, rather than condemned or mocked for, this association.

Conclusion

In this chapter I have discussed some of the 'facts of life' in thoroughbred breeding, believing them to be central to how people imagine both humans and horses are related. What is 'natural' in Newmarket has been identified as the inheritance of ability through parental blood. The asymmetry of the male and female contributions to their offspring is evident in the literary form taken by the pedigree, in the price of yearlings and in their assessment by phenotypic resemblance to their sire.

AI is 'unnatural' because it frees 'blood' from procreation and in doing so threatens old certainties. Furthermore, it raises the possibility that blood may be lost, which is frightening because this is 'noble' blood that has been honed to perfection by more than two centuries of human endeavour. By 'natural' means, of course. The export of stallions similarly suggests a loss of blood, because who knows what will happen once it leaves these shores? The export is resisted because the blood of the English thoroughbred belongs to the English. The pedigrees of the founding stallions of the breed express this point clearly, by running *forwards* to the English thoroughbred, rather than backwards to the Barb, Turk or Arabian.

Some of the certainties threatened by AI were brought into even sharper relief by the suggestion that Cigar, the American wonderhorse, was to be cloned. The story began with his infertility, which was reported in jocular tone, referring to him as a 'Jaffa' (seedless). In some ways, people seemed almost happy that the horse had failed, since he had gone to stand for the Coolmore organisation, which is perceived as having a monopoly over all the best thoroughbred blood:

Cigar, but no smoke signals . . . Human fertility experts have volunteered to help out . . . and phials of Cigar's semen are being examined all over the world. In addition, many of Cigar's fans, who have presumably suffered the same problems, have written with suggestions, including acupuncture and massage. If nothing works, there is talk Cigar could move down the road to the Kentucky Horse Park to join another favourite American horse, John Henry – a gelding! (Smurthwaite 1997c: 5)

Sterility seemed quite amusing in what was, after all, an American horse owned by Coolmore. However, the enhanced reproductive possibilities of cloning were not greeted with the same sort of response:

The Jockey Club poured scorn on the idea. World-wide rules prevented such breeding a spokesman said. 'Quite a few barriers would have to come down before cloning became a reality. It's highly unlikely.' . . . Hamish Anderson . . . said, 'In the meat and livestock business uniformity might be an advantage, but in racing variation is vital.' (Varley 1997: 18)

When I pointed out to a breeder that even in a race of clones there would be a first, second and so on, his response was to boom 'EXACTLY!!' Cloned racehorses would create races exactly the same as those involving racehorses born 'naturally'. In a sense, all thoroughbred blood would be lost, since it would be static, no longer travelling through generations according to a route mapped out by breeders, an image implicit in the nightmarish *Guardian* headline: 'Sterile wonder-horse may run on for ever as former owner pursues race of clones' (Varley 1997: 18).

This chapter has sought to support the claim by Strathern that, 'ideas about kinship offered a theory, if you like, about the relationship of human society to the natural world' (1992c: 5). In the case of racing society, what is natural is that one should 'breed the best to the best to get the best', that horses are 'in the blood', that ability is transmitted as a 'spark' during copulation and that blood can be lost through improper management or the interference of impostors or technology. These ideas support an image of human society constituted by groups of people associated with each other through ties of substance and hereditarily inclined to excel in a particular role. It is thus impossible to think about racehorses without also thinking about class.

NOTES

1 On the continent, the controlled breeding of horses classified as 'warmbloods' arose from the need to provide a strong cavalry. 'In the case of England, the small size of the land forces meant that the state had a correspondingly modest interest in breeding horses for military purposes . . . Thus in eighteenth century England, wealthy, self-confident and politically dominant aristocrats took the lead in breeding Thoroughbreds for racing' (Clarke 1995: 15). Accordingly the breeding of cavalry horses on the continent and of racehorses in Britain developed in diametrically opposite directions – from stringent performance testing on the continent to bloodlines in Britain. The horses are thus of wholly different types, stout versus fragile, consistent versus brilliant in flashes. Their breeding philosophies contain a wealth of corresponding contrasts

2 Compare the racecourse test, with its enormous number of variables, to the extensive performance tests undergone by Hanoverian stallions, a type of warmblood sports horse, '[Stallion] licensing begins with a veterinary inspection . . . The colts are then loose jumped and shown in hand. Following licensing privately owned colts must pass a 100-day ridden performance test with marks of at least 90, while the state-owned sires must complete eleven months of testing. The first crop of foals are also inspected, and if they do not reach the required standard, the sire may still be removed from the breeding stud book' (Wallin 1995: 53–4).

3 For an overview see Willett 1975: 49–61. Willett describes Bruce Lowe's Figure System that traced all of the pedigrees of all of the mares included in the GSB back to the original foundation mares. Lowe found that around fifty mares had contemporary representatives and ranked these 'families' according to the number of classic winners they had produced. He argued that mating decisions should combine blood from particular successful families. Willett concludes that, 'breeding racehorses by the figure system is nonsense' (1975: 51), and is similarly dismissive of all of the alternatives, 'Galton's Law has little of value to offer the breeder' (1975: 56), Friedrich Becker

talked 'mainly through his hat' (1975: 53), 'The telling criticism of the dosage system is that it is scientifically unsound' (1975: 58), and J. B. Robertson 'was not ruthless enough in confronting his prejudice with his scientific knowledge' (1975: 61). In other words, even Willett finds little to impress in a selection of so-called 'breeding theories'.

4 Ideas concerning the relative contributions of dam and sire have varied historically, and Tesio's views represent the most extreme form of asymmetry I have encountered. More conservative bloodstock theorists such as Willett assert the equality of contribution, 'Since a foal receives half of its make-up of genes from its sire and the other half from its dam, it is obvious that the two parents are potentially of equal importance, and a prepotent mare may transmit important characters to her offspring just as surely as a prepotent stallion' (1975: 101). However, the extra attention paid to the female line by equality theorists derives not from an idea that the mare's contribution is equally qualitatively valuable, but the opposite, 'In bloodstock breeding . . . the superior specimen (the stallion) is mated to the mean or subnormal (brood mares)' (Leicester 1957: 125). Moreover, this weakness is 'the key to the generally accepted principle, amongst breeders, that the tail female line is of the utmost importance' (Leicester 1957: 144).

5 Borneman mentions a similar idea in his work on horse-breed classification in America, 'An old aphorism says: The mare contributes the disposition, the stallion the conformation' (1988: 37).

6 I mention this unsubstantiated story because it strikes me as ironic that there is a possibility that some of the original Arabian stock that produced the modern thoroughbred may themselves have been produced by the illicit technique of AI. The first documented successful use of AI was by an Italian physiologist, Spallanzani, in 1780 (Bearden and Fuquay 2000: 152).

10   Conclusions

Introduction

In these conclusions I ask, 'What sort of place is Newmarket?' and 'What sort of people claim allegiance to its windswept Heath and horse-dominated way of life?' To some degree this book responds to my desire to 'make strange' the sometimes taken for granted and homogenised notion of 'British culture':

> Much has been written recently of the dangers to anthropologists of essentialising visions of non-western societies. Less has been written recently of the dangers to people in the West of their essential visions of themselves. (Carrier 1990: 706)

Though some aspects of racing society may seem utterly 'foreign' to outsiders, there is also much which finds resonance amongst a wider British audience. The ideas encompassed by the saying of: 'like father, like son', for example, the inheritance of sporting talents and the explanation of traits as 'in the blood', are common to many contexts outside racing. The difference seems to me that within the racing industry these ideas are worked out more fully, albeit in the guise of another species.

In 1988 Borneman related race, ethnicity, species and breed to horse-breed classification in America and concluded that:

> The mythical systems produced through classificatory devices, while experienced as innocent speech, are in fact constructed first, by a plagiarism of the social world, and second, by a harmonisation of that world with its dominant discourse. This kind of myth is neither simply a charter for reality nor is it an invention of pure thought. It is both a language for analogically representing another reality – an hierarchical system of human differentiation – and a means by which that reality can be validated. (1988: 48)[1]

This book has described the ideological sleight of hand whereby inequality can be naturalised by appeal to a system credited with its own independent existence – the breed of thoroughbred racehorse. The myths of the breed are many, and made concrete in a number of different embodied and literary forms that have been discussed in the preceding pages: the General Stud Book, the sales catalogue, the jockey's disciplined body, the trainer's family tree, the owner's silks, the horse's names. All refer to the 'hierarchical system of human differentiation' played out perfectly by the thoroughbred.

The rest of these conclusions pull together the two most powerful structuring principles at work in Newmarket amongst racing professionals: risk and pedigree. It is the potency of these two principles when combined which accounts for the resilience of this way of life. In the first section of this chapter I concentrate on the people of Newmarket, and their ideas of 'class'. I shall then describe the presence of risk in almost all of the significant roles within the racing industry, from breeder to lad, from jockey to punter. The final section seeks to acknowledge my debt to a group of anthropologists who may not automatically consider themselves to be part of the intellectual landscape of horseracing. It contextualises my attempt to describe racing society in Newmarket within important debates in contemporary anthropology.[2]

Inequality

As one might expect of a place in which the class structure is so strikingly out of step with the majority of the rest of the surrounding communities, Newmarket is a place that quickly lulls one into its daily rhythms and routines. The proximity of Cambridge (twenty minutes away) always struck me as amazing, and even formed a local explanation of the character of Newmarket itself:

> it's being so close to Cambridge that has preserved Newmarket. No one notices New-market and we go on as before, whilst Cambridge is always changing, from too much attention. We don't generally get busybodies like you. (Stud hand)

The conventions of Newmarket seem contrived to make one take the status quo for granted. For example, having been racing as owner, trainer's assistant and lass, each experience seemed definitive at the time. As the guest of an owner I was invited to lunch and we spent the entire afternoon at the races, drinking, eating, betting, watching the races and relaxing. Whilst assisting the trainer we arrived in time for 'our' race, saddled the horse, instructed the jockey, watched the race and came home, all in a state of nervousness and anxiety.

Going racing as a lass is different again. Arriving at the track three hours before the race, I had often ridden three horses and mucked out their stables before leaving. Almost every lad and lass with whom I travelled could sleep in virtually any position and for any period of time. I learnt quickly and could sleep leaning against even the most pungent of old lads, ignoring cigar smoke and other fumes. An hour and three quarters before the race the horse is prepared, and an hour later the horse leaves the racecourse stables and enters the paddock. The horse returns to the stables after the race and is washed down, given a drink and allowed to recover before travelling home again. Despite having come racing as a friend of both owner and trainer and enjoyed days at the races and elsewhere with both, when I came racing as the lass, I did not interact with them in the same way. I spent the majority of the time asleep in the horse lorry, only participating in the race meeting to the extent that my 'lead up' demanded. When I did come into contact with owner and trainer in the saddling box before the race I was treated entirely differently, and asked, 'How is he?' (of the horse), rather than 'How are you?'

The ability of racing society to naturalise such differences in status and respect was considerable, although there were informants who sought to puncture this ideology:

I operate in the more common sphere where more or less people judge you on your own merits. I'm an educated woman and mostly I'm treated accordingly. But because I won't adhere to the fixed class infrastructure I'm not accepted because I won't tug my forelock. (Stud groom's wife)

The work of the stud hand is often monotonous and physically demanding, and is mainly directed towards maintaining the appearance of the stud. A typical day as a stud hand was thus spent mowing, strimming, sweeping, raking and scrubbing. Although sit-on mowers and petrol-powered strimmers have undoubtedly improved the lot of the stud hand, much of the work is still arduous and boring. The stud landscape obviously reflects more than the desire of the breeding industry to impose its will upon nature, it is also dependent upon a particular class structure:

Stud hands are born into it and don't know how to do anything else. A lot of people get trapped, they couldn't stick a factory job and so they stay with the horses, although I've had people go into transport and things. Half the problem with stud work is that it takes advantage of people because you live on the stud. You are 'lucky enough' to have tied accommodation! And especially if you've got a family, which all of us have, you don't want to lose it. (Stud groom)

Whilst on the stud I listened to many complaints from the stud hands, particularly regarding the shortage of labour and poor working conditions. When I asked why they stayed on, many stud hands gave the same reason; their accommodation. In particular, it became obvious that tied accommodation had been turned into the family home by most of the hands' wives and children. These houses were decorated with ornaments, photographs, extensions, new carpets, furniture and curtains. Gardens were packed with kennels, rabbit hutches, paddling pools and bicycles. The idea of leaving represented a considerable wrench to the hands and their families. It was noticeable, by contrast, that younger hands without families moved between studs quite freely. The restrictions of tied accommodation obviously hampered the movement of some hands. However, hands also exhibited a sense of pride regarding their work, epitomised by their description of polo ponies as 'second class citizens' and their pity for me and my academic life:

Well, you see, I've got a hand in the royal family, the thoroughbred, and there's nothing like him is there. You wouldn't catch me having anything to do with those old ponies, I don't know why you bother! And as for all those books, what can they tell you about life? You've all you need to learn about right here in the barn, standing looking at you! Nothing in the world comes close to him. (Stud hand)

Stud hands valued work with thoroughbreds above work with other horses, and work with horses above all other forms of manual labour that they perceived as alternatives to their work on the stud. The idea that stud hands are 'born into it' fits ideas of heredity in Newmarket, and also detracts from the fact that although the stud groom is a manager, and may therefore consider himself to be more mobile, he also lives in a tied house. However, in addition to these structural restrictions, stud hands are also motivated by their admiration for the thoroughbred, and their valuing of the breed above all other creatures.

I have rejected the idea that lads were stuck in their jobs as a result of their 'breeding' or their lack of skills. A large number of lads also occupied tied accommodation, and shared with the stud hands a reluctance to move on despite poor pay or conditions. Lads are devalued by those inhabitants of Newmarket who are outsiders to racing, as well as by many of their superiors within racing. The considerable embodied skills of many of the lads are not valued. However, it was not just the physical labour of the lads that condemned them to low status in Newmarket, but also their place in the racing hierarchy and the outsider's perception of this hierarchy. Outsiders saw racing as 'feudal', and blamed the lads themselves for the perpetuation of this system on the grounds of their inability to mobilise industrial action.

Though some younger lads seemed in awe of their trainers, and to have internalised the lessons of the British Racing School ('do not speak unless spoken to by the boss, and keep replies to "yes sir" or "no sir"'), amongst some older, more experienced lads, respect went no deeper than a job requirement:

To be honest Rebecca, you just heard me thissing and thatting to him, 'yes sir' and that, and it doesn't bother me. It's the way it is, but I know the way it is. I know my job, and I could tell him more about that filly on one trip up the sand than he could ever tell me.

I encountered many lads who did not conform to the popular image according to which they are lazy, unambitious and trapped. In particular, lads who rode work described the experience as one of considerable personal and financial empowerment:

I walk into breakfast and pick up the [*Racing*] *Post*, and likely as not, I know more about the day's runners than the boss. I know Bob's ridden this or that, Sam's had a sit on one filly or another. Something might be pinging, something else might be over the top. It's the work riders who know what's going on in Newmarket.

Even among the less accomplished, the possibility of looking after a 'good horse' kept lads in the business.

There are many positive explanations for remaining a lad, it is not just a default position occupied by the unskilled, as their image within Newmarket suggests. The strength of this image is such that lads often underplay the rewards of the job, as if to indicate that they are not foolish enough to attempt to justify involvement in such a dead-end occupation. Where this is the case, lads will tell you of their skills and achievements within racing along with their plan to 'get out'. Typically, the attitude the lads expressed towards their work was determined by the questions I asked. When I showed admiration by asking about a technical detail of their work they responded with pride. When I asked them about early mornings and low wages they distanced themselves from the job by demeaning its tasks and communicating their desire to leave the industry. The lads reproduce the negative image the rest of Newmarket thrusts upon them; however, they also maintain alternatives that are easily prompted by more positive enquiry.

It becomes clear that although 'breeding' is used by all classes of racing society in order to explain talent or ability in both humans and horses, alternative explanations are also apparent. These explanations take two forms; they may be structural, as in the case of tied housing, or the age of apprenticeship that prevents higher education. They may also take the form of positive motivations to remain in racing as offered by lads and stud hands themselves; these included a pride taken in dealing with valuable livestock, the possibility of dealing with a 'good horse', and the intrinsic pleasure of becoming skilled in a demanding embodied practice.

Among 'real' Newmarket families, the 'connection' has come to signify both object and relationship. Being connected in and to Newmarket is essential for success. And if success should somehow come before connections have been made? Well, then they will be discovered in retrospect. As in many small-scale elite societies members of racing families fetishise connections. The more prestigious the connection in question the further the trail will extend in order to claim it. I interviewed a woman with an entire room dedicated to her (very) distant cousin's husband Lester Piggott, for example. In my own case, Irish ancestors came to light in the imagination of my informants. Family trees provide the 'proof' of these claims. The trees I plotted during fieldwork were emblematic of these interests. Huge chunks of highly detailed tree recorded racing families, that dwindled to nothing on the fringes, which could be dismissed as a kind of wasteland, referred to as, 'out of racing'. Those individuals who chose not to uphold the family tradition were effectively eliminated by their racing relatives by virtue of the diagonal pencil line placed through their locus on the tree. It was not the family that they were interested in plotting, but heredity itself.

A similar sort of discounting applied to outsiders, those who could not find a place in any of the intricate webs of connections by which members of this society are able to navigate. Without connections it is very difficult to find success in Newmarket, and without success no connections will be made. As I was told of a trainer who had trained on the Hamilton Road for fifteen years, 'He's never been anyone'. This unfortunate individual receives the equivalent of a diagonal pencil line through his existence. And so one can see the inherent conservatism of such a system that is nepotistic not only in practice, but also in principle.

Risk[3]

Every significant feature of the racing and bloodstock industry can be extrapolated from the basic uncertainty that governs which horse will finish first, second and third (and last!). Despite the sport's long history of record keeping and changes in technology, there is no such thing as a racing 'certainty'.[4] Unlikely winners romp home regularly, and similarly, short-priced favourites get turned over all the time. Each race is a unique combination of an infinite number of variables, most of which are not measurable in any sense. It is not enough to say that the abiding attraction of horseracing lies in this uncertainty. It is more that this uncertainty is what racing is. As journalist Foden says, 'Racing teaches you about risk' (1996: 14).

Every horserace is a microcosmic reproduction of all of the risks taken by the various contributors to the sport. Each runner has been bred by someone who believes that a particular mating will produce a valuable or talented yearling. Mare owners pay a nomination fee and this fee and the forsaken chance to mate the mare to a different stallion is the stake in their particular gamble. The gamble is played out in the auction ring or, for breeders who race their own stock, on the racecourse. If the horse has been sold to a new owner then this owner's stake has been paid at the auction. They might cash in either on the racecourse (prize money) or in the breeding shed (nomination fees or offspring). Punters have the shortest time scale from stake to winnings (or losses). The finish line marks the end of their involvement. In all of these gambles, the contributors must also be content merely to have taken part, to have played the game. Because otherwise, they would spend their money differently.

Racing is so saturated with risks that it has even developed a number of dialects in which its professionals may discuss their business. Odds and slang are used to express the likely chances of each horse in a race at the racecourse and in the betting shop: 'Berlington Bertie 100-30' or 'Double Carpet 33-1'. Bloodstock auctioneers cajole their bidders with the idea that by ceasing to bid they risk losing out, 'All done, quite sure? Hammer's up, comes down quicker! Just look at him walk, *he could be anything*. Happy to lose him?'

Whilst auctioneers and bookmakers trade openly in risks, other members of racing society cultivate the impression that they are in control. In the case of the professional punter, the racing pundit and the bloodstock agent the appearance of knowledge replaces uncertainty. The professional punter attempts to assert his control over uncertainty by treating punting as 'work', by acting alone at the racecourse and therefore denying his communion with the crowd, and by remaining stony faced whatever the outcome of the race.

Racing pundits describe races in such a way that every possible outcome is contained within their pre-race ramblings. They are the masters of hedging. For example:

This horse is coming off a nice win at Beverley and should have the measure of a lot of these others, but he might just find the ground a bit firm for his liking. This filly has the makings of a good horse and whatever she does today I think she'll go on to better things. She might just not get things her own way today. This colt would have to improve to take a hand in the finish, but he's got form on this track.

Each explanation for the victory of any horse in the race is combined with a ready explanation for its failure.

The stance of the bloodstock agent is an embodied statement of his expertise. And looking at him one is led to believe that there is nothing uncertain in buying racehorses, it is just that what this man is doing is extremely difficult. What does the bloodstock agent tell his client about risk?

Well obviously I let them know that buying racehorses isn't an exact science. Then I hand them a colour print out of the winners I bought last season! But seriously you have to tell them that any horse could turn out to be useless. But you don't want to push that too far . . . if you do then your more astute client might say 'Well, what am I paying *you* for then?' And then you're on really sticky ground. (Bloodstock agent)

Taking risks is, in Newmarket, a way of life. From the lads who get the leg up onto some or other piece of explosive horseflesh every morning, to the high rolling punter who stakes his status and his cash on Nobby's Delight in the 3:40. From the bloodstock agent who signs the chit for a million-dollar yearling with a trembling hand, to the jockey who goes for a gap with two furlongs to go . . .

Denaturalising Newmarket, denaturalising class?

The risks provided by the sport of horseracing rarely constitute a threat to the established inequalities that structure its production. A small-time punter may land the odds on a long shot but his success will only very rarely translate into connections with the producers of racing. He remains a consumer, and the supply and demand sides of racing are kept separate by connections and their absence, and by distinctions based upon appearance, language and shared experience. A badly bred champion racehorse will only be relatively badly bred, the flexibility of the pedigree system and the narrow gene pool available ensures that good blood can be 'read' backwards into the horse's ancestry. A beautifully bred failure will be explained by recourse to any number of factors: an accident, a character flaw, or even an excess of fine blood, requiring an injection of 'rough'. None of these 'blips' prompts a review of the system itself. During my fieldwork in Newmarket it was matters of equine fertility that led to the most far-reaching discussions of first principles, and it is to this discussion that I now turn.

Racing society is currently undergoing processes of 'literalisation' and 'displacement' (Strathern 1992a: 4) brought about by increased pressure to open the General Stud Book to progeny produced through AI and more explicitly by the possibility of cloning racehorses. These processes make evident the supporting ideas of the ideology of pedigree. Examining resistance to new equine reproductive techniques reveals the processes by which, in Newmarket, 'power appears natural, inevitable, even god-given' (Yanagisako and Delaney 1995: 1).

Racing society is a productive locus of study for these concerns because it has a strong self-image; despite internal variations, members of racing society were all keen to identify more closely with each other than with anyone outside their society. A sense of 'peripherality' and suspicion of 'outsiders' is part of this self-image. Thus generalisations across racing society do not require the caveats forced upon those who take 'English kinship' as their frame of reference. Furthermore, racing society has an origin story explicitly endorsed by all its ranks, which I would suggest can be linked to the 'natural facts' of reproduction implicit in Newmarket's form of monogeneticism.

In racing, 'the stallion is king'. The stallion is the central focus of the entire bloodstock industry. In myriad ways, stallions are credited with a disproportionate influence over the breed of English thoroughbred, from its inception in the late eighteenth century to the present day. This influence is, moreover, different in kind from that of the thoroughbred mare. The three male progenitors of the thoroughbred breed are still thought to exert an influence over the breed.

The 'natural facts' of reproduction in thoroughbred breeding cast the mare as 'empty', waiting to be 'covered' by the 'entire' 'sire'. The mare is capable of passing on those qualities perceived as typically feminine by racing society, defects and a hot temper, whilst the stallion provides the essential spark of life. The mare can only detract from the stallion's unquestioned quality, the most valued foal resembles its sire, thus reflecting its disproportionate inheritance of his desirable attributes of speed, stamina and heart. The price of a yearling will be most strongly influenced by its sire and its resemblance to that sire.

In Newmarket, these are not just the natural facts about racehorses. Facilitated by the capacity for analogic thought and the ability of racehorses to become signs and thus 'stand for' other things, these 'natural facts' influence ideas of human relatedness also. The 'rub' is that even where informants' ideas regarding human reproduction were based upon sophisticated knowledge of genetic contribution that contradicted monogeneticism, they still used this model to explain the life path of an adult individual. The 'facts of life' according to the modern medical profession were known but did not interest racing society to the extent that ideas about heredity governed by male-dominated pedigree did. I would suggest that this is because monogeneticism makes sense of a sexual and class-based division of labour.

The insulation of 'nature' from 'culture' is no longer a given (Strathern 1992a, Latour 1993, Descola and Palsson 1996).[5] Racing society is both arch monist and arch dualist in this regard. Racehorses are treated as family members, granted complex 'person'alities and pedigrees and gendered traits explain both equine and human lived trajectories. However, thoroughbred racehorses are also 'man's noblest creation', the object of the 'science' of selective breeding, nature controlled. Thoroughbred breeders depend upon dualism in order to claim the prestige associated with the manipulation of a sphere conceived in opposition to society, and therefore ostensibly outside human control. It depends upon monism in order to allow cultures of relatedness most fully worked out amongst an equine population to function as a guiding axiom of human society. Crucially, racing society depends on the ability to elide the two meanings of nature (as both all powerful and also dominated) in racehorse breeding in order to blur the outcome as both man-made and beyond man's control. In addition, eliding the two meanings provides a means of creating a boundary between racing society and the rest of society, in that only racing society has the pedigree necessary to control this part of nature.

In Newmarket, 'nature' (for the moment) retains its status as the 'grounding' of all meaningful articulations of the relationship between that which is fixed and that which is variable. In addition, selective breeding, the status quo, is also 'natural' in relation to the alternatives of AI and cloning, in the sense of being a threatened present regarded nostalgically. Why should this be? Despite the motivation for selective breeding being the control of nature, I would suggest that AI offers too much control, relieving nature of its potency and thus making its control less attractive:

What is in crisis here is the symbolic order, the conceptualisation of the relation between nature and culture such that one can talk about one through the other. Nature as a ground for meaning of cultural practices can no longer be taken for granted if Nature itself is regarded as having to be protected and promoted. (Strathern 1992a: 177)

In addition, AI is a literalisation. The casualties of AI are numerous and include the separation of sex from reproduction and the consequent displacement and exposure of the pedigree theory of heredity outside its supporting 'natural facts'. Pedigree without monogeneticism is a weakened justification for nepotism and chauvinism, just as the British Racing School is seen as a threat to the practice of a 'proper' apprenticeship whereby talent is discovered, rather than created.

AI is a mechanism for unpacking the 'natural facts' of equine reproduction. This being the case, cloning is anathema to racing society. The relationship between AI and cloning was described to me as similar to that between 'the speed of light and warp factor ten'. I was told that what AI had loosened cloning would 'blow away'. AI has loosened the connection between sex and reproduction and thus pedigree and society. Cloning would eradicate pedigree because individuals would no longer be unique according to this criterion. Factors other than breeding would determine an individual's characteristics. To racing society this would be a world in which that which was thought to defer individuality was held constant, only for individuality to find an alternative source. Cloning is the 'control' experiment for the operation of pedigree and is therefore a threat to the basic governing principle of racing society.

This process is not without precedent in Newmarket, because where pedigree is threatened by technology, risk has been threatened by money, the other catalyst capable of achieving this 'flattening' effect. The bloodstock industry was transformed by events in the seventies and eighties, and, in particular by the actions of Robert Sangster and the Maktoum brothers. In 1975 Robert Sangster, heir to the Vernon's Pools fortune, decided to make a business out of horseracing and breeding. He recruited the exceptional trainer Vincent O'Brien and the premier stallion master of Ireland, John Magnier, and went to Keeneland in Kentucky to buy yearlings with fashionable American pedigrees, notably colts by the stallion Northern Dancer, who he hoped would grow into priceless stallions. In 1977, the year in which the first generation of purchases entered their three-year-old campaigns, Sangster was the leading owner in Britain. More importantly, he owned Alleged and The Minstrel, two champion racehorses in great demand as stallions.[6]

Sangster's strategy to overcome the huge risk involved in buying yearlings as potential stallions was to buy lots of them, in the knowledge that a small number of successful stallions would pay for a large number of failures. This trimming of the odds, seen as indiscriminate and motivated by profit, has been condemned by those members of racing society who maintain a fierce affection for the sporting ethos of what they see as the golden years of English racing. Their anguish is summed up in the reaction of journalist de Moubray, 'Once a symbol of power and grace, the racehorse has become little more than a fragile symbol of money' (1985: 3).

An equally important revolution began with the victory of Hatta at Brighton in June 1977. Sheikh Mohammed's first British winner marked the beginnings of an interest in English racing that shows no signs of abating. In 1982 the Maktoum brothers spent £27 million on yearlings, in 1983 they spent £50 million, including $10.2 million on one horse, Snaafi Dancer, who was too slow ever to run in a race. Initial reaction to what has been referred to as the 'Arab invasion' was predictably hostile (the irony of what Sheikh Mohammed described as a reclaiming of Arab blood was lost on English racing society). However, racing now depends upon Middle Eastern money to such a degree that any hint of a reduction in this investment is met with panic. Before this investment 'trickled down' so that almost everyone in the business was affected by it, Middle Eastern buyers were regarded as 'perverting' the sport, by buying so many horses that they could hardly lose. I was told that it was not 'in the spirit of the game' to 'hedge your bets' to such an extent. By buying a large proportion of each generation of yearlings and the best broodmares, the Dubai ruling family ensured that they had an extremely high chance of owning at least a few talented racehorses.

Constraining uncertainty to this degree goes against the central ethos of horseracing and undermines all of the major roles in racing. The bloodstock agent is employed on the grounds that he is capable of identifying those yearlings who will make good racehorses. The stud manager is employed on the basis that he can predict which stallion will 'get' a good foal from a particular mare. Each does so on the grounds of their connections and their resultant inherent abilities. Buying all of the available yearlings in order to guarantee winners subverts this process by squeezing the risk out of success. Expressed within the racing industry's own particular idiom of morality, it was 'just not cricket'.

Following initial hostility, resentment and resistance, the British racing industry has now softened its response, describing the endeavour as, for example, 'Making a science out of an art' (Down 1998: 13), but criticism is still to be found amongst those who believe that racing should be about risk, and therefore opportunity. As in the case of AI and cloning, too much control spoils racing, by upsetting the balance between fixed and variable factors. Maintaining this balance is the major preoccupation of each member of racing society, visible at the auction, on the racecourse, on the stud farm and at the training yard.

Conclusions

My consideration of racing society in Newmarket is an attempt to respond to Haraway's invitation, 'to remap the borderlands between nature and culture' (1989: 15). The apparent boundary between humans and animals is becoming ever fuzzier. New technologies including xenotransplantation and gene therapy as well as zoonoses such as Bovine Spongiform Encephalopathy and variant Creutzfeldt-Jakob Disease demand that we think creatively about our relationships with animals. Recasting these ideas depends upon an awareness of their present trajectories of meaning.

Meanings of 'nature' in Newmarket are imbued with class, and offer a mechanism by which people and animals may be categorised according to ideas whereby some are innately superior to others by virtue of their breeding. This image depends upon the symbolic associations of the horse, and in particular the English thoroughbred racehorse, the aristocrat of the horse world. The English thoroughbred is at the centre of British horseracing, and all of racing's consumers engage, to varying degrees, with the symbolic value of this animal. The royal and aristocratic associations of racing and of the thoroughbred enable owners, trainers, lads, breeders, stud grooms, stud hands, racegoers and even punters to gain prestige. In Britain, the world to which racing pays homage is not so long gone, as the late jockey and trainer Gordon Richards states, 'racing is a form of public life' (quoted by Bowen 1994: 36), where that life still includes the navigation of hierarchies of class and of gender. This most dynamic and yet conservative society accommodates all comers with its unique combination of the fixed and the variable. Risk offers opportunity, breeding preserves stability. Any challenge to this society can be deflected by recourse to one or other of these explanatory mechanisms. And so the world of racing trundles on, principles intact. 'All are equal on the turf and underneath it', or so I'm told. Oh yes, and 'blood will tell'.

NOTES

1 I should add that Borneman's characterisation of the horse in America as a 'democratic ideal' (1988: 31) is based upon an analysis of light-horse breed classification and therefore explicitly excludes the American thoroughbred that is bred on precisely the same (blood) lines as the English thoroughbred. Both are governed by the rules of the International Stud Book.

2 These debates often acknowledge a common origin in the work of David Schneider (Yanagisako and Delaney 1995: 2). Schneider's critique of the study of kinship suggested that the 'facts of life', as described by biology, were 'not always and everywhere the basis of kinship' (1968, 1984). He argued that the basis of kinship theory in sexual reproduction was a reflection of 'European folk models' and did not therefore offer a sound basis for comparative analysis. Schneider's solution to this impasse was to abandon kinship theory, whilst later theorists have since suggested that critical treatment of 'the facts of nature' may enable a new and improved form of kinship theory to prosper (see Carsten 1999).

3 The study of risk and the perception of risk is a growing field (see, for example, Beck 1992, Douglas 1992, Lash, Szerszynski and Wynne 1996). Beck, in particular, has described the 'risk society' of advanced modernity in which 'the social production of wealth is systematically accompanied by the social production of risks. Accordingly, the problems and conflicts relating to the distribution in a society of scarcity overlap with the problems and conflicts that arise from the production, definition and distribution of techno-scientifically produced risks' (1992: 19). Beck defines risk as a 'systematic way of dealing with hazards and insecurities induced and introduced by modernisation itself' (1992: 21). The risks that I am discussing in relation to Newmarket do not succumb to this analysis. On the contrary, they are often presented as an opportunity for the individual to exercise short-term control. Criticisms of the new preoccupation with the unanticipated consequences of technological progress are similarly unsuited as an explanation for behaviour in Newmarket. Furedi, for example, condemns the 'worship of safety' (1997: 8), and bemoans the fact that 'Economic life

today is clearly oriented towards the avoidance of risk' (1997: 2). People in New-market have a different perception of risk because it is one of the idioms by which they progress within the context of their lives in racing.

4 Some forms of technology such as veterinary expertise are available to all trainers and would not affect the ability to predict the outcome of the race. Other improvements such as cameras that can track the field and sectional timing should, theoretically, make it easier to make accurate judgements about the relative merits of individual horses. However, as I mentioned in chapter five, horses have days when they might just feel a bit sore, although show no outward signs of discomfort. They may also have days when, for whatever unfathomable reason, they just don't feel like giving their all.

5 Studying racing society as a 'nature' as well as a 'culture', breaks down the separation between nature and society which Latour refers to as the 'Internal Great Divide' (1993) making it possible to examine racehorses and racing people as hybrids. It also facilitates the comparative study that has been made illegitimate by the 'one nature' model of science assimilated by anthropology. I have chosen to reject an arbitrary distinction made between biology and culture in order to ask what, in Newmarket, are the 'natural facts' of reproduction, and how does their being framed in this way enable them to sustain racing society.

6 Sangster's plunge coincided with a change in taxation that made Ireland a more attractive base for stallions than ever before, enabling him to set up the world-famous Coolmore stallion station in County Tipperary. Coolmore currently stands more than fifty stallions on five continents, including four of the top ten stallions by earnings in the UK.

References

Adamson, C. 1996. 'Small town poisoned by inner city plague: It happens to be the world capital of flat racing', *The Evening Standard*, 10 December, 12–13.

Alcock, A. 1978. *They're Off! The Story of the First Girl Jump Jockeys*, London: J.A. Allen.

Appadurai, A. 1986. 'Introduction: commodities and the politics of value', in A. Appadurai (ed.) *The Social Life of Things: Commodities in Cultural Perspective*, 3–63, Cambridge: Cambridge University Press.

Armytage, M. 1997. 'Ghostly inspiration', *The Daily Telegraph*, 27 July, 30.

Ashforth, D. 2001. 'Go Racing and the BHB: A done deal at last: the £307 million TV deal is agreed', *The Racing Post*, 23 June, 6.

2000. 'Owner follows victor's destiny', *The Racing Post*, 8 May, 13.

Atwood Lawrence, E. 1985. *Hoofbeats and Society: Studies of Human–Horse Interactions*, New York: Indiana University Press.

'Audax' 1996. 'Lynch gives polished performance', *Horse and Hound*, 29 August, 31.

Bale, J. 1994. *Landscapes of Modern Sport*, Leicester: Leicester University Press.

Barclay, H. 1980. *The Role of the Horse in Man's Culture*, London: J.A. Allen.

Barnes, R. and J. Eicher (eds.) 1992. *Dress and Gender: Making and Meaning in Cultural Contexts*, Oxford: Berg.

Barnes, S. 1997. 'Bred for the job', *Horse and Hound*, 5 June, 24–5.

Barth, F. 1975. *Ritual and Knowledge among the Baktaman of New Guinea*, New Haven: Yale University Press.

Baudrillard, J. 1981. *For a Critique of the Political Economy of the Sign*, trans. C. Levin, St Louis: Telos Press.

Bearden, H. and J. Fuquay, 2000. *Applied Animal Reproduction*, London: Prentice Hall.

Beck, U. 1992. *Risk Society: Towards a New Modernity*, trans. M. Ritter, London: Sage.

Beer, G. 1983. *Darwin's Plots. Evolutionary Narrative in Darwin, George Eliot and Nineteenth Century Fiction*, London: Routledge and Kegan Paul.

Bellman, B. L. 1984. *The Language of Secrecy: Symbols and Metaphors in Poro Ritual*, New Brunswick, NJ: Rutgers University Press.

Bender, B. (ed.) 1993. *Landscape: Politics and Perspectives*, Oxford: Berg.

Berenson, B. 1953. *Seeing and Knowing*, London: Chapman & Hall.

Bernard, J. and H. Dodd, 1991. 'Sizing up a filly', in J. Bernard and H. Dodd (eds.) *Tales from the Turf*, 52–65, London: George Weidenfield & Nicolson.

Birley, D. 1995. *Land of Sport and Glory: Sport and British Society 1887–1910*, Manchester: Manchester University Press.

Black, R. 1893. *The Jockey Club and Its Founders*, London.

Bland, E. (ed.) 1950. *Flat Racing since 1900*, London: Andrew Dakers Ltd.

Blyth, H. 1969. *Hell and Hazard*, London: Weidenfeld & Nicolson.

Bolus, J. 1994. *Royal Blood: Fifty Years of Classic Thoroughbreds*, Lexington, Kentucky: The Blood-Horse Inc.

Borneman, J. 1988. 'Race, ethnicity, species, breed: totemism and horse-breed classification in America', *Comparative Study of Society and History*, 30 (1), 25–51.

Bott, E. 1957. *Family and Social Networks: Roles, Norms, and External Relationships in Ordinary Urban Families*, London: Tavistock.

Bouquet, M. 1996. 'Family trees and their affinities: the visual imperative of the genealogical diagram', *Journal of the Royal Anthropological Institute*, 2 (1), 43–67.

1993. *Reclaiming English Kinship: Portuguese Refractions of British Kinship Theory*, Manchester: Manchester University Press.

Bourdieu, P. 1990 (1980). *The Logic of Practice*, trans R. Nice, Cambridge: Polity Press.

1984 (1979). *Distinction*, trans. R. Nice, London: Routledge and Kegan Paul.

1977 (1972). *Outline of a Theory of Practice*, trans. R. Nice. Cambridge: Cambridge University Press.

Bowen, E. 1994. *The Jockey Club's Illustrated History of Thoroughbred Racing in America*, Boston and London: Little, Brown & Co.

Bowling, A. 1996. *Horse Genetics*, London: CAB International.

Brailsford, D. 1991. *Sport, Time and Society: the British at Play*, London: Routledge and Kegan Paul.

Brenner, R. with G. Brenner, 1990. *Gambling and Speculation: A Theory, a History and a Future of Some Human Decisions*, Cambridge: Cambridge University Press.

Briggs, R. 2000. 'Background to a partnership both feared and revered', *The Racing Post*, 15 September, 13.

Briggs, R. and D. Lawrence, 1997. 'Trainers are up in arms', *The Sporting Life*, 21 February, 2.

British Horseracing Board Annual Reports, 1993, 1994, 1995, 1996, 1997.

Broen, M. 2001. 'First past the post', *The Guardian* (Media section), 25 June, 6–7.

Brown, D. 1979. *Berenson and the Connoisseurship of Italian Painting; a Handbook to the Exhibition*, Baltimore: National Gallery of Art.

Budiansky, S. 1997. *The Nature of Horses: their Evolution, Intelligence and Behaviour*, London: Weidenfeld & Nicolson.

Burke, P. 1995. 'Introduction', in P. Burke and R. Porter (eds.) *Languages and Jargons: Contributions to a Social History of Language*, 1–21, Cambridge: Polity Press.

Carrier, J. 1997. 'Introduction', in J. Carrier (ed.) *Meanings of the Market: the Free Market in Western Culture*, 1–67, Oxford: Berg.

1990. 'The symbolism of possession in commodity advertising', *Man*, (n.s.) 25 (4), 693–706.

Carsten, J. (ed.) 1999. *Cultures of Relatedness: New Approaches to the Study of Kinship*, Cambridge: Cambridge University Press.

Cashman, R. and M. McKernan, 1979. *Sport in History: the Making of Modern Sporting History*, Queensland: Queensland University Press.

Chinn, C. 1991. *Better Betting with a Decent Feller: Bookmaking, Betting and the British Working Class 1750–1990*, London: Harvester Wheatsheaf.

Clark, K. 1974. *Another Part of the Wood: A Self Portrait*, London: John Murray.

Clarke, J. 1995. 'The warmblood approach to breeding', in D. Wallin, J. Kidd and C. Clarke (eds.) *The International Warmblood Horse: A Worldwide Guide to Breeding and Bloodlines*, 14–22, Addington: Kenilworth Press.

Clutton-Brock, J. 1994. 'The unnatural world: behavioural aspects of humans and animals in the process of domestication', in A. Manning and J. Serpell (eds.) *Animals and Human Society: Changing Perspectives*, 23–35, London: Routledge and Kegan Paul.

Cohen, A. (ed.) 1990. 'The British anthropological tradition, otherness and rural studies', in P. Lowe and M. Bodiguel (eds.) *Rural Studies in Britain and France*, trans. Henry Buller, 203–21, London: Belhaven Press.

  1986. 'Of symbols and boundaries, or, does Ertie's greatcoat hold the key?' in A. Cohen (ed.) *Symbolising Boundaries: Identity and Diversity in British Cultures*, 1–19, Manchester: Manchester University Press.

  1982. *Belonging: Identity and Diversity in British Rural Cultures*, Manchester: Manchester University Press.

Comaroff, J. 1985. *Body of Power, Spirit of Resistance: the Culture and History of a South African People*, Chicago: University of Chicago Press.

Csordas, T. 1994. 'Introduction: the body as representation and being-in-the-world', in T. Csordas (ed.) *Embodiment and Experience: the Existential Grounds of Culture and Self*, 1–24, Cambridge: Cambridge University Press.

Davis, G. 2001. 'Spicing up the betting game', *The Guardian*, Online section, 22 March, 12–13.

Delaney, C. 1991. *The Seed and the Soil: Gender and Cosmology in Turkish Village Society*, Berkeley and Oxford: University of California Press.

  1986. 'The meaning of paternity and the virgin birth debate', *Journal of the Royal Anthropological Institute*, 21 (2), 494–513.

De Moubray, J. 1987. *The Thoroughbred Business*, London: Hamish Hamilton.

  1985. *Horse-Racing and Racing Society: Who belongs and How it Works*, London: Sidgwick and Jackson.

Descola, P. and G. Palsson (eds.) 1996. *Nature and Society: Anthropological Perspectives*, London: Routledge and Kegan Paul.

Dickerson, M. 1984. *Compulsive Gamblers*, Hong Kong: Longman.

Dilley, R. 1992. 'Contesting markets: a general introduction to market ideology, imagery and discourse', in R. Dilley (ed.) *Contesting Markets: Analyses of Ideology, Discourse and Practice*, 1–34, Edinburgh: Edinburgh University Press.

Douglas, M. 1992. *Risk and Blame: Essays in Cultural Theory*, London: Routledge.

  1957. 'Animals in Lele religious symbolism', *Africa*, 27, 46–57.

Down, A. 1998. 'Making a science out of an art', *The Sporting Life*, 10 January, 13.

Du Bourg, R. 1980. *The Australian and New Zealand Thoroughbred*, London: Michael Joseph.

Edwards, J., S. Franklin, E. Hirsch, F. Pine and M. Strathern (eds.) 1993. *Technologies of Procreation: Kinship in the Age of Assisted Conception*, Manchester: Manchester University Press.

Edwards, J. and M. Strathern, 1999. 'Including our own', in J. Carsten (ed.) *Cultures of Relatedness: New Approaches to the Study of Kinship*, 149–66, Cambridge: Cambridge University Press.

Edwards, P. 1988. *The Horse Trade of Tudor and Stuart England*, Cambridge: Cambridge University Press.

Evans-Pritchard, E. 1940. *The Nuer: a Description of the Modes of Livelihood and Political Institutions of a Nilotic People*, Oxford: Clarendon Press.

Firth, R., J. Hubert and A. Forge, with the team of the 'London Kinship Project', 1969. *Families and Their Relatives: Kinship in a Middle-Class Sector of London*, London: Routledge and Kegan Paul.

Fisher, S. 1993. 'The pull of the fruit machine: a sociological typology of young players', *Sociological Review*, 41 (3), 446–74.

Fitzgeorge-Parker, T. 1968. *The Spoilsports*, London: Andre Deutsch.

Foden, G. 1996. 'Tote, hope and glory', *The Guardian*, 26 July, 14–15.

Forest Heath District Council. 1994. 'Local plan inquiry topic paper: horse racing industry in newmarket', Unpublished Policy Paper.

Fox, K. 1997. *The Racing Tribe: the Social Behaviour of Horsewatchers*, The Social Issues Research Centre, Oxford.

Fox, R. 1978. *The Tory Islanders: a People of the Celtic Fringe*, Cambridge: Cambridge University Press.

Franklin, S. 1997. *Embodied Progress: a Cultural Account of Assisted Conception*, London: Routledge and Kegan Paul.

Furedi, F. 1997. *Culture of Fear: Risk Taking and the Morality of Low Expectation*, London: Cassell.

Gallier, S. 1988. *One of the Lads: Racing on the Inside*, London: Stanley Paul.

Geertz, C. 1973. 'Deep play: notes on the Balinese cockfight', in C. Geertz, *The Interpretation of Cultures*, 417–52, New York: Basic Books.

Geismar, H. 2001. 'What's in a price? An ethnography of tribal art at auction', *Journal of Material Culture*, 6 (1), 25–47.

Giddens, A. 1973. *The Class Structure of Advanced Societies*, London: Hutchinson.

Goffman, E. 1969. *Where the Action is: Three Essays*, London: Allen Lane.

Gorer, G. 1955. *Exploring English Character*, Harmondsworth: Penguin.

Gow, P. 1995. 'Land, people and paper in Western Amazonia', in E. Hirsch and M. O'Hanlon (eds.) *The Anthropology of Landscape: Perspectives on Place and Space*, 43–53, London: Oxford University Press.

Gray, J. 1984. 'Lamb auctions on the Borders', *European Journal of Sociology*, 25 (1), 59–82.

Green, G. 2001. 'Threat: major tracks on guard as they seek to avoid threat from drug problem', *The Racing Post*, 25 May, 6.

    1999. 'Owner calls for agents to have code of conduct: High Court victor Heywood wants more openness', *The Racing Post*, 15 November, 4.

Griffiths, R. and D. Yates, 2000. 'Collapse of the doping trial: doping case was "a fiasco"', *The Racing Post*, 20 October, 6.

Haraway, D. 1989. *Primate Visions: Gender, Race, and Nature in the World of Modern Science*, New York and London: Routledge and Kegan Paul.

Hargreaves, J. 1994. *Sporting Females: Critical Issues in the History and Sociology of Women's Sports*, London: Routledge and Kegan Paul.

    1982. *Sport, Culture and Ideology*, London: Routledge.

Herman, R. 1967. *Gambling*, New York: Harper & Row.

Hill, C. 1988. *Horse Power: the Politics of the Turf*, Manchester: Manchester University Press.

Hirsch, E. and M. O'Hanlon (eds.) 1995. *The Anthropology of Landscape: Perspectives on Place and Space*, London: Oxford University Press.

Hislop, L. 1997. 'Agreement sought over AI', *The Sporting Life*, 9 January, 17.

Hoffman, H. 1984. 'How clothes communicate', *Media Development, Journal of the World Association for Christian Communication*, 4, 7–11.

Hoggart, R. 1957. *The Uses of Literacy: Aspects of Working-Class Life with Special Reference to Publications and Entertainments*, London: Chatto and Windus.

Hore, J. 1886. *The History of Newmarket and The Annals of the Turf (Vols. I, II, III)*, London: A. H. Baily.

Horserace Betting Levy Board and Horserace Totaliser Board, 1996–2001. *Annual Reports, Thirty-fifth* to *Fortieth*.

Huggins, M. 2000. *Flat Racing and British Society 1790–1914: a Social and Economic History*, London: Frank Cass.

Ingold, T. 1994. 'From trust to domination: an alternative history of human–animal relations', in A. Manning and J. Serpell (eds.) *Animals and Human Society: Changing Perspectives*, 1–22, London: Routledge and Kegan Paul.

1988. 'Introduction', in T. Ingold (ed.) *What is an Animal?*, 1–16, London: Routledge and Kegan Paul.

Jackson, A. 1987. *Anthropology at Home*, London: Tavistock.

Jamieson, L. 1998. *Intimacy: Personal Relationships in Modern Societies*, Cambridge: Polity Press.

Jockey Club Annual Reports, 1995, 1996, 1997.

Jockey Club History, 1997. Unpublished Report.

Kennedy, A. 1998. 'Courage', letter to *The Racing Post*, 21 May, 8.

Kuper, A. 1988. *The Invention of Primitive Society: Transformations of an Illusion*, London: Routledge and Kegan Paul.

Lash, S., B. Szerszynski and B. Wynne (eds.) 1996. *Risk, Environment and Modernity: Towards a New Ecology*, London: Sage.

Latour, B. 1993. *We Have Never Been Modern*, trans. Catherine Porter, London: Harvester Wheatsheaf.

Lave, J. and E. Wenger, 1991. *Situated Learning: Legitimate Peripheral Participation*, Cambridge: Cambridge University Press.

Le Wita, B. 1994. *French Bourgeois Culture*, trans. J. Underwood, Cambridge: Cambridge University Press.

Leach, E. 1972 (1963). 'Animal categories and verbal abuse', in P. Maranda (ed.) *Mythology*, 39–67, Harmondsworth: Penguin.

Leach, J. 1970. 'The Pie Kid's party', in R. Bloomfield (ed.) *Heard in the Paddocks*, 14–28, London: Stanley Paul.

Leicester, Sir Charles, 1983 (1957). *Bloodstock Breeding*, second edition, revised by H. Wright, London: J.A. Allen.

Lesh, D. 1978. *A Treatise on Thoroughbred Selection*, London: J.A. Allen.

Lévi-Strauss, C. 1966 (1962). *The Savage Mind* (trans.), London: Weidenfeld & Nicolson.

1963. *Totemism*, trans. R. Needham, Boston: Beacon Press.

Löfgren, O. 1985. 'Our friends in Nature: class and animal symbolism', *Ethnos*, 50, 184–213.

Lovesey, J. 1994. *Ready to Ride: Winning Fitness*, London: Sporting Types.

Lurie, A. 1983. *The Language of Clothes: The Definitive Guide to People-Watching Through the Ages*, London: Hamlyn.

Lyle, R. 1945. *Royal Newmarket*, London: Putnam.

Lyng, S. 1990. 'Edgework: a social psychological analysis of voluntary risk taking', *American Journal of Sociology*, 95 (4), 851–86.

MacCormack, C. and M. Strathern (eds.) 1980. *Nature, Culture and Gender*, Cambridge: Cambridge University Press.

Maclean, N. 1984. 'Is gambling "bisnis"? The economic and political functions of gambling in the Jimi Valley', *Social Analysis*, 16, 44–59.

Mahon, G. 1980. 'Inbreeding and infertility in the thoroughbred horse', unpublished PhD thesis, Dublin University.

Manning, A. and J. Serpell (eds.) 1994. *Animals and Human Society: Changing Perspectives*, London: Routledge and Kegan Paul.

Masters, R. and G. Green. 2001. 'Anger as trainers of horses in race-fixing inquiry face fines', *The Racing Post*, 19 January, 4.

McDonald, M. 1987. 'The politics of fieldwork in Brittany', in A. Jackson (ed.) *Anthropology at Home*, 121–38, London: Tavistock.

Miller, D. (ed.) 1995. *Acknowledging Consumption: A Review of New Studies*, London: Routledge and Kegan Paul.

1993. 'Appropriating the state on the council estate', in N. Cummings (ed.) *Reading Things*, 80–113, London: Chance Books.

Mitchell, W. 1988. 'The defeat of hierarchy: gambling as exchange in a Sepik society', *American Ethnologist*, 15, 638–57.

Morreau, D. and M. Taylor. 1997. 'Swinburn: my crisis', *The Sporting Life*, 28 March, 1.

Morris, T. 1998. 'Newmarket', in *Newmarket Stud Farmers Association Directory 1998*, Cambridge: World Racing Network.

1997. 'A collector's item to cherish: a look at the latest edition of the General Stud Book', *The Racing Post*, 30 December, 10.

1996. 'Bloodstock Diary', *The Racing Post*, 28 November, 15.

1990. *Thoroughbred Stallions*, London: The Crowood Press.

Mullins, M. 1999. 'Mirrors and windows: sociocultural studies of human:animal relationships', *Annual Review of Anthropology*, 28, 201–24.

Munting, R. 1996. *An Economic and Social History of Gambling in Britain and the USA*, New York and Manchester: Manchester University Press.

Napier, M. 1975. *Breeding a Racehorse*, London: J.A. Allen.

National Lottery Commission website, 29 February 2000, natlotcomm.gov.uk

Newby, H. 1979. *The Deferential Worker: A Study of Farm Workers in East Anglia*, London: Penguin.

Newman, O. 1968. 'The sociology of the betting shop', *British Journal of Sociology*, 19, 17–33.

Newmarket Open Day Programme, 1996.

Newmarket Stud Farmers' Association. 1998. *Directory*, Cambridge: The Cloister Press.

Oaksey, Lord J. 1978. 'Foreword', in A. Alcock, *They're Off! The Story of the First Girl Jump Jockeys*, London: J.A. Allen.

O'Ryan, T. 1997. 'Battling is a way of life', *The Sporting Life*, 6 December, 10.

Oldman, D. 1978. 'Compulsive gamblers', *Sociological Review*, 26, 349–71.

Onslow, R. 1990. *Royal Ascot*, Marlborough: The Crowood Press.

Orchard, V. 1953. *Tattersalls: Two Hundred Years of Sporting History*, London: Hutchinson.

Ortner, S. 1995. 'Ethnography among the Newark: the Class of '58 of Wacquahic High School', in S. Yanagisako and C. Delaney (eds.) *Naturalizing Power: Essays in Feminist Cultural Analysis*, 257–73, New York and London: Routledge and Kegan Paul.

    1974. 'Is female to male as nature is to culture?', in M. Rosaldo and L. Lamphere (eds.) *Woman, Culture, Society*, 67–88, Stanford: Stanford University Press.

Paulick, R. 2000. 'Offers quickly roll in for Fusaichi Pegasus', *Bloodhorse*, 20 May.

Phillips, S. 1986. 'Natives and incomers: the symbolism of belonging in Muker parish, North Yorkshire', in A. Cohen (ed.) *Symbolising Boundaries: Identity and Diversity in British Cultures*, 141–54, Manchester: Manchester University Press.

Potts, A. 1995. *Against the Crowd: The Methods of a Modern Backer*, Oswestry: Aesculus Press.

Racing Industry Statistical Bureau, Statistics 1996.

Rae, G. 1990. *The Sporting Life Guide to Owning a Racehorse: A Handbook for Present and Future Owners*, London: The Sporting Life.

Reith, G. 1999. *The Age of Chance: Gambling in Western Culture*, London: Routledge.

Riches, D. 1975. 'Cash, credit and gambling in a modern Eskimo economy: speculations on the origins of spheres of economic exchange', *Man*, (n.s.) 10, 21–33.

Ritvo, H. 1997. *The Platypus and the Mermaid: and Other Figments of the Classifying Imagination*, Cambridge, Mass. and London: Harvard University Press.

    1995. 'Possessing Mother Nature: genetic capital in eighteenth century Britain', in J. Brewer and S. Staves (eds.) *Early Modern Conceptions of Property*, 413–26, London: Routledge.

    1987. *The Animal Estate: The English and Other Creatures in the Victorian Age*, Cambridge, Mass. and London: Harvard University Press.

Rivers, W. 1968 (1910). 'The genealogical method of anthropological inquiry', in *Kinship and Social Organisation*, L.S.E. Monographs in Social Anthropology No. 34 (with commentaries by Raymond Firth and David E. Schneider), 97–109, London: The Athlone Press; New York: Humanities Press.

Robinson, P. with N. Robinson, 1993. *Horsetrader: Robert Sangster and the Rise and Fall of the Sport of Kings*, London: Harper Collins.

Rosaldo, M. and L. Lamphere (eds.) *Woman, Culture, Society*, Stanford: Stanford University Press.

Ruff's Guide to the Turf. 1996. London: Weatherbys

Russell, N. 1986. *Like Endgend'ring Like: Heredity and Animal Breeding in Early Modern England*, Cambridge: Cambridge University Press.

Schechner, R. and W. Appel (eds.) 1990. *By Means of Performance: Intercultural Studies of Theatre and Ritual*, Cambridge: Cambridge University Press.

Schneider, D. 1984. *A Critique of the Study of Kinship*, Ann Arbor: University of Michigan Press.

    1968. *American Kinship: a Cultural Account*, Chicago: University of Chicago Press.

Scott, J. 1990. *Domination and the Arts of Resistance: Hidden Transcripts*, New Haven and London: Yale University Press.

Sharpe, G. 1996a. 'Quotes of the year', *The Sporting Life*, 23 December, 4.

    1996b. 'More quotes of the year', *The Sporting Life*, 24 December, 4.

Slaughter, T. and S. 1994. *Go Racing in France*, London: Tor Communications.

Smurthwaite, T. 2000. 'Why there's no hello Dolly at the National', *The Racing Post*, 4 December, 6.

1997a. 'More research into pedigrees', *The Sporting Life*, 9 January, 17.

1997b. 'AI problem still present', *The Sporting Life*, 16 January, 7.

1997c. 'Cigar, but no smoke signals', *The Sporting Life*, 17 June, 5.

1997d. 'TV watch on jockey diets', *The Sporting Life*, 29 May, 22.

Stewart, M. 1997. *The Time of the Gypsies*, London and New York: Westview Press.

Strathern, M. 1993. 'A question of context', in J. Edwards, S. Franklin, P. Hirsch, F. Price and M. Strathern (eds.) *Technologies of Procreation: Kinship in the Age of Assisted Conception*, 1–19, Manchester: Manchester University Press.

1992a. *Reproducing the Future: Essays on Anthropology, Kinship, and the New Reproductive Technologies*, Manchester: Manchester University Press.

1992b. *After Nature: English Kinship in the Late Twentieth Century*, Cambridge: Cambridge University Press.

1992c. 'Parts and wholes: refining relations in a post-plural world', in A. Kuper (ed.) *Conceptualising Society*, 75–104, London: Routledge and Kegan Paul.

1982. 'The place of kinship: kin, class and village status in Elmdon, Essex', in A. Cohen (ed.), *Belonging: Identity and Social Organisation in British Rural Cultures*, 72–100, Manchester: Manchester University Press.

1981. *Kinship at the Core: An Anthropology of Elmdon, a Village in North-west Essex in the Nineteen-sixties*, Cambridge: Cambridge University Press.

1980. 'No nature, no culture: the Hagen case', in C. MacCormack and M. Strathern (eds.) *Nature, Culture and Gender*, 174–222, Cambridge: Cambridge University Press.

Tambiah, S. 1969. 'Animals are good to think and good to prohibit', *Ethnology* 8 (4), 423–59.

Tarlo, E. 1996. *Clothing Matters: Dress and Identity in India*, London: Hurst & Co.

Tattersalls, 2000. '1999 Houghton Yearling Sales Results', Tattersalls website, www.tattersalls.com

The Racing Industry Statistical Bureau Statistics 1996, London: Weatherbys.

Tesio, F. 1958. *Breeding the Racehorse*, trans. E. Spinola, London: Allen and Unwin.

Thomas, K. 1983. *Man and the Natural World: Changing Attitudes in England 1500–1800*. London: Allen Lane.

Thomas, W. 1901. 'The gaming instinct', *American Journal of Sociology*, 6, 750–63.

Thompson, L. 1997. *Lamtarra: Quest for Greatness*, London: J.A. Allen.

1996. 'Big yen for fresh blood', *The Guardian*, 11 October, 6–7.

Underwood, J. 1998. *Review of 1997: Stallion Statistics, Fees, Group and Listed Winners in Europe, Yearling Averages etc.*, London: European Racing and Breeding Digest.

Vamplew, W. 1988. *Pay Up and Play the Game: Professional Sport in Britain 1875–1914*, Cambridge: Cambridge University Press.

1979. 'The sport of kings and commoners: the commercialisation of British horse-racing in the nineteenth century', in R. Cashman and M. McKernan (eds.) *Sport in History: The Making of Modern Sporting History*, 307–25, Queensland: Queensland University Press.

1976. 'One for the rich and one for the poor: the law and gambling', in *The Turf: A Social and Economic History of Horse Racing*, 199–212, London: Allen Lane.

Varley, N. 1997. 'Sterile wonder-horse may run on for ever as former owner pursues race of clones', *The Guardian*, 14 March, 18.

Varola, F. 1974. *Typology of the Racehorse*, London: J.A. Allen & Co. Ltd.

Vodafone Derby Official Racecard, 1997.

Wacquant, L. 1995a. 'The pugilistic point of view: how boxers think and feel about their trade', *Theory and Society*, 24 (4), 489–535.

1995b. 'Pugs at work: bodily capital and bodily labour among professional boxers', *Body and Society*, 1 (1), 65–93.

1992. 'The social logic of boxing in black Chicago: toward a sociology of pugilism', *Sociology of Sport Journal*, 9, 221–54.

Wallin, D. 1995. 'The Hannoverian', in D. Wallin, J. Kidd and C. Clarke (eds.) *The International Warmblood Horse: A Worldwide Guide to Breeding and Bloodlines*, 51–72, London: Kenilworth Press.

Walwyn, P. 1997. 'True horsemanship', *The Sporting Life*, 6 January, 4.

Willett, P. 1996. 'Heads you win', *Horse and Hound*, 25 July, 27.

1991. *A History of the General Stud Book*, Wellingborough: Weatherbys.

1981. *The Classic Racehorse*, London: Stanley Paul.

1975. *An Introduction to the Thoroughbred* (second edition), London: Stanley Paul.

1966. *An Introduction to the Thoroughbred*, London: Stanley Paul.

Willis, P. 1977. *Learning to Labour: How Working Class Kids get Working Class Jobs*, London: Saxon House.

Willis, R. (ed.) 1990. *Signifying Animals: Human Meanings in the Natural World*, London: Unwin Hyman.

Willmott, P. and M. Young 1960. *Family and Class in a London Suburb*, London: Routledge and Kegan Paul.

Winters, L. 1939. *Animal Breeding*, New York: John Wiley.

Wolff, K. 1950. *The Sociology of Georg Simmel*, New York: The Free Press.

Wolfram, S. 1987. *In-Laws and Outlaws: Kinship and Marriage in England, 1800–1980*, New York: St Martin's Press.

Woodburn, M. 1982. 'Egalitarian societies', *Man*, 17, 431–51.

Wright, H. 2000. 'New cash plan as Britain trails in owners' league', *The Racing Post*, 17 October, 6.

1999. 'Self-help is the answer', *The Racing Post*, 24 March, 9.

Yanagisako, S. and C. Delaney (eds.) 1995. *Naturalizing Power: Essays in Feminist Cultural Analysis*. New York and London: Routledge and Kegan Paul.

Zimmer, L. 1987. 'Gambling with cards in Melanesia and Australia: an introduction', *Oceania*, 58, 1–6.

Zola, I. 1967. 'Observations on gambling in a lower-class setting', in R. Herman (ed.) *Gambling*, 19–31, New York: Harper and Row.

Index